A Short History of British Architecture

By the same author

A City at Risk
Landlords to London
Companion Guide to Outer London
The Battle for the Falklands (with Max Hastings)
Images of Hampstead
The Market for Glory
The Selling of Mary Davies
Against the Grain
Accountable to None
England's Thousand Best Churches
England's Thousand Best Houses
Mission Accomplished
Thatcher and Sons
Wales
A Short History of England
England's 100 Best Views
England's Cathedrals
Britain's 100 Best Railway Stations
A Short History of Europe
Europe's 100 Best Cathedrals
A Short History of London
The Celts: A Sceptical History

A Short History of British Architecture
From Stonehenge to the Shard

SIMON JENKINS

PENGUIN
VIKING

VIKING

UK | USA | Canada | Ireland | Australia
India | New Zealand | South Africa

Viking is part of the Penguin Random House group of companies whose addresses can be found at global.penguinrandomhouse.com

Penguin Random House UK,
One Embassy Gardens, 8 Viaduct Gardens, London SW11 7BW

penguin.co.uk
global.penguinrandomhouse.com

Penguin Random House UK

First published 2024
001

Copyright © Simon Jenkins, 2024

The moral right of the author has been asserted

Picture credits (numbers refer to image numbers on inset pages): 123RF: 17, 63; 4Corners Images: 1 (Maurizio Rellini), 12 (Alessandra Albanese), 25 (Corrado Piccoli); Alamy: 2, 4, 5, 7, 11, 13, 15, 16, 20, 21, 23, 24, 29, 34, 35, 37, 39, 43, 51, 55, 59, 67; Bigstock: 10, 30, 45, 52, 66; Bridgeman Images: 22 (Sandro Vannini), 26 (Christie's Images), 27 (Yale Center for British Art, Paul Mellon Collection), 33 (Norwich Castle Museum & Art Gallery), 36 (courtesy of the Trustees of Sir John Soane's Museum, London), 49 (Luisa Ricciarini), 54 (London Metropolitan Archives); British Museum: 3 (© The Trustees of the British Museum); British Pathé: 58 (Glasgow Today & Tomorrow, 1949); Byker Community Trust: 61; Dreamstime: 62; Geograph: 6 (Michael Garlick, CC BY-SA 2.0); Getty Images: 9, 41, 48, 65; © Ian Grundy: 57; John Robertson Architects/Max Alexander: 53; © Dom Jones: 56; David Pringle: 38; RIBA Collections/Martin Charles: 46, 47; Royal Commission on the Ancient and Historical Monuments of Wales: 18 (© Crown copyright, RCAHMW); Shutterstock: 8, 28, 31, 32, 40, 42, 44, 50; St Mary's Church, Beverley: 19; Ministry of Transport, HMSO: 60 (Colin Buchanan, Traffic in Towns, 1963); University of Cambridge, Judge Business School: 64; Wikimedia Commons: 14 (Photo by David Iliff, CC BY-SA 3.0).

No part of this book may be used or reproduced in any manner for the purpose of training artificial intelligence technologies or systems. In accordance with Article 4(3) of the DSM Directive 2019/790, Penguin Random House expressly reserves this work from the text and data mining exception

Set in 12/14.75pt Dante MT Std
Typeset by Jouve (UK), Milton Keynes
Printed and bound in Great Britain by Clays Ltd, Elcograf S.p.A.

The authorized representative in the EEA is Penguin Random House Ireland,
Morrison Chambers, 32 Nassau Street, Dublin D02 YH68

A CIP catalogue record for this book is available from the British Library

ISBN: 978–0–241–67495–6

Penguin Random House is committed to a sustainable future
for our business, our readers and our planet. This book is made from
Forest Stewardship Council® certified paper.

To Marcus Binney

Contents

Introduction: Let the Buildings Speak ... 1

1. Stonehenge to Rome (3000 BC–AD 400) ... 11
2. The Saxon Era (400–1066) ... 18
3. Norman Britain (1066–1170) ... 24
4. Gothic Dawn (1170–1245) ... 31
5. The Glory of Decorated (1245–1348) ... 41
6. Perpendicular Climactic (1348–1500) ... 49
7. Tudor Prodigies (1500–1616) ... 59
8. Inigo Jones to Christopher Wren (1616–1688) ... 74
9. Burlington versus Baroque (1688–1750) ... 89
10. The Golden Age (1750–1810) ... 101
11. Nash and the Italianate (1810–1825) ... 113
12. The Battle of the Styles (1825–1850) ... 128
13. Palaces of Prosperity and Faith (1850–1870) ... 143
14. Sweetness and Light (1870–1900) ... 155
15. Fit for Empire (1900–1920) ... 166
16. Homes for Heroes (1920–1930) ... 179
17. Modernism Emergent (1930–1940) ... 191
18. Modernism Triumphant (1940–1965) ... 199
19. The Dawn of Hesitation (1965–1973) ... 213
20. The Conservation Counter-Revolution (1973–1986) ... 229

Contents

21.	The Age of Spectacle (1986–2020)	244
22.	Conclusion: Full Shard Ahead	259
	Glossary	269
	Further Reading	271
	Acknowledgements	277
	Index	279

Introduction: Let the Buildings Speak

My first awareness of British architectural style came when walking through Sicily in my youth. High on Monte Bàrbaro, I came across the Grecian temple of Segesta. Its sturdy columns and triangular pediments had been left, isolated and unfinished, some two and a half thousand years ago. They now lay enveloped by trees and wildflowers. What surprised me was not Segesta's survival but something quite different, its familiarity. I had spent my childhood near Regent's Park in London, and my early meanderings took me past the Nash terraces, whose facades fascinated me. Here they were again, perched on a Sicilian hilltop. What could Regency London possibly have in common with fifth-century-BC Sicily? What bond united them?

The answer was classicism. A similar surprise occurred early in my writing of this book. A vertical white strip rises up the brick facade of my Victorian terrace house in London, apparently marking its boundary with its neighbour. I noticed for the first time that it was not paint but the ghost of a column flat against the wall, a so-called pilaster ending in a near-invisible capital beneath the roof. This column was repeated evenly four times down the terrace. It served no purpose but was a decorative echo of those same Greek columns at Segesta. What was it doing on a humble London terrace?

Such symbols of classicism have recurred throughout my life – as they do for most Britons if they care to notice. We encounter them on schools, libraries and universities. If we sit on the top deck of a bus or visit the centre of any British town or city, we see Segesta clones looming at us from churches, museums, theatres and public buildings. Classicism's pediments, fluted columns and scrolls survived in Britain for two millennia, challenged by only two other architectural languages: Gothic and modernist. But classicism has not vanished. It is in our architectural bones.

Architecture is not the same as building, engineering or fortification. These are about structure, a utilitarian response to our need for shelter and protection. Architecture is about how we choose to clothe that structure with meaning or delight. Such clothing has occurred since the dawn of time. The urge to beautify utility is a basic human desire. The Victorian architect George Gilbert Scott called his profession the 'decoration of necessity'. Architecture has been said to start where building stops, where the mason lays down his measure and allows imagination and art to take over his craft.

Most of this book records my interest in how this imagination has evolved over centuries. I cannot leave home and walk down a street without noticing how its buildings look. One reason is that this appearance can be beautiful, another that it may be interesting, controversial. Style has caused many, often bitter, arguments throughout history. The reality is that buildings surround us, yet to most people they are a mystery. Few can say why they look as they do, and what their differences signify. Few speak architecture.

This book is my attempt to remedy this mystery. Most young people are taught the rudiments of art, drama, music and literature, but curiously few study architecture. It exists in a lost aesthetic realm somewhere between art and engineering. As tourists, we eagerly seek out old buildings, but generally for their antiquity. A building is not a painting, a sculpture or a piece of music, our contact with it confined by space and time. It is like an exhibition that is ubiquitous and inescapable. Yet works of architecture are rarely subject to the same public critique as a new painting, play or film. We are not permitted to take them or leave them. We must take them, as if they were imposed on us by some anonymous power.

Introduction: Let the Buildings Speak

I derive pleasure from those buildings that make me pause and hear what their designers are trying to tell me. This is particularly true of old ones because, like old pictures and old music, they are messengers of memory. They take us to times past and lend context to times present. Eighteenth-century Britons – those who could afford it – took architecture sufficiently seriously to send their young to Italy, often for years, to study the legacy of classicism. For a brief period, the British establishment became seriously conversant with architecture. The outcome was reflected in the appearance of Georgian Bath, Brighton, Cheltenham, Edinburgh and the London square.

Of all aesthetic concepts, that of style has been the hardest to define. When the art historian John Ruskin said we wanted architecture both to shelter us and to speak to us, he did not reveal what it should say. In his 1963 radio lecture series *The Classical Language of Architecture*, the historian John Summerson traced its rises and falls, its variations and rebirths since the Roman Empire in Britain. He told of a classicism that originated in ancient Greece, was adapted by the Romans and spread across Europe and later the world as the hallmark of cultural imperialism. Its buildings are to be found from Moscow to San Francisco and from Cape Town to Hong Kong. Classicism came close to being a truly global style.

The Edwardian William Lethaby was one of the few historians to analyse the possible meanings of architectural style. He searched ancient ruins for answers in the relics of mysticism and magic. Others delved into the trees worshipped by Druids. The Roman writer Vitruvius in the first century BC suggested that the three Greek designs known as 'orders' at the top of classical columns were derived from the branches of trees propping up ancient roofs. To him the simple discs of a Doric capital had 'the proportions, strength and grace of a man's body'. His sixteenth-century apostle Sebastiano Serlio suggested Doric was suitable only for columns in churches dedicated to male saints. It became the order of military architecture and, in its later Tuscan variant, of commercial buildings.

As for the dignified scrolls of an Ionic capital, Vitruvius gave them female attributes, hence suited to temples of the muses and places of culture. The third capital, Corinthian, is composed of acanthus leaves, clearly derived from vegetation. The Renaissance architect Donato Bramante even designed a column in Milan in Corinthian's honour, with shrubs poking out of its drums. The Romans combined Corinthian with Ionic into a style called Composite.

What none of this explains is the potency, the quasi-religious significance, that these orders and their enveloping architecture acquired. They were initially symbols of an eastern Mediterranean religion. Yet they were adopted by Rome and bequeathed to, and wholeheartedly accepted by, Christianity. The citadel of Catholicism, St Peter's in Rome, was to be fronted by the portico of a pagan temple, as was St Paul's in London. Two thousand years later, the British architect Edwin Lutyens professed to see the orders as commandments of a Christian God. The orders are present somewhere in virtually every British city street, from the grandest town hall to the meanest corner pub.

When the Romans left Britain in the early fifth century their architectural ideas might have been expected to go with them. But Rome left behind the Christian faith, and that faith retained its loyalty to classicism in the tentative form of north European Romanesque. When in the seventh century the Synod of Whitby decided Britain would worship in the Roman rite, all British churches were ordered to be designed 'after the Roman fashion'. It was to be the fashion of British ecclesiastical architecture for some five hundred years.

From the mid-twelfth century to the sixteenth, Europe, at least outside Italy, wavered from the classical tradition and adopted

Introduction: Let the Buildings Speak

Gothic. The crowning of an opening with a sharp angle rather than a curve had long been practised in the Islamic world and the Levant. It enabled weight to be transferred more efficiently to the ground, lightening walls, expanding windows and raising roofs. In 1144 Abbot Suger of Paris boasted that his new choir of St-Denis released worship from Romanesque gloom into 'the light of God received in splendour'. Gothic architecture soared as Roman never did. In England, Lincoln's now vanished cathedral steeple out-topped even the pyramids of Egypt and was probably once the tallest structure on earth.

Britain's Gothic era ended, or at least hibernated, at the dawn of the sixteenth century. Aristocratic architecture moved hesitantly towards a hybrid 'English Renaissance' seen in Tudor mansions such as Longleat and Burghley. This was transformed under the early Stuarts with the return of the remarkable Inigo Jones from his studies in Rome, bringing with him a passion for a conservative classicism that was to influence British architecture into the eighteenth century.

The baroque interplay of columns, towers and domes flowered briefly under Christopher Wren, Nicholas Hawksmoor and John Vanbrugh. But Britain was denied the full baroque genius of a Bernini or Borromini. Instead, the Georgians remained loyal to the Vitruvian tradition as dictated by Jones and adopted by the patrons of the grand tour of Italy. It was championed by the architect/aristocrat Lord Burlington and his followers Colen Campbell, William Kent and William Chambers. Only towards the end of the eighteenth century was it challenged by such innovators as Robert Adam and James Wyatt, followed by the Regency's John Nash and John Soane.

Architecture now became the source of extraordinary professional dispute. What began as an argument between strict and fluid classicism evolved into a series of running 'battles of the styles', Greece versus Rome, classical versus Gothic revival. The argument, obscure or at best unimportant to the layman, had much to do with the elite nature of patronage. Most people could understand a Shakespeare play, a Handel concerto or a Van Dyck painting. Few understood building style. Should classical Belgravia be adorned with a Gothic church? Should the new railway speak Great Western Tudor or London and Birmingham Greek? A building's appearance seemed impregnated with significance to its designer, but so what?

Under the Victorians the debate between classical and a re-invigorated Gothic became one over patriotism. An argument in 1834 over the design of the new Palace of Westminster concluded that British meant Gothic rather than classical. Fifteen years later the same argument over a new Foreign Office concluded the reverse. Manchester's town hall was to be Gothic, but Leeds was classical. Liverpool's Anglican cathedral was Gothic so its Catholic counterpart was initially classical (though later modernist). As we shall see, these arguments were often fierce.

By the 1870s many architects sought refuge in a vernacular revivalism. The Arts and Crafts movement was described by the poet Matthew Arnold as the architecture of 'sweetness and light'. Inspiration was found in diversity, in Italianate classical, Queen Anne, Dutch and French Renaissance. Yet the turn of the twentieth century led to a renewed outburst of neoclassicism for public buildings, and a retreat into suburban 'Tudorbethan' for private ones. Edwardian eclecticism delivered Liverpool's Three Graces and Cardiff's civic centre as well as the domesticity of Letchworth Garden City and Romford's Gidea Park.

The interwar period saw that eclecticism spiced by a smattering of stylistic novelty. Continental influences produced innovative buildings in art deco and early modernism. The latter, aggressively politicized by the Swiss-French architect Le Corbusier, was intensely influential among a younger generation of interwar architects. It extended far beyond the design of individual buildings to a call for a crusade of comprehensive urban renewal, one

Introduction: Let the Buildings Speak

that found fertile soil in Britain in the aftermath of the Second World War.

This ideological modernism – as distinct from the modernist style – captured the commanding heights of British national and local government patronage in the 1940s and 50s. It briefly brought swathes of Britain's cities to the brink of destruction. The ambition, to replace the totality of the urban environment, was to tear apart communities and displace hundreds of thousands of Britons from their homes. It attracted no debate or protest at the time and was accepted planning doctrine for two decades after the war. It was ended by its sheer scale and cost of reconstruction. The scars remain in the downtown areas of Glasgow, Liverpool, Birmingham and Newcastle.

The collapse of the modernist revolution was aided in the 1970s by what amounted to a counter-revolution, that of building conservation. This argued that old cities were not by definition 'obsolete'. Cars need not be the rulers of urban planning. Renewal did not require destruction and existing fabric should be recognized as integral to townscape. By the end of the twentieth century, town planning was slowly transformed from state power harnessed to social ideology to the exercise of compromise and sensitivity.

This counter-revolution took place when I was working as a planning journalist and seeing these often bitter conflicts at close quarters. I have tried to stand back in retrospect, but I can only repeat what I thought at the time, that I was witnessing an architecturally traumatic moment. The scale of the postwar revolution and counter-revolution has rarely been recognized or analysed. I therefore believe that the weight I give them here is not disproportionate. Those battles were to determine why most British cities look as they do now.

Architecture has a rare history in that we can encounter it first hand and face to face. It is a history whose evolution is ever-present. I thus try always to mention buildings that readers can see and appreciate for themselves. Of the oldest, this mostly means churches, as they are buildings whose style carries meaning and which survive through being of stone. I deal less with castles and other fortifications as they are primarily buildings of utility rather than style, though I appreciate this is not always the case.

London features prominently for the simple reason that, at least from the sixteenth century and apart from certain aristocratic properties, British architecture was dominated by the growth of the capital. It led the country in both size and fashion. By 1700 it was seven times bigger than Britain's next largest cities: Norwich, Bristol and York. Its churches, houses and streets led the course of change. Its controversies and conflicts dominated debate.

Only with the industrial revolution of the late-eighteenth and nineteenth centuries did architecture start to transform the appearance of provincial townscapes, with cities such as Manchester, Liverpool, Edinburgh and Glasgow in the lead. The buildings of Scotland in particular merit a history of their own, as does Wales's extraordinary burst of chapel architecture. Ireland does not feature in this book as it is not part of Britain.

Not until after the Second World War did the status of architecture enter the nation's political realm. Only then was it realized that the entirety of the buildings of Britain were the creation of a select group of people, the owners of property and elite architects, planners and engineers, operating with only the most rudimentary democratic oversight. Those whose lives were conditioned by their decisions were never asked for their opinion or offered a choice.

I have always regarded this as a most extraordinary power. Arbiters of style have felt entitled to encompass other people in surroundings from which they have no escape – unless they are rich. As we shall see, this power had wide consequences, economic, sociological and psychological. These consequences are

Introduction: Let the Buildings Speak

today at last the subject of controversy, and that is welcome. I make no apology for entering into that controversy and appreciate that many readers may not agree with my judgements. I hope only that I have been fair to all sides in the ongoing argument. This argument features so prominently in the final third of the book because it has determined the appearance of most of the buildings we see around us every day. It has been little discussed in recent architectural histories.

This is a book by a lay observer for the general reader, so I have tried to avoid technical terms. Those that are unavoidable I have listed in a glossary. The dating of buildings is difficult. Since the story of style can be fast-moving, building dates, where given, are usually those when a work was designed or begun rather than completed.

This is not an academic history and sources are given in the text where appropriate. The Further Reading section includes those works that I have found most useful. As for chapter headings, the dividing of historical narrative is always controversial, and in matters of style near impossible. I have tried to parcel the text into periods of dominant architectural styles and the dates of their most notable buildings.

My intention above all is to inform what should be a public debate on the future appearance of Britain's built environment. I believe people will only join this debate if they can understand its history and language. That is why they must learn to speak architecture.

1.
Stonehenge to Rome (3000 BC–AD 400)

The view of Stonehenge from the A303 is one of the most exhilarating in England. It straddles known history. From Stone Age construction to internal combustion it embraces humanity's attempt to harness nature's materials and give them purpose. I must have seen that view a hundred times, a privilege shared with some ten million people a year on the road to or from the south-west.

Stonehenge is by general agreement Britain's first work of architecture. There are earlier buildings. The Mesolithic huts of Skara Brae on Orkney, tiny rooms buried in sand dunes by the sea, possibly dating from 3100 BC, are among the first known settlements to survive in Europe. They stand as relics of a Stone Age culture, abandoned and buried by some sudden crisis. But if architecture is defined as the desire to give meaning to structure, Stonehenge must take primacy. Its earliest features are believed to date from the early third millennium BC.

Close to, the monument loses none of its magic. Its uprights, lintels, mounds and post-holes sit as they have – give or take some re-erection – for some five millennia, asking silent questions and giving no answers. It is unlikely to have served as living quarters or had a military use. Microscopic inspection of markings on the lintels indicates that the builders understood wooden joinery and could adapt that joinery to stone, even without metal tools. We know the stones are aligned to the solstices and so must have had to do with seasons, and thus probably agriculture. We know that the inner ring of bluestones, originating in Wales, were scraped for their dust, which has been found in burial pouches and thus may have been thought therapeutic. Adjacent tracks such as the nearby three-kilometre-long Neolithic Greater Cursus look as if intended for some sort of sport or entertainment. But of this and of the stones' supernatural significance we know nothing.

Stonehenge is contemporary with the earliest Sumerian civilizations of Mesopotamia and predates the pyramids of Egypt. It implies a society sufficiently ordered to transport large stones a hundred miles across land and water from south Wales, and then raise lintels and erect trilithons to a considerable height. Bones retrieved from surrounding tombs indicate long periods of habitation. The nearby Amesbury burial site shows there were visitors from as far away as Kent and even Switzerland. There are stone circles elsewhere in northern Europe and a possible precursor to the henge has been discovered in the Preseli hills of west Wales, to which the bluestones have been traced. None has Stonehenge's complexity or grandeur.

In the seventeenth century the architect Inigo Jones was asked by the ever-curious James I to investigate and explain. Jones declared the stones of Roman origin and indeed classical in inspiration. He dubbed Stonehenge the 'founding creation' of British architecture. The stones were first studied in detail later in the same century by the antiquary John Aubrey and attributed to the Iron Age Druids. The Georgian antiquary William Stukeley agreed. A similar theme was taken up by the creator of Georgian Bath, John Wood, who declared the stones 'architecture handed down by God'. He used the cursus as model for his Circus, hub of the Bath terraces. He even crowned his classical facades with Druidical acorns in honour of 'the priests of the hollow oak'. He bequeathed the word 'circus' that follows Piccadilly and Oxford in London, and that describes traffic roundabouts nationwide.

Stonehenge has never been at peace with its celebrity. In her 2008 account of Stonehenge's afterlife, the historian Rosemary

Stonehenge to Rome (3000 BC–AD 400)

Hill charted successive attempts to place it in a European context. Romantics found it a place of mystery, even violence and horror. William Wordsworth asked, 'What does it more than while the tempers rise, / With starless glooms and sounds of loud dismay, / Reveal with still-born glimpse the terrors of our way?' Here priests 'like a thousand Gods mysterious council hold'. Artists depicted the stones variously as a backdrop to Shakespeare's tragedies, Turner's thunderstorms and Blake's 'Jerusalem'. They were cited as an influence by Henry Moore and Barbara Hepworth. Modern Druids have claimed the stones as their own. Twentieth-century hippies, particularly at solstice time, made them their temple.

An appealing feature of Stonehenge is that it has always seemed incontrovertibly British, a rare characteristic in the islands' architecture. Its legacy today is a dispute over whether the stones should continue to be visible from the A303 or whether the congested road should be put in a tunnel and the site accessed via a visitor centre. The latter would clearly damage the site and deprive millions of what remains one of the most electrifying views in the country, albeit from a car. A simple dual carriageway would suffice.

After Stonehenge, British architecture embarked on a great silence. As the Stone Age mutated into the Bronze Age – the 'industrial revolution' of European prehistory – there are few equivalent advances in the realm of architecture. On Orkney, apart from Skara Brae there are numerous passage tombs and hall houses. These can be reconstructed and efforts made at envisaging such ancient settlements. But wood vanishes over time and evidence relies on fragments of stone or signs of the movement of earth. We have nothing on the scale of the Wiltshire henge.

Little by way of architecture came with the Iron Age of the first millennium BC. Over 3,300 British hill forts have been excavated, some defensive, others probably gathering-places of agrarian tribes for winter shelter. The most intact and exciting is Tre'r Ceiri – 'Place of Giants' – dating from 200 BC high on a mountain ledge on the

Llŷn peninsula in north Wales. I first visited it after a trip to Peru and considered it to rank as a British Machu Picchu. Six hundred metres in circumference and with walls and gateways intact, Tre'r Ceiri has breathtaking views over Snowdonia and Cardigan Bay. Its 150 huts, once probably thatched, appear to have been inhabited through the Roman occupation. They were partly demolished by looters in the nineteenth century following rumours that they concealed hoarded gold.

A smaller settlement survives at Chysauster (*c*.400 BC), on a hillside overlooking St Michael's Mount in Cornwall. It has a more modest layout of circular stockades, with single rooms and storage huts arranged round small courtyards. Each has a doorway facing east, away from the prevailing wind. Chysauster would have had an excellent view of the tin- and copper-trading vessels arriving and departing during the pre-Roman period. Various other Iron Age settlements have a similar plan, usually with ceremonial halls, presumably those of tribal chieftains.

The invasion of Britain by Julius Caesar in 55 BC and then by the emperor Claudius a century later opened its recorded history. Battles are fought, individuals named, trade develops, forts, roads and towns are built. Much of this can now be dated by scientific archaeology, as can the skeletons of their occupants. A triumphal arch was erected in AD 85 where the Romans first landed at Richborough on Kent's Thanet river. With its Corinthian columns and giant attic it was said to be a copy of the Arch of Titus in Rome, its marble from Carrara in Italy. Though the arch was later demolished, it clearly indicated a people who meant to stay.

The arrival of Roman legions began four centuries of alien rule over what became Britannia. The Roman occupation saw a building boom as intense as anywhere in the empire, to ensure the security of the new province in the face of initially rebellious tribes. The province extended over all of England and Wales but only briefly southern Scotland. Both the Scottish Picts and the

Irish posed a persistent threat. Military forts and other settlements were linked by some 2,000 miles of roads, from Isca Dumnoniorum (Exeter) in the south to Pons Aelius (Newcastle) in the north. They were paved, drained and kept in repair, becoming the defining phenomenon of Roman rule. It was said that a message would never again travel as fast across land until the post roads of the eighteenth century.

To the north, Hadrian's Wall was to be the longest such structure in Europe, marking as it did the empire's northernmost boundary. Within the first century of Roman occupation, twenty-eight new towns were founded throughout England and Wales, though it is not known who populated them other than colonists from elsewhere in the Roman Empire. British servants and slaves occupied adjacent compounds. Other towns were bases for tribal communities. One such was Caerwent for the Silures of south Wales – where Corinthian capitals have been found – and another was York, home to the initially troublesome Brigantes.

Searching Britain for relics of these settlements is not easy as almost all above ground have disappeared. Some of the towns were walled and fortified – substantial fragments surviving in London, York and Colchester – and most had stone buildings of a quality unlike any seen in Britain before. They were in the style of settlements found throughout the empire, a rectangular grid of streets round a basilica or town hall, a forum and baths. We can assume that public buildings would have been fronted by arcades, using classical orders on their columns. Almost everywhere, even a simple fort had an amphitheatre, used for gladiatorial contests, plays, ceremonies and executions. That at Caerleon in south Wales had an estimated capacity of 5,000, not equalled until modern times.

Since most Roman towns have vanished beneath later buildings, the finest examples of their architecture are the colonists' villas. Many are in isolated country, safe thanks to Roman law and order. They enjoyed extraordinary comforts, with reception rooms and bathrooms with hot and cold running water, all warmed by a plumbing system that fed underfloor ducts. So efficient was this heating that fireplaces were rare. The villas were built not just of wood and stone but of brick, lime mortar and plaster, their floors decorated with pictorial mosaics and their walls with murals. Some had simple glass windows. Pitched and red-tiled roofs were not unlike those in modern Italy. The native population would be in outhouses of mostly circular thatched huts, though over time many intermarried and graduated to 'Romano-British' status.

The most impressive surviving villa is at Fishbourne in Sussex, though three-quarters of the site still lurks beneath the A27. It was begun as early as AD 75, reputedly as the mansion of a local tribal chief favoured by the Romans. It is thought to have had a hundred rooms, including a large assembly hall and fifty mosaic floors, making it the largest known Roman villa north of the Alps. Whether it is on the scale of Sicily's palatial Casale remains to be seen when, perhaps one day, the A27 can be persuaded to reveal all. Another villa, at Lullingstone in Kent, includes a room converted into an early chapel. Its Chi-Rho Christograms and wall-paintings appear to be of Christians at prayer, one of the earliest depictions of Christianity in Britain.

Of the surviving villas my favourite is Chedworth, reached up a winding lane from the old Fosse Way in the Cotswolds. The buildings lie round a courtyard, underpinned by a most elaborate plumbing system feeding sauna and plunge baths. Walls carry murals and floors pictorial mosaics, offering clues to Roman lifestyle in everything from women's clothes to Christian worship. The loveliest mosaic is a celebration of Spring, dancing scantily clad and carrying a basket of flowers and a bird.

The most vivid recreation of a Roman villa is not far from Chedworth at Villa Ventorum. It was constructed in 2021 on mid-fourth century foundations on The Newt estate in Somerset by a

South African couple, Koos Bekker and Karen Roos. Careful research of surviving mosaics and other fragments allowed the archaeologist Nicola du Pisanie to re-erect an imagined facsimile. That it looks as if furnished by Ikea may reflect a timeless reality.

These new towns and villas cannot have had much relevance to the native population. Only some 15 per cent of Britons during the Roman period are thought to have lived in Roman buildings, occupying hutted Iron Age encampments with only the most primitive of facilities. But there had arrived on Britain's shores a practice of building – the mixing of clay, cutting of stones and tiling of roofs – that remained an example to later generations of builders. Its architecture was to live on above all in the design of churches, deferentially reborn in the style later to be known as Romanesque.

2.

The Saxon Era (400–1066)

In the year 410 the leaders of a now-integrated class of Latin-speaking Romano-Britons wrote to Emperor Honorius in Italy. They requested military aid to resist continuing Saxon and Pictish raids down England's east coast. The letter reflected the decay of order in the northern Roman Empire as its boundaries fell to incoming raiders and refugees. Honorius refused the request. Instead he withdrew his existing legions and told the Britons they were now a people on their own.

What happened in the former province of Britannia – present-day England and Wales – over the course of the fifth century remains obscure. England was once thought to have suffered a series of quasi-genocidal invasions from north Germany which destroyed or drove westwards an indigenous Celtic people and their language across the British mainland. This thesis was based on one sixth-century source, a Welsh monk named Gildas, fiercely hostile to what he saw as bloodthirsty newcomers from eastern parts. He became the source for all subsequent chroniclers, including the Venerable Bede in the eighth century.

There is no other literary or archaeological evidence of such an existential trauma and it is now generally discredited, notably in *The Emergence of the English,* by the historian Susan Oosthuizen. England clearly suffered raids, as it had long done from Scotland and across the North Sea, but none that constituted a systematic invasion. Nor was there evidence of military disruption or tribal uprising, of massacres, looting or ethnic flight.

The Saxon Era (400–1066)

DNA archaeology indicates some inflow of Germanic stock fleeing post-Roman turbulence in northern Europe. We know also that many former Roman colonies such as Colchester had long been settled with German veterans.

What appears to be the case is that England and Wales reverted to an Iron Age lifestyle as experienced before the Romans arrived. Where a town- and villa-dwelling aristocracy went into decline, they were supplanted by tribal chiefs and migratory warlords. We know that many magistrates remained in post, probably protected by armed bands or militias. But Roman roads, basilicas and amphitheatres fell into disuse, with no imperial authority to maintain or even need them. The sense must have been of an era departed. In a rare record, an eighth-century observer gazes on the relics of ancient Bath and tells of the splendour of the masonry: 'The fates destroyed it, strong buildings crashed. The work of giants moulders away. The roofs have fallen, the towers are in ruins.'

The result is that we can glean only the most scant evidence of British architecture in this period. Whatever their origins, the inhabitants of the eastern side of Britain lived in wooden buildings – even the Anglo-Saxon word for building was 'timbrian' or timber – few of which survive. Evidence has been excavated from this period in Yeavering in Northumberland and similar houses have been reconstructed in West Stow in Suffolk. They are simple huts of wood and thatch, devoid of architectural detail.

One building style that was bequeathed by the Romans was that of the Christian church. While it is clear that paganism took hold of much of eastern England – possibly influenced by Germanic migrants – what became known as Celtic Christianity survived in the west. It flourished in Wales and Cornwall (and Brittany) and extended beyond the boundaries of the Roman empire in Ireland. Whether there was a Celtic church distinct from that of Rome is now questioned, but there was clearly a sense of mission emanating from monastic foundations in Wales and Ireland. Figures such as St Patrick, St Ninian and St Columba nurtured a faith that spread across western Britain in the fifth and sixth centuries – dubbed the Age of Saints in Wales – even as it dimmed with the incursion of paganism in eastern Britain.

What Rome left of churches we do not know, since Saxon churches were regularly rebuilt over the centuries and almost all were altered or extended. Of the thousands that were probably built between the sixth and the eleventh centuries, scholars estimate that some fifty still exist, with a further two hundred displaying Saxon traces. Added confusion arises from the early practice of new churches reusing stones and sometimes entire doorways and windows from derelict Roman sites.

Most Saxon churches adopted the rectangular plan of the Roman basilica, often with an east wall bulging to form a circular passage or apse, perhaps above a crypt. A less common plan was that of the 'tower/nave' or turriform church, arranged round a central shrine with a tower rising overhead. It might add transepts and become cruciform. This was the plan of eastern Byzantine churches, copied in Italy's Ravenna and by Charlemagne for his chapel at Aachen. That it should have occurred as far north as Britain is remarkable, presumably the influence of migrant missionaries.

The earliest church in Britain is assumed to be St Martin's Canterbury, fragments of which suggest it may have been the chapel of Queen Bertha of Kent, host to Augustine's first mission to England in 597. When he first landed his party were treated as aliens in what was a pagan part of England. Bertha, a French-born Christian, was clearly a determined woman. She welcomed Augustine and secured the conversion of her husband, Aethelbert of Kent. We assume she instigated the foundation of St Martin's, although like two other churches in the cathedral enclave it shows traces of Roman brickwork and thus the tantalizing possibility of a link back to Roman places of worship.

The Saxon Era (400–1066)

An early church retaining its original appearance is St Peter's Bradwell-on-Sea in Essex, lost in a lonely meadow adjoining the ruin of a Roman seaside fort. It was reputedly founded in 654 by St Cedd on a mission to bring the Ionian rite of Lindisfarne to southern England. This was at a time of rivalry with Canterbury's Roman rite, soon to be resolved in Rome's favour at the Synod of Whitby (664). The building was saved for posterity as a barn but has since been restored and is a most moving survivor of early Christianity. Another survivor is the tiny St Laurence in Bradford-on-Avon, its foundation possibly dating from 709 or earlier. Its exterior carries relief decoration known as blind arcading, possibly of the early eleventh century.

England's finest Saxon church is that of Brixworth in Northamptonshire, thought to date from the eighth century. Its size indicates that it was almost certainly a monastic foundation. Even from a distance the view of All Saints Brixworth on its hill is exceptional. The brickwork looks Roman in its simplicity. The interior has an eerie dignity, an orderly space of rounded arches embracing a spacious choir and apse. Most significant is that the arches and window surrounds reuse Roman bricks, some traced to as far away as Leicester. In few places have I enjoyed such a sensation of architectural continuity, of masons practising a style and with materials in use over some four centuries since the departure of the Romans.

There is no greater contrast than the church of Llandanwg, buried in sand dunes near Harlech in Wales. It boasts a foundation of 453, based on the authority of a fifth-century standing stone. I first came across this single-cell structure on a wild winter's evening. It was lit only by candles with the surf of Cardigan Bay roaring in the background. A notice declared it 'a refuge of solace, simplicity and peace'. The church fabric is near impossible to date as it was long derelict and unroofed until restored by the Society for the Protection of Ancient Buildings in 1884. If only in its solitude, Llandanwg carries us back to this earliest period of British faith. Its secular message is for all time.

This architecture illustrates how a hierarchical church enabled Rome's ecclesiastical authority to exert a continued influence over post-Roman Britain. Contact did not cease with the withdrawal of the legions. Leaders went on regular pilgrimages to Rome. When describing the churches built by Abbot Benedict Biscop of Northumbria, the Venerable Bede described them as 'in the Roman manner which [Biscop] always loved' when on his visits to Rome. He is recorded as bringing his own masons from France. After Whitby, Pictish Christians asked in York for advice on their new churches. The monks told them to design 'in the Roman fashion'.

These regular references to Rome are clear in their inference. To the builders of churches – principal custodians of architectural tradition – the legacy of Rome was ubiquitous. It was typified at Biscop's Monkwearmouth, where each of the tower stages took stones from an adjacent Roman site. A British Library manuscript of the period depicts the building of the Tower of Babel, looking remarkably like Monkwearmouth. Most distinctive is the precious survival of early crypts in the north's Hexham and Ripon and in the mausoleum at Repton in Derbyshire. Dating from the eighth century, Repton's underground chamber is a glade of arcades, crude capitals and grooved columns. To walk through them is to sense the power of the Roman tradition living on from centuries before.

Little is known of the impact of the Vikings on British architecture. The word 'window' is of Norse derivation, while the few round-towered churches of East Anglia are said to originate with the Danes in the first half of the tenth century. The Anglo-Saxon chronicle remarked that they were peaceable and 'ploughed to support themselves'. They converted to Christianity in what became known as 'church-towns' or kirkbys.

The Saxon Era (400–1066)

The most significant event of the period was the coronation in 1043 of Edward the Confessor (r.1042–66) as king of a by then united England. A contemporary account had him 'of outstanding height, with milky white hair and beard . . . always walking with eyes downcast, graciously affable to one and all'. Though his father was a Saxon, Edward was French-speaking and raised by a Norman mother. He moved his throne from Winchester, ancient capital of Wessex, to the nation's biggest city, London, but he wanted no truck with its potentially hostile Anglo-Danish citizenry. He based himself and his court upstream at Westminster.

This creation by Edward of a bipolar capital determined the development of London for all time. Westminster was a royal colony, comprising a palace, abbey and monastery. We know little of the palace but much of the abbey, which survived and was recorded into the Middle Ages. Its design had little in common with Saxon churches elsewhere in England and derived from the abbey of Jumièges in Normandy, the king's childhood home. The nave was lined with Norman arcades, concealing aisles and rising to a row of windows above the arcade and beneath the roof known as a clerestory. The new abbey was only partly built by the time of Edward's death in 1066, but was used for William I's coronation after the Battle of Hastings a year later.

3.

Norman Britain (1066–1170)

The River Wear at Durham curves gently through a sudden wooded ravine. I watched the morning sun picking out an oarsman gliding his craft downstream. The scene was idyllic. Yet from the riverbank, it was two cliffs of stone rising into the sky that held the view. Even today, Durham's castle and cathedral are the unmistakable architecture of power. Their raw stone expresses military authority and the authority of faith alike.

William the Conqueror's campaign for the English throne in 1066 had been opposed by many of his barons as outside their feudal obligation. He had to promise any who came with him rich rewards from an England that was larger and richer by far than Normandy. Conquest therefore turned from the customary homage and tribute to occupation and plunder. Within months virtually all England's Saxon earls had been dispossessed of their estates. Bishops were toppled from their thrones. Some 90 per cent of productive land passed to Norman ownership.

In northern England, the result in 1069 was a Northumbrian revolt and brutal suppression, the 'harrowing of the north'. Durham's castle was begun in 1072 as the episcopal residence and work on its cathedral started in 1077. The castle hall contained the most sumptuous of Norman arches while the cathedral, and particularly its interior, was to be in the van of European architecture. It symbolized William's ambition that his newly expanded realm be seen as both secure and splendid. The round-arched nave arcades rise like giant oaks, alternately fluted and chevroned, tall enough to convey an almost Gothic elegance. The arches rest on simple cushion capitals but are decorated with the signature of Norman architecture: courses of zig-zag and dog-tooth.

Durham's roof was not wooden, like that of Ely and most other cathedrals at the time, but of stone. This war on innovation would have astonished visitors in the early 1100s. The roof was composed of ribs rising to a central ridge, thought to be the first such 'pointed' vault on this scale in Europe. Durham was a radical work of medieval engineering, produced at the periphery of the Christian world and testament to that world's coherence. It remains the glory of Britain's pre-Gothic age.

Historians emphasize that early Norman architecture was pre-dated by much that was already taking place in Saxon England before 1066. What was new about the Normans was their unleashing of a building frenzy more extensive probably than any prior to the industrial revolution. Though only 8,000 Normans are thought to have migrated to join some two million Saxon inhabitants, they represented a new aristocracy that was determined to settle. Like their Viking predecessors they integrated well, albeit continuing to speak French. But William was creating a new nation state and needed visible manifestations of his authority. Above all he needed military bases in a land that had not been heavily fortified, at least since Rome's departure.

The result was the hasty erection of castles across England's south-east and the border with Wales. The first were at Porchester, Dover, Rochester and Hedingham but within twenty years some fifty castles followed. Most were simple structures, comprising earth mounds or mottes, surmounted by a wooden palisade protecting a house or keep. Many would be later rebuilt of stone. Wales did not initially submit to William's rule and here he turned to his most loyal friend and follower, William fitz Osbern, who had funded much of the invasion fleet. When William suffered a bad fall at the initial landing, it was fitz Osbern who declared to the army that their commander had merely seized England and anointed it with his blood.

Fitz Osbern's reward was the earldom of Hereford and land from the south coast of England north to Herefordshire and the Welsh border. The historian John Goodall records him founding castles from Carisbrooke on the Isle of Wight to Berkeley, Monmouth, Wigmore and the great tower of Chepstow, where he also built a monastery. Much of Chepstow was built with repurposed Roman bricks. An impressive tower of this period survives at Exeter, its windows more Anglo-Saxon than Norman, as do castles from the late 1060s in Warwick, Lincoln, Oxford and York.

London's White Tower, begun in 1075, was exceptional. It was a palace within a castle, surrounded by two lines of fortification. It embraced state chambers, dormitories, wash-houses, a chapel and a prison. Another palatial tower followed at Colchester, with others at Norwich and Richmond in Yorkshire. In general, castles in stone rather than perishable brick were built for strength over architectural subtlety. William's were to determine the style of English castles for the next three centuries.

The spiritual wing of the conquest saw William embark on an ambitious rebuilding of virtually all England's cathedrals and enhancing hundreds of its churches. With almost every Norman baron there arrived a Norman bishop, intent on evicting the 'rude unlearned' Saxon clergy. The only Saxon bishop to keep his job was Wulfstan of Worcester, but even he could not save his cathedral. As the Saxon structure came crashing down he complained that 'we have destroyed the work of saints. We neglect our souls so that we can build up stones.'

To reform the Saxon Church, William appointed his senior clergyman, Lanfranc of Caen, as archbishop of Canterbury. Lanfranc reorganized what became seventeen dioceses. No fewer than a dozen cathedrals were immediately demolished and subjected to reconstruction. At Canterbury, Lanfranc obliterated the

Saxon building and imported Norman masons and even Norman stone for its replacement. Of the new cathedral all that survives today is the crypt, its entrancing column capitals depicting nature, animals and humans, sacred and profane.

The former minster of Winchester was treated even more drastically. This is vividly illustrated by the old church's footings today lying excavated in the grass, overawed by the new one next to it. The latter was comparable in size to the cathedrals of Ottonian Germany or even St Peter's Rome. Only the Norman transepts remain today but they make their point. Formed of tiers of naked arches and window openings, they are like the walls of a military keep, supremely evocative of conquest.

The threat to William's new state was chiefly from Danes, Picts and local rebels down the eastern side of England. Here alongside his castles he commanded a line of monumental cathedrals, surviving in whole or part at Ely, Norwich, Lincoln and Durham. At Norwich the new bishop, Herbert de Losinga, was shameless in his extravagance. On moving from his seat at Thetford, he seized and demolished a third of the town to make way for his cathedral. The tower is panelled in relief carving that dates from the early 1100s and depicts portholes and geometrical shapes. To the north at Lincoln, the west front is all that remains of the Norman church but its wall of masonry seems to be expecting an imminent siege.

In Wales three new dioceses were created, at Llandaff, Bangor and St David's, the last crucial in securing the south Welsh March at a time when north Wales had not yet acknowledged Norman rule. The ancient shrine of St David in Pembrokeshire was visited by William in 1081, indicating its strategic importance opposite Ireland. A new cathedral was begun in the 1130s but this was succeeded by another after just fifty years. This was to be the last major Norman church in Britain, built as it was after the Gothic style was well established in England. It is thought that the Welsh masons may have been deliberately rejecting the new fashion to assert their distance from England.

What is certain is that St David's represents Norman architecture at its most developed. In his *Romanesque Architecture and Sculpture in Wales*, the historian Malcolm Thurlby has listed twenty-two different versions of the style's signature chevron motif in its interior. Under Henry II (r.1154–89), penitent for the murder of Becket, the pope allowed two pilgrimages to St David's to equal one to Rome, an accolade of immense value to the cathedral. Today, lost in its wooded valley and far from any urban bustle, the cathedral looks down to the seashore, still evocative of the age of pilgrimage.

William's burst of cathedral building was equalled by his promotion of monasteries. A total of forty British monasteries in 1066 had risen to 700 by 1200. The initial beneficiaries were Normandy's Benedictines, invited to evict and supplant their Saxon brethren. The new abbeys were of cathedral splendour, notably at Tewkesbury, Bury St Edmunds and Castle Acre in Norfolk. The west front of Tewkesbury (1123) was composed of a single six-shafted Norman arch rising to the apex of the facade, claimed to be the tallest arch in Christendom. The hospital of St Cross outside Winchester (1136) boasted a chapel of equally episcopal dimensions. The hospice was charged with caring for thirteen poor men and dispensing 'a morsel of bread and a horn of beer' to passing strangers. This so-called wayfarer's dole remains a charitable obligation to all who apply at the gate. Determined hikers still successfully put it to the test.

The most determined newcomers were the Cistercians. Arriving in the 1120s, they were disciplined, hard-working and well organized, soon with an extraordinary fifty-four foundations in Britain. These included the majestic Rievaulx and Fountains abbeys in Yorkshire, Forde in Dorset and no fewer than thirteen in Wales. They formed an ecclesiastical freemasonry outside the formal Church hierarchy. Through their wealth they were able to pioneer – or bring from France – a new quality of collegiate living.

Norman Britain (1066–1170)

Monastic enclaves comprised cloisters, dormitories, halls and private quarters of a luxury that England had not seen since Roman times. Monasteries constituted a new Norman middle class, benefiting from advancement by merit rather than birth.

How immediate was the rebuilding of parish churches is not clear, but it was drastic. There had been some 650 Saxon churches in the county of Norfolk alone, of which few survive. What is certain is that many buildings rivalled cathedrals in their craftsmanship. The chancel arch at Tickencote in Rutland comprised an ostentatious repetition of six distinct mouldings. Each was different, zig-zag, beak-headed, crenellated or adorned with heads of humans and monsters in abundance.

Another example is the modest church of Kilpeck in Herefordshire (*c.*1140). Its architecture may be humble Norman, but its eaves carry no fewer than eighty-five sculpted corbels, as rich in pagan and mythological symbols as in Christian ones. The subjects are biblical, bawdy, animal and human. There is even a rare sheela na gig, a sculpture of a woman with her legs apart. The south doorway is adorned with a gathering of beasts, snakes, birds and monsters dancing attendance on a tree of life. Here, in a tiny village that was once in Wales, we find carving that would do credit to a metropolitan cathedral. British architecture was never again to display such decorative invention as in the arches of Norman churches.

As in Wales, so in Scotland, wholly beyond the reach of the conquest, church architecture flourished. Dalmeny church outside Edinburgh (1160) boasted a zig-zag-coated south door and a chancel arch with 'beast-head' corbels. Far to the north on Orkney, Kirkwall Cathedral was built by its Norwegian rulers from Trondheim in 1137, though its masons' marks are said to indicate craftsmen who had also worked on Durham.

By the early years of the twelfth century, church building was joined by advances in domestic architecture. The Conqueror's flamboyant son William Rufus (r.1087–1100), England's possibly first and certainly most extravagant gay monarch, ordered two remarkable buildings. One was a new ceremonial hall for his palace at Westminster, its ancient walls surviving to this day. The other was Norwich Castle (1097), intended to rival London's White Tower. Though its interior has since been gutted its exterior remains a marvel of early Norman design, sharing relief panels with those on the tower of Norwich Cathedral. Royal castles followed at Corfe in Dorset, Kenilworth in Warwickshire and Bamburgh in Northumbria. Away from this grandeur almost no Norman domestic building survives, merely monastic fragments and the ghost of a facade to Lincoln's charming Jews House.

Norman architecture no longer reflected the necessities of invasion and conquest. France and England were increasingly one nation culturally as well as politically. Monarchs, aristocrats and priests moved back and forth across the Channel, absorbing influences from France as well as from Germany and Italy. The result, seen in the vaults of Durham, the portals of Tewkesbury and the sculptures of Kilpeck, was architecture of a quality to equal any in Europe.

4.
Gothic Dawn (1170–1245)

While William and his sons were building a new Anglo-Norman state, new forces were stirring in another part of their native France. The Île-de-France region round Paris was experiencing what came to be called the twelfth-century Renaissance. This centred on the city's abbeys and cathedral schools, following a debate between the radical rationalist Peter Abelard, lover of Héloïse, and the conservative Cistercian monk Bernard of Clairvaux.

The stability and prosperity of the Paris region at the time led to a burst of cathedral building, similar to that seen in England under the Conqueror. The style of its architecture was conventionally Romanesque. This changed dramatically in 1144 when Abbot Suger of St-Denis outside Paris unveiled his new choir to a gilded assembly of French royalty and bishops. He showed them a chamber ablaze with light. Its novelty lay in redistributing the weight of a roof onto pointed arches and buttresses and freeing the walls to carry larger windows.

Suger was doing more than displaying a new engineering. He was expressing the philosophy of Abelard and his followers in architectural terms. He asserted that 'the dull mind rises to truth through that which is material', and by material he meant the built church. Architecture's contribution to truth was 'the use of light in abundance'. In a Romanesque church worshippers had been expected to bow their heads submissively in mystic darkness. In Suger's church they lifted them up to heaven. They sought 'the light of God received in splendour'. The implication for architecture was clear.

The thesis had its critics. Bernard was shocked at this interpretation of worship. He replied in a tract that he 'deemed as dung whatever shines with beauty, charms the ear and delights through fragrance'. He deplored a church 'that clothes her stones with gold but lets her sons go naked'. The argument over the extravagance of church architecture would obsess Christians for centuries. For the time being, Suger won. Bishops dispersed from St-Denis eager to follow his example and spread the word abroad.

The pointed arch had appeared in Burgundy and elsewhere in the early years of the twelfth century, possibly brought back from the Levant by crusaders. Suger's novelty was to convert it into a complete programme of church design. He created what became a frenzy of flying buttresses, soaring vaults, gables, turrets and windows. These were soon to be seen in Chartres and Notre-Dame and across the Île-de-France as bishops vied with each other in architectural splendour.

England at the time was under the same rule as much of western France. The empire of the Plantagenet Henry II combined with that of his wife, Eleanor of Aquitaine, stretched from the Scottish border to the Pyrenees. King and queen would travel regularly across the Channel, attended by a French-speaking court as alert to events in France as in London. England had already seen fifteen of its cathedrals rebuilt in the Norman style, their dioceses prospering from the surging wool trade with the continent. The monasteries had followed suit, in particular the Cistercians.

The earliest use of the pointed arch in Britain is thought to have been in an abbey, possibly at Byland or Rievaulx in Yorkshire, in the mid-twelfth century, or at St Bartholomew's church in London's Smithfield. The symbolic catalyst for its arrival was the murder in 1170 of Thomas Becket in Canterbury Cathedral.

Gothic Dawn (1170–1245)

What was a political trauma for Henry II – accused of ordering the murder – was a commercial opportunity for the monks of Canterbury. Within weeks, reports of miracles associated with Becket turned their cathedral into a pilgrimage destination. The monks eagerly promoted their new saint, declaring that garments dipped in his carefully preserved blood would 'make the blind see, the dumb speak, the lame walk, the sick . . . whole'. Tens of thousands came to Canterbury from across Europe.

The crowds needed an appropriate shrine. This problem was solved when in 1174 another disaster afflicted Canterbury, the gutting of its eastern presbytery by fire. Tenders were invited for its reconstruction and the job went to a French mason, William of Sens, whose own cathedral had recently been rebuilt in the pointed style. He was bidden 'to do the work in a different fashion from the old', employing the 'broken arch' but preserving side chapels and the Norman crypt below. In other words, unlike his contemporaries in France, he had to work the Gothic style into a Romanesque frame, as was the case with much of early English Gothic. As a result it rarely soared like the churches in the Île-de-France.

Work on Canterbury began at once, but William returned to France after an accident and was replaced by an English mason, also William, of whom we know little. He appears among the 'greats' of architecture on the frieze of the Albert Memorial in Hyde Park. The new presbytery was in a transitional style. Its gently pointed arches strained upwards, above arcades that, in the Trinity Chapel, were slender and of polished Purbeck marble. The column capitals had composite acanthus leaves and scrolls, as if echoing a now archaic classicism. Overall, Canterbury's new east end had the solidity of Romanesque yet with a Gothic elegance.

The shrine formed the climax to the endeavour of pilgrimage. Visitors would have progressed from entry in the transepts, bypassing what was still a dingy Norman nave as well as the site of Becket's murder. They would have gazed up at medieval windows telling the Bible story in dazzling detail – in colours they might never have seen before – and then reached the Trinity Chapel. Here the saint was honoured with what became a colossal mound of gold and precious donations, of which some 2,200 were listed in 1307. During Henry VIII's dissolution in the sixteenth century, twenty carts were needed to remove the hoard to London. A single Protestant candle is all that remains today.

Beyond the shrine lay a separate Corona Chapel housing a fragment of Becket's skull, its columns of pink marble to honour the archbishop's spilled blood. The chapel was guarded by old-fashioned Norman arches, decorated with zig-zag and attributed to the English William. Pilgrims would then have moved down into the candlelit gloom of the crypt. This was a cathedral within a cathedral, a gallery of Norman capital carvings and murals, chapels and shrines. The cathedral was and is a textbook example of the transition from Norman to Gothic in English architecture.

Canterbury was soon imitated. In the West Country the canons of Wells, long averse to sharing their diocese with Glastonbury and Bath, decided in the 1170s to rebuild their cathedral in the wake of the Canterbury fire. Here there was no doubt over style. Wells's sharply pointed nave arcades rise to a triforium of blind arcading and above it a tier of clerestory windows, bathing the nave below in light. The same happened at Lincoln, where Hugh of Avalon arrived in 1186 as bishop, eager for his own glory and, in particular, posthumous sainthood. This he assumed would reward a great work of architecture. In 1185 the old Norman cathedral was mostly destroyed by an earthquake and once again the chapter took the opportunity to switch to Gothic. The new Lincoln became a monument to the pointed arch, here the work of a French mason, Geoffrey de Noyes.

Gothic Dawn (1170–1245)

Hugh's most intriguing decision was to leave in place the old west front and three Norman arches of its 'gateway to heaven'. This respect for the past leaves most English cathedrals as catalogues of each period in their history, where continental ones were more often rebuilt. More bizarre was Hugh's 'crazy vault' in the choir, with its lopsided transverse ribs. They were assumed to represent 'birds stretching out their wings to fly'. Experts claim there is a pattern, but anyone who can understand Pevsner's account of it deserves a medal.

The west front of Peterborough is a startling Gothic overlay of a Norman facade. Here three giant doorways with pointed arches take up the entire facade, half concealing the previous west front behind. They were erected to welcome pilgrims after the local abbot claimed to have acquired a Becket relic from Canterbury, a valuable acquisition. Forty years later came the serene consummation of early English Gothic in the west front of Ripon Cathedral (1160) in Yorkshire. Here the facade is entirely of lancet windows, quiet and elegant above three modest doorways, Gothic at its most sedate.

The style in England reached its apogee at Salisbury. Here in 1219 the canons asked Rome if they could move their cathedral from Old Sarum on its hill to a site adjacent to the river below. In what must be the most poetic of planning permissions the pope replied, 'Let us spread joyfully to the plains . . . where the fields are beautiful and there is freedom from oppression.' Salisbury is the new Gothic at full stretch. Arches now have multiple mouldings. The triforium ripples with trefoils and quatrefoils. Black Purbeck marble arcades are sleek and handsome. Only the famous steeple was not built for another century.

Throughout this period, cathedrals and abbeys remained the chief arenas of architectural innovation. They were joined by parish churches, those that had not been rebuilt by the Normans. The often highly ornamented Norman doorways were supplanted by plain arches. Churches became taller and more slender. Decoration was standardized according to masons' patterns. Of these the most common was the 'stiff-leaf' column capital. This took the form of acanthus leaves growing from the tops of columns to encircle their crowns. Each leaf was carefully bent back, concealing its stalk and thus forming a bowl to support the architrave above.

These leaves were a delightful introduction of nature into the formality of church liturgy, as if to symbolize its marriage to the living world outside. They had one variation, in which the leaf tilted to the side to become 'windblown stiff-leaf'. This new English church at the turn of the thirteenth century, with its plain arches, capitals and lancet windows, had a simple dignity that made it a favourite among Victorian Gothic revivalists. Its style was dubbed 'Early English' or 'first pointed' and was much recommended for new suburban churches in the nineteenth century.

One feature of Gothic now largely forgotten was its use of colour. When the nineteenth-century architect George Gilbert Scott came to restore Salisbury Cathedral, his workmen found traces of medieval paint behind carvings and beneath whitewash. The black stone of the arcades was contrasted with chiaroscuro red and white of walls and ceilings. Vaulting ribs, Scott recorded, were 'decorated in full colour while the inter-spaces were occupied by medallions in which red is again the predominating tint'. We cannot imagine the impact such colouring must have had on medieval parishioners and pilgrims. By Scott's day, colour could be seen everywhere and the role of the church in brightening the lives of worshippers was no more.

Ever since the Reformation ordained that Gothic should be white or grey, only the most daring of Victorians dissented (such as the polychromist William Butterfield). The employment of colour continues to be the medieval feature that has defied all attempts at revival. Apart from the interwar restorations of the

Gothic Dawn (1170–1245)

architect Ernest Tristram at Exeter and Bristol, the nearest approximation to the appearance of a true medieval cathedral is the annual illumination of the west front of Amiens Cathedral outside Paris. Its precision lighting brings doors, vaults and carvings to life and transforms our appreciation of the true nature of the Gothic style. The technique has also been applied to the west front of Westminster Abbey.

Of buildings other than churches, the most prominent were the domestic arrangements attached to them, notably cloisters, chapter houses and monastic dormitories. At the same time the stability of the Norman state, at least in England, meant less need for the security of the walled castle and keep. Military structures thus mutated into dynastic and family houses. As the architectural historian John Goodall has pointed out, the concept of the 'real' castle fused with the eagerness of aristocrats seeking 'to live in buildings that made manifest their wealth, advertised their vocation and articulated their power' by continuing to reside in them. It was an eagerness that has survived to the present day. Throughout English history royalty and aristocracy have clung to medieval ceremony.

The romanticism of chivalry obsessed the long reigns of Henry III in the thirteenth century and Edward III in the fourteenth. A castle was the natural setting for chivalric display and with it went a craving to 'crenellate' even the most unmilitaristic dwelling. Since castles indicated territorial power, permission to fortify one's house rested with the monarch and thus became a source of royal revenue. Some 500 licences to crenellate are recorded over the Middle Ages. It often meant little more than the building of superfluous gatehouses, walls and battlements and the digging of moats. Little attention was paid to a capacity to resist a siege.

Only along England's borders with Scotland and Wales was there felt to be a need for properly fortified residences. The inner gatehouse of Gilbert de Clare's moated Caerphilly Castle in south Wales (1268) was the grandest and also the most fortified of private castles. It is equalled by the dramatic Powis Castle in Montgomeryshire, a mid-thirteenth-century fortress, now rising above landscaped terraces and with magnificent Tudor and Jacobean interiors. In Scotland, political insecurity led to the continued building of habitable keeps throughout the Middle Ages. Lesser grandees built what were called 'pele' towers. These were usually modest towers or keeps attached to ordinary houses, to which a family could retreat in times of trouble. The ultimate pele tower is Appleby Castle, ancestral seat of the Clifford family since the Middle Ages, comprising a seventeenth-century mansion with a passage to its adjacent twelfth-century keep.

Many of these structures borrowed features from France. Caerlaverock in Dumfries has a massive gatehouse and is built on a triangular plan inside a moat, unlike any castle in England. These houses became the natural residences of the rich and powerful, evolving a style now known as 'Scots baronial'. It was defined by corner towers, crenellated parapets and robust front doors, preferably with a cannon or two in sight. The style survived much enhanced into the nineteenth century.

Of surviving domestic architecture, the most distinctive is the hall house. This was developed round a central (or 'great') hall, a place of social receiving, eating and entertaining. In medieval times it was where the lord of the manor and his family ate publicly with their relatives, friends and tenants, a ceremony that was considered a feature of feudal cohesion. Lady Anne Clifford in the seventeenth century was said to have reverted to the tradition by travelling with her retinue round her various castles, dining publicly with her tenantry in their halls.

The hall itself would be entered through a side door at one end of the facade onto the courtyard. This led into a passage separated from the hall by an ornamental screen, possibly with a minstrels' gallery above. Known as a screens passage, this conserved heat in the hall itself. In early times the fire would be in the centre of the hall with smoke escaping through louvres in the roof. By the thirteenth century this configuration had been replaced by a fireplace and side chimney, the fireplace surround becoming a focus of family insignia.

At the far end of the hall from the entrance would be a raised dais lit by a prominent, sometimes two-storey bay window. Here would be the 'high table' at which the head of the family ate or conducted business. Behind the dais wall would be the 'smart' end of the house, the owner's private chambers and possibly an upper floor known as a solar. At the other end of the hall behind the screen passage would be the kitchens and service quarters. Over time, the smart end grew ever grander and the service end ever more expansive, each wing extending round courts and back yards.

The plan proved resistant to change down the centuries. It marked the owner as someone of local distinction and longevity. This antiquity compensated for any lack of grandeur. The greatest accolade P. G. Wodehouse could pay to Lord Emsworth's Blandings Castle was not its architectural splendour but that it was 'one of the oldest-inhabited houses in England'. A typical hall house could not be dated, being as old as the lordship it served. More to the point, its plan was flexible. It could be expanded – or if needs be contracted – without losing its dignity. Some of the greatest houses to survive from the Middle Ages, such as Knole and Penshurst in Kent, are built round hall houses.

Over this period another English tradition was also embedded, that of the informal medieval street plan, notably in the City of London. The city had been recolonized after the abandonment of Roman Londinium in the fifth century. But new buildings went up not on the former Roman grid but along tracks and passages that had led across the City's waste ground during the Dark

Ages. These tracks, soon lined with timber-framed cottages and tenements, became the new London. This led to the anarchic pattern of rights of way that has ruled much of City planning to the present day. It has dictated access to ancient churchyards and impeded the footings of skyscrapers. This in turn has held at bay the frigid grid pattern of most modern city centres, bequeathing a modicum of intimacy to even the most gargantuan London property developments.

5.

The Glory of Decorated (1245–1348)

The reign of King John (1199–1216) and the collapse of England's Plantagenet realm in France began the separation of Britain as a nation from continental Europe. John's concession of Magna Carta to his barons in 1215 and the revolt of Simon de Montfort against his successor Henry III (r.1216–72) in 1264 gave birth to the eventual rule of law and the rise of parliament. They demonstrated the emergence of a distinctive political identity for the people of Britain. For Henry this identity was rooted elsewhere in a personal fixation with his distant predecessor Edward the Confessor. Henry spent the latter part of his reign seeking to rebuild Edward's most lasting creation, Westminster Abbey, as a shrine to his forebear. And just as Edward in the eleventh century had looked to France for architectural inspiration, so now did Henry, though it would be wrong to think English masons were unaware of developments on the continent.

The Paris region at the time was engaged in a frenzy of episcopal building not unlike that seen after Bishop Suger's initiative in the 1120s. The new French *rayonnant* style had been introduced, again at Suger's old abbey of St-Denis in 1231. Its defining features were rose windows and giant clerestories. Height was everything. Walls became lightweight frames for ever greater expanses of glass, while vaults and buttresses likewise soared upwards. In 1267 the choir at Amiens reached 42 metres, driving Beauvais in 1272 to 48 metres. Soon even the smallest towns of the Île-de-France were erecting churches of an ostentation far beyond their needs.

The climax of *rayonnant* was the Sainte-Chapelle in Paris, built in the 1240s. This small rectangular cage of stone was almost entirely walled by stained-glass windows. It obsessed Henry III after a visit and became the model for St Stephen's Chapel in his palace at Westminster. This in turn became what was called Gothic's court style. In 1245, Henry's master mason, Henry de Reynes, began work on Westminster Abbey, possibly using elements from Rheims Cathedral in France, though his link with it is not established. It initiated what the Victorians called the Decorated Gothic period.

Decorated lasted roughly from the start of Westminster Abbey in the 1240s to the Black Death of 1348. It liberated Gothic from its 'Early English' straitjacket, giving a sense of visual movement to windows, doors, arcades and towers. The new Westminster was clearly French in inspiration. The vault was higher than any in England. The windows and clerestory were exceptionally tall in relation to the nave's width.

The most distinctive innovation of Decorated was the dividing of windows by stone bars, giving support for far more glass than the simple lancet. It extended the load-bearing properties of a wall and admitted more light. Probably first used at Binham Abbey in Norfolk in the early 1240s, it gave window tracery a sculptural form. The tops of windows were filled with three-leaf and four-leaf patterns. Later tracery turned curvilinear, bars repeating themselves like the cells of a fishing net in a style called reticulated. The west window of York Minster contains a shape dubbed the 'heart of Yorkshire', beneath which Yorkshire couples are traditionally photographed. The French enthusiasm for rose windows was widely copied.

Finest of the new Decorated cathedrals was Exeter. Its chapter levied on their clergy reputedly England's first income tax to pay for it, helpfully keeping records of the progress of the work. The two original Norman towers were left flanking a new nave, like

The Glory of Decorated (1245–1348)

bodyguards supporting the longest continuous medieval roof in England. This was the work of a master builder, Thomas of Witney, from 1313 to 1342, who was followed by William Joy until the Black Death. Thomas's west front is a lofty gallery of Gothic statuary built in front of a west window rich in tracery. Its animated figures are eroded beyond recognition. If we can restore medieval tracery then why not medieval statuary?

Inside, an arcade of columns stretches eastwards, each composed of sixteen shafts of Purbeck marble. Arches of the creamiest limestone rise to a clerestory of cooler Caen stone. Above is a vault of eleven ribs to each bay, meeting at a roofline adorned with celebrated bosses of biblical scenes interspersed with foliage. Overlooking the nave is a loft of colourful angels playing their instruments, an invaluable record of medieval music-making.

Exeter delights in this fusion of architecture and sculpture, requiring a table mirror to see it from the nave below. The chancel screen of 1324 dances with animal and human faces. The cathedral's final treasure is the retrochoir and Lady Chapel, blessed with one of the few attempts to restore medieval colouring, by E. W. Tristram in the 1930s. He gives us an all-too-brief glimpse of how these great churches might have looked in their prime – and we can only hope might one day look again.

Other cathedrals seized on the new inventiveness. At Wells the crossing at the east end of the nave in 1338 acquired huge scissor arches to keep it from collapsing, a striking work of medieval engineering. They concealed what is a gallery of some 200 carved capitals dating from the mid-thirteenth century. These turned from the biblical and religious subjects familiar on a cathedral's west front to scenes from everyday life. A farmer chases a fox, boys steal fruit, a cobbler repairs a shoe, a man has toothache. Each is a vernacular masterpiece, fit to stand comparison with the crypt at Canterbury. The toothache man peers above the tomb of a bishop, who duly became an informal patron saint of toothache.

Wells Cathedral shared with Exeter the skills of Thomas of Witney. His serene east end of the 1320s, its retrochoir and Lady Chapel, reflect in their vaults Thomas's known fascination with geometry. The Gothic historian Olive Cook compared the pattern of ceiling ribs with classicism's evolution of the baroque. It 'reminds us, despite the difference of idiom, of the affinity between the two great architectural expressions of the same faith'. Adjacent lies the cathedral's chapter house. A spacious staircase curves upwards to open into a chamber whose circular vault rises like a giant palm tree from a central trunk. The vault has sixteen shafts that splay outwards to form thirty-two ribs, touching those from the surrounding bays. Windows are everywhere. It is a vivid reminder of the putative origins of the Gothic style in the trees and other wonders of nature.

A similar sense of English Gothic at an aesthetic climax is found in another chapter house, that of Southwell Minster in Nottinghamshire (c.1300). Here the sculptors adorned their building with the fruits of woods and fields. They took the stiff-leaf of early Gothic and unstiffened it. Leaves are bent, twisted, undercut and bunched into capitals and arch mouldings. Stone appears to have become fertile and borne fruit. Botanists have detected a dozen species of leaf in these capitals, but none are of plain-leaved limes or beeches. All are of complex maple, oak, hawthorn, ivy, hop and vine. In other words, the carvers were clearly eager to show off their talents as sculptors, not botanists.

The carved leaves of Southwell so moved the historian Nikolaus Pevsner that he wrote an entire book on them. They were created in the early fourteenth century at a time when Europe was making new discoveries about nature and the scientific world. To Pevsner they were 'carved in that spirit which filled the saints and poets and thinkers of the thirteenth century with the spirit of religious respect

The Glory of Decorated (1245–1348)

for the loveliness of created nature . . . one of the purest symbols surviving in Britain of Western thought, our thought, in its loftiest mood'. He went so far as to compare Southwell's leaves 'with the Greek art of the Parthenon'.

Southwell's nave displays a more advanced form of Decorated than its chapter house. Here the choir screen is less moving, though it is Gothic carving at its most delicate and accomplished. Stone imitates not nature but lace, a hundred foliated capitals and finials encased in 'flying ribs'. Here too we find another innovation of late Decorated, the convex/concave S-bend of the ogee arch, which in its most elaborate form 'nods' forward from its base.

Another albeit bruised example of late Decorated was undertaken at Ely in the 1320s. At the time, the chapter was building a Lady Chapel to honour the growing cult of the Virgin Mary. The chamber is more glass than stone, with alcove seats running beneath the windows as in a chapter house. Each is crowned with an ogee gable and contains carvings of scenes from the Virgin's life. The chapel suffered at the hands of Puritan iconoclasts, the stained glass smashed and the statues beheaded.

As this chapel was being built in 1322 a disaster occurred. Ely Cathedral's Norman central tower crashed to the ground, caused by what the monks thought must be an earthquake. They replaced the tower with an octagonal vault that rose not to a new tower but to a lantern beneath another octagonal vault. This composition was designed and executed by a local monk, Alan of Walsingham, in a work of medieval engineering that continues to defy experts.

The crossing at Ely is one of English Gothic's most uplifting creations. The splaying of ribs within the two superimposed vaults forms a visual explosion, similar to that of the Wells chapter house. The upward swirl craves musical accompaniment. Visitors with a head for heights can view it from the lantern gallery above. Here we can turn from Gothic intensity to gaze out over the Cambridgeshire fens as they recede towards the horizon. There are few such moving spectacles in all of British architecture.

While Gothic towers had long been crowned with wooden pyramids, the addition of spires was new. It was not until 1310 that Salisbury Cathedral finally commissioned Richard of Farleigh to erect a tower and spire over its crossing. Its elegant proportions in relation to the body of the cathedral rising from its tree-lined setting brought Salisbury widespread celebrity, making it the most reproduced of all cathedrals. Constable depicted it a reputed 300 times, and it must have appeared on countless jigsaw puzzles and chocolate boxes. William Golding's novel *The Spire* was based on its construction.

Where cathedrals led, parish churches followed. Over the course of the late thirteenth and fourteenth centuries steeples – defined as a tower plus a pointed spire – indicated a community's confidence and wealth. Patrons competed to fund them and raise them high. They became features of competitive riding and later gave their name to steeplechases. Two of the most splendid are at Raunds and King's Sutton in Northamptonshire, designs much copied by Victorian revivalists.

At the same time, windows acquired ever more elaborate tracery and filled with stained glass. Choir stalls were dressed with carved bench-ends and misericord seats. Naves were divided from chancels by elaborate carved screens. Ottery St Mary in Devon borrowed features from neighbouring Exeter Cathedral, possibly using the same craftsmen. The builders of the nave at St Patrick's in Patrington, Humberside, the 'Queen of Holderness', are thought to have been masons from York.

A feature of Decorated was its capacity to innovate. The north porch of St Mary Redcliffe in Bristol has an oriental arch of seven points, a design allegedly brought back from the Near East by

The Glory of Decorated (1245–1348)

local traders. The church guide attributes it to 'the luxuriance of Seljuk portals in Asia Minor or the stuccowork of Islamic Spain'. The only similar doorway I know is in equally maritime Cley next the Sea in north Norfolk.

An original creation of the inventive late thirteenth century was Bristol Cathedral. It was built in the 1290s by the Berkeley family, treating it almost as the family's 'downtown' chapel. The chancel was in the form of a nave with side aisles of the same height, precursor of the Reformation's hall churches. Such designs were common in Germany and the Low Countries, where congregations and a preaching clergy were starting to share the same space. The cathedral walls are a celebration of Gothic decoration, framing doors, niches and tombs, at times like an oriental palace.

The development of secular architecture showed perhaps less originality. Under Henry III the sale of licences to crenellate boomed, but in only one region was the building of castles a military rather than a status activity. The independence of the rulers of north Wales was a long-standing bone of contention. The refusal of the Welsh prince, Llywelyn ap Gruffudd, in 1274 to pay appropriate fealty to Henry III's son, Edward I (r.1272–1307), swiftly escalated into war. The belligerent Edward decided to enforce what has been called the first English empire, that of England over the Scots, Welsh and Irish. The invasion of north Wales in 1277 was conducted in effect by two English armies, one of soldiers and another of masons. The first defeated Llywelyn's army and the second led to the finest collection of medieval castles in Europe.

Those erected by Edward at Caernarvon, Beaumaris, Conwy and Harlech were unmatched in their scale and extravagance. They were accompanied by a further dozen English and restored Welsh castles. The supervising architect was James of St George, a Savoyard reputedly involved in the construction of crusader castles in the Levant. Caernarvon displayed echoes of the Roman walls of Constantinople, perhaps an indication of Edward's imperial ambition. Its polygonal west towers reflect Edward's wife Eleanor's homeland of Castille. Modest Rhuddlan Castle cost more than half that of his palace adjoining the Tower of London. So vivid was the Edwardian conquest to Welsh identity that a Welsh tourism minister once told me he refused to promote the castles to English visitors. I wondered if England should refuse to promote Norman Dover to the French.

No other corner of Britain boasted such displays of English might. Edward's reign ended with a similar attempt to conquer Scotland, in the course of which he died. His son Edward II (r.1307–27) was humiliated at Bannockburn in 1314 and Scotland saw no English castle-building to compare with that in Wales. None the less, ongoing Anglo-Scottish conflict and internal clan feuds meant the castle remained the default residence of Scottish aristocrats. It was also favoured by English grandees south of the border. The Clifford family mentioned above sustained castles at Brougham, Brough, Appleby and Skipton as well as others to which, it was said, they had no claim.

The English Decorated style had borrowed initially from French *rayonnant*, though it was more disciplined and less ostentatious. As time passed it did not veer into the *flamboyant* style that was to galvanize – and to some vulgarize – French and Spanish Gothic in the fifteenth century. While Henry III might have craved the Gothic of France for his Westminster Abbey, ten years into the reign of Edward III (r.1327–77), England and France were at war. Contact diminished, hostility increased and, from the mid-fourteenth century, English Gothic moved in a different direction. A truly British architecture was stirring into life.

6.

Perpendicular Climactic (1348–1500)

The Black Death of 1348 is thought to have wiped out possibly a third of Britain's population. It led to a crisis in farm labour but also to a rise in agricultural efficiency and, in the longer term, standards of living. There is little evidence of this being reflected in secular architecture. Houses big and small remained in what the Victorians would later term 'the native English vernacular'. The fifteenth-century Renaissance that was gradually influencing architectural taste in Italy and France had as yet made little headway in England, though it had in Scotland.

Of Britain's continued prosperity there was no doubt. The wealthy continued to build in the style familiar to them. The concept of the castle retained its appeal, particularly in the north and near the Scottish and Welsh borders. Ancestral families did as they had always done, adapting previously fortified buildings into domestic ones, preferably with no loss in the imagery of status. The Nevilles turned Raby Castle into a moated palace. The Percys expanded Alnwick and recreated Warkworth as a mansion on the plan of a Greek cross. If Renaissance traces were to be found anywhere before the sixteenth century, it was as a decorative motif round a doorway or fireplace or on a church tomb.

While castles might be domesticated, a distinctive aspect of the traditional hall house was to take on one feature of the castle. This was the fashion for the fortified gatehouse. Once merely the entrance to a courtyard, gatehouses added a touch of grandeur to even the most modest hall house, as if implying the presence of a grander building behind. Even monasteries and Oxford and Cambridge colleges built themselves gatehouses. Over time, the gatehouses gradually took on a personality of their own.

An early instance of this was when the royal treasurer, Lord Cromwell, in 1443 planned the building of Tattershall Castle in Lincolnshire. It was in effect a palace arranged vertically inside a keep, as in Norman Colchester or Norwich castles. Grandiose gatehouses later appeared at Oxborough in Norfolk (1482) and Hadleigh in Suffolk (1490s). At Richmond in 1501 the parsimonious Henry VII (r.1485–1509) replaced his palace after a fire. We have only a vague idea of its appearance but the few surviving prints suggest a fantasy-like confection of courtyards, turrets, pinnacles and domes, overseen by twelve rounded and octagonal towers. It was destroyed in the Civil War but its modest gatehouse survives.

A spectacular form of house enrichment was taken in the peaceful surroundings of Kent at Knole. Here a series of owners in the fifteenth century added one court after another to the original hall ranges as their needs grew, erecting a crenellated gatehouse on the front. Inside, the house eventually comprised an extraordinary seven courtyards with a reputed 365 rooms, some palatial. It now sits in its sylvan landscape like a hill town in Umbria. Likewise the Manners family's Haddon Hall in Derbyshire and the Berkeleys of Berkeley Castle. None felt in need of bravura architecture. They merely added new wings to the hall ranges of medieval castles. One feature of these houses that did change over the fifteenth century was the ubiquity of glass. Medieval bay windows had traditionally illuminated only the high-table end of the hall. Now windows erupted across entire facades. The royal palaces of Richmond and Greenwich were feasts of glass.

Perhaps the most celebrated example of an unaltered fifteenth-century mansion is Ockwells near Maidenhead in Berkshire. Built

Perpendicular Climactic (1348–1500)

from the 1440s, though much restored, it remains gabled, half-timbered and surrounded with large oriel windows. It marks the move from the expansive medieval courtyard and hall house to a more compact style, often with over-sailing upper floors, as became common in urban streets throughout England. The so-called half-timbered style attracts the adjectives that have made such houses so popular down the ages: cosy, reassuring, timeless, comfortable. Ockwells exemplifies the architecture that was to be craved by English suburban homeowners over the course of the twentieth century. When it went on the market in 2019, it was priced at £10 million. The brochure added understandably that it was 'convenient for Eton'.

Where the Black Death had an immediate impact was on church building. It traumatized the Christian faith and led to a new emphasis on sin and redemption and the patronage of church alterations. While French Gothic was progressing from *rayonnant* to *flamboyant*, English Gothic moved if anything in the opposite direction. Walls flattened and were consumed by ever more glass. Columns faded into walls, shafts and relief pilasters. Display took over from architecture. Interiors were crowded with the celebration of local worthies, guilds and historical events. The Victorians called the style Perpendicular.

This stylistic evolution was stimulated, like so many previous ones, by events at court. The murder of Edward II in Berkeley Castle in 1327 led his son, Edward III, to build for him a tomb in neighbouring Gloucester Cathedral. Edward's sainthood was applied for, though not granted. Pilgrims were nonetheless encouraged by reports of miracles to pay homage, while the young king lavished money on a new choir, built under the direction of royal masons sent from London.

What emerged at Gloucester in the 1340s and 50s was a genuine departure. What is sometimes called the court style had long taken a lead from Paris's Sainte-Chapelle and from St Stephen's

Chapel Westminster. The royal masons were working on new chambers for Windsor Castle, but the south transept and choir at Gloucester were on a different scale. The transept is today a confused mix of earlier Norman and late-Gothic fabric, with intruding buttresses propping up a new tower overhead. At one point a tower buttress slams like a javelin through the whole composition.

The choir beyond is a single, breathtaking chamber. Completed in 1350, it has none of the visual depth of three-dimensional Decorated. Instead the walls, arcading and clerestory flatten to become vertical frames to the windows. The east wall, eventually completed in the 1360s, is one huge window, claimed when built to be the largest expanse of glass in the country if not the world. The wall edges are even splayed to make the window actually wider than the church. It was named the Crécy Window to celebrate Edward's victory over the French in 1346. The glass contains the first image of a man playing golf, while a choir stall contains the first known depiction of a game of football.

Greater wonders were to come. Gloucester crowned its status as birthplace of the new Gothic with a cloister entirely vaulted with ribs arranged as fans. Created in the 1350s, the vaults were low and formed a phalanx of waving umbrellas for the monks strolling below. There are few lovelier corners of an English cathedral than Gloucester's cloister when sunshine filters through the stained glass onto its paving stones. Meanwhile, overhead hovers the cathedral's late-Perpendicular tower (1450). Its crenellated crown of Cotswold stone radiates silver or gold depending on the angle of the sun. It might be an oriental fantasy when seen from the Cotswolds across the Severn valley.

Perpendicular naves were now being built wherever Norman ones had been left unimproved. The appeal of the English church was no longer that of mystery and saintly shrines. It was that of preachers and sermons, not chanting the liturgy but extolling the Bible message. Congregations were occupying ever more space as

Perpendicular Climactic (1348–1500)

they flocked to hear evangelical friars. Canterbury Cathedral demolished its Norman nave in 1378 and erected a Perpendicular one of great elegance, designed by the royal mason, Henry Yevele. Columns became bunches of shafts. Capitals all but disappeared, while mouldings vanished upwards into clusters of ribs and liernes.

Ten years later it was Winchester's turn. Replacing its nave became an exercise in manic Perpendicular, resulting in the longest Gothic nave in the world. To sit in this cathedral is to wonder where it ends. We almost expect to see mist forming. Its master mason, William Wynford, enjoyed sufficient status to be granted lifelong 'dining rights' at the table of his patron, William of Wykeham. The day of the celebrity architect was at hand. Winchester is best seen with its ceremonial banners unfurled down its length like a glorious tent.

Neither Canterbury nor Winchester chose to copy Gloucester's fan vault, which must have been costly to create. Richard Winchcombe in the 1430s designed fan vaults for Oxford University's Divinity School, where they were decorated with hanging stone cones or pendants. The first church fan vault appeared at Sherborne Abbey in Dorset in 1437. This is delightful in that its fans do not overlap or touch but seem to wave in unison. Both St George's Chapel Windsor and Bath Abbey acquired fans by the brothers William and Robert Vertue around the turn of the sixteenth century. William Vertue is said to have told Bath's bishop of his vault that 'there shall be none so goodly, neither in England nor in France'. Fans can also be found in a handful of enterprising, or wealthy, parish churches, such as Ottery St Mary and Cullompton in Devon.

These vaults were English Gothic at the extremity of invention, found nowhere else in Europe. The style was perfected in two masterpieces. The chapel of King's College Cambridge was the favoured project of successive monarchs during the fifteenth-century Wars of the Roses. Henry VI (r.1422–61/1470–71), Edward IV (r.1461–70/1471–83), Richard III (r.1483–85) and Henry VII in succession contributed to its completion, as if to sanctify their monarchical status. Work on the chapel was intermittent throughout the conflict and it was not until 1509 that the master mason John Wastell began work on the roof, with William Vertue known to have been consulted. Funds for its completion were left in Henry VII's will.

The chapel, venue for the annual Christmas festival of nine lessons and carols, has one of England's loveliest interiors. Its undivided volume rises on walls almost completely of glass. Walls and glass seem flattened onto a two-dimensional plane, adorned only with crowns in honour of their patrons. Light is refracted by stained glass, giving the interior space an aura of serenity. The vault comprises splaying ribs, like ball gowns swirling the length of the roof in search of music. It is equally beautiful when bathed in sun by day or lit from inside by night. Finally, as if nodding to the future, a chapel screen was added in 1533. This is not Gothic at all but Renaissance, probably by a French sculptor. It seems rather overawed.

If King's said farewell to Gothic with a dance, Westminster Abbey did so with a trumpet. This is the abbey that greeted Gothic's arrival under Henry III three centuries earlier and now bade farewell in style. The new eastern extension is a Lady Chapel, intended first in honour of Henry VI and then a memorial to Henry VII, who died in 1509. It was scheduled to sing 10,000 masses for his soul. The chapel roof was again attributed to William Vertue.

This vault is astonishing. The ascent of the roof ribs is interrupted by a parade of gold-tipped pendants that seem to defy gravity by floating in air. There can be no more extraordinary roof in all architecture. The walls mostly comprise windows while the choir stalls are replete with heraldry and ceremonial banners. Every ledge and niche carries carvings, of saints, kings, animals and heraldic devices.

Perpendicular Climactic (1348–1500)

As with the screen in King's Chapel, the centrepiece of the Henry VII Lady Chapel is another Renaissance calling card: Henry's tomb lying alongside that of his wife, Elizabeth of York. It was carved in 1512 by Pietro Torrigiano, an Italian chiefly famous for breaking Michelangelo's nose in a fight. The sombre tomb stands amid so much Perpendicular ostentation like a Puritan at a fancy-dress ball. Unobtrusive in a corner of the chapel lies another foretaste of the future, the tomb of a far greater monarch, Elizabeth I.

We should remind ourselves where England stood at this stage in Europe's cultural history. Vertue must rank among the masters of British architecture. He was designing buildings of the most intense and innovative craftsmanship a full century after Filippo Brunelleschi's conventionally classical church of San Lorenzo in Florence. At the very least he might have been thought to presage a new era of British Gothic design. Yet it was not to be. His King's College and Henry VII chapels were to prove dead ends. Nothing remotely like them was to follow, not even under the Gothic revival of the nineteenth century. Rarely can a style have departed so completely yet in such a blaze of glory.

Elsewhere, Perpendicular was serving an ever more prosperous middle class. Churches were benefiting from wool and wool cloth traded across Europe through markets in London and Calais. The Lord Chancellor sat on a sack of wool. Church towers soared over the limestone hills of the Cotswolds at Cirencester, Chipping Campden and Northleach. They strode across the lowlands of East Anglia at Boston, Louth and Salle. They became four square and sturdy, topped no longer by spires but by pinnacles and castle-like battlements.

Districts short of stone produced delicate patterns in flint known today as flushwork, as at Suffolk's church at Eye. The handsome west front of Beverley Minster, built in the 1360s, and regarded as among the finest in England, showed how far English style had now diverged from French. Its two elegant towers would in France have been riotously flamboyant.

Perhaps the most remarkable of this peculiarly English form were the towers of Somerset, a county that was to Perpendicular what Northampton was to Decorated. The group comprising Taunton, Bishops Lydeard, Isle Abbots and Wells St Cuthbert were characterized by corner buttresses and roof battlements of delicate openwork. Taunton had a massive solidity as its five horizontal stages piled ever upwards. It differs conspicuously from nearby Wells, where the elongated belfry panels occupy a single stage that rises virtually the entire height of the tower. We must assume some deep-seated masonic rivalry.

Inside, churches were filled with a new decorative carpentry. Worshippers were no longer content to stand or lean against the wall. They now expected benches, pews and choir stalls. Bench-ends and chancel screens became galleries of carving and painting. Much of this was lost at the Reformation, notably any depiction of the crucifixion. But a glimpse of what must have existed can be seen in the surviving screen at Ranworth on the Norfolk Broads. The dashing, debonair Saints Michael and George are medieval painting at its most accomplished, attributed to an unknown Spanish artist.

Wales, a country more resistant to Reformation than England, suffered less at the hands of the iconoclasts. Many of its exquisite rood screens were thus able to survive, as at Patricio and Llananno in Powys and Llanegryn in Gwynedd. They rank, according to the scholar of Welsh screens, Richard Wheeler, 'among the finest achievements of the medieval woodworker'. Hunting down Welsh screens is one of the most satisfying pursuits of the dedicated church crawler.

Nowhere was carpentry more spectacular than in the reversion to wood rather than stone vaulting for roofs. Here Perpendicular

1. In the beginning: Stonehenge

2. Britain's Machu Picchu: Tre'r Ceiri, *c.*200 BC

3. Early Christian ornament at Lullingstone, *c.* fourth century

4. Saxon Robust: the tower of All Saints, Earls Barton, *c.*970

5. Echoes of Rome in All Saints, Brixworth, seventh or eighth century

6. The Saxon mausoleum at Repton, *c.* eighth century

7. Tickencote's Romanesque splendour, 1130–50

8. Durham: the architecture of supremacy

9. Freestyle Norman: Canterbury crypt, *c.*1100

10. Canterbury's twelfth-century east end: Gothic arrival

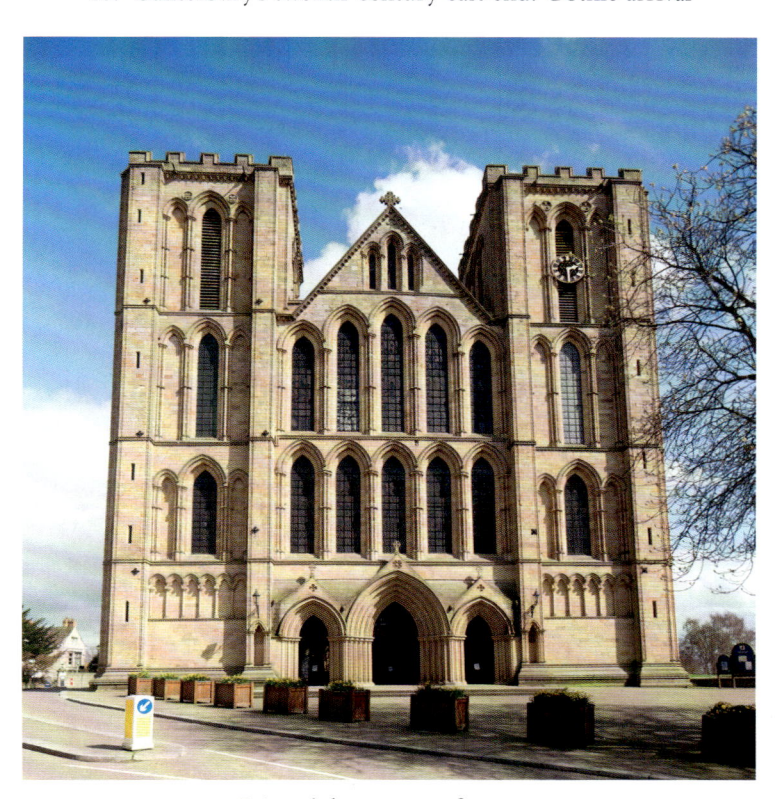

11. Ripon's lancet west front, *c.*1160

12. Edward I's imperial Caernarvon, 1283

13. Caerlaverock's Scots Baronial, *c.*1220

14. Vaulted serenity: Ely's fourteenth-century crossing

15. The leaves of Southwell, *c.*1300

16. Toothache at Wells, mid-thirteenth century

offered a uniquely English device, the hammerbeam roof truss. This involved using a beam jutting out from the wall on which a subsidiary arch could be erected, possibly repeated upwards twice or even three times. Used by Richard II to create an uninterrupted roof over the ancient Westminster Hall, it brought wood back to centre stage. The hammerbeams of East Anglia became home to clouds of sculpted angels, notably at Cambridgeshire's March and Suffolk's Needham Market.

The end of the fifteenth century saw a boom in the sponsorship of furnishings. Local patrons funded towers, aisles, chapels and chantries to pray for their souls in Purgatory, an early form of death duty. Effigies of the great if not good fill Gloucestershire's Tewkesbury with Despensers and de Clares, and Yorkshire's Harewood with Aldburghs and Gascoignes. To wander round Harewood's mausoleum of a church and look at the youthful tomb dates is to realize the carnage of England's Roses wars. The one and only consolation was to be magnificently remembered. Only a few decades separate these tombs from those of the Bedingfield family chapel at Oxborough in Norfolk of *c.*1530. Here what looks at first sight like another Gothic chantry is now coated with Renaissance pilasters and motifs, a taste of things to come.

The quality of much late-Gothic art was superb, if mostly confined to churches. Winchester's retrochoir is like a harbour with episcopal chantries as ships lying at anchor, each a distinctive essay in Perpendicular. In St Mary's Warwick the tomb of Richard Beauchamp (*c.*1439) is a magnificent work of Gothic sculpture, equalled only by the earlier effigy of Blanche Mortimer (*c.*1347) in Herefordshire's Much Marcle. I have rarely been so enraptured by a woman of stone, surely the truest masterpiece of English Gothic. Meanwhile just two English churches, Fairford in Gloucestershire and St Neot's in Cornwall, retain their full complement of medieval windows. That they are such glorious survivals reminds us of what has been lost.

This last period of ecclesiastical building saw churches treated ever more as civic institutions. Local guilds, lodges and societies funded but also took virtual possession of chapels and upstairs rooms. Thus the 'guild chamber' in the village of Croscombe in Somerset was set aside for the use of webbers, fullers, archers, hogglers (labourers), yonglyngs (young men), maidens and wives. An adjacent storeroom served as the local prison. When St Mary Beverley's nave was rebuilt, the sponsors were thanked by being depicted in person on the nave capitals. Those of the musicians' guild look uncannily like the four Beatles, instruments and all.

We have traced the evolution of Britain's architecture for nearly a millennium, largely through its principal patron, the Church. The reason is unavoidable. Outside the realm of work the local church played an overwhelming role in the lives of ordinary citizens. It did so not just as home to their faith but as a prominent visual presence located almost always at the community's heart. On a quiet September evening I once visited the tiny settlement of Up Marden on a crown of the Sussex downs. Its tiny church would have sat isolated on what would have been a barren upland. Villagers would have climbed each week to shelter within its walls. To them these walls had for centuries offered a unique solace, an emotional comfort in a hard life and a promise of salvation in a life to come. Now, at the conclusion of the fifteenth century, churches were to lose this pre-eminence.

7.
Tudor Prodigies (1500–1616)

The coming to the English throne in 1509 of the seventeen-year-old Henry VIII (r.1509–47) promised an uncertain beginning. The new men of Tudor England were different from the nobility that had survived the Roses wars. They were concerned less with military glory, more with trade and money. The universities of Oxford and Cambridge were outward-looking and open to the debates taking place within the Catholic Church, leading to increasingly embittered divisions. The Dutch scholar Erasmus was a frequent visitor to England. Henry himself had studied theology before he became heir to the throne. He was well read, intelligent and extrovert, but on taking power he was above all eager to cut a dash on the European stage.

A high point in Henry's early reign came in 1520 with the Field of Cloth of Gold. This was an Anglo-French conference promoted by his chief counsellor, Cardinal Thomas Wolsey. The venue was a field outside Calais – then an English colony – to which Henry brought a 5,000-strong retinue. His intention was to impress Francis I, the French monarch whose talents were matched by his arrogance. Francis had been playing host to Leonardo da Vinci and the Italian architect Sebastiano Serlio (d.1554), and his palace at Fontainebleau was soon to be rebuilt in a grand Renaissance style. The egos of Henry and Francis soon clashed, a difference resolved in part by a wrestling match that Francis won. One thing was clear. Henry's medieval pavilion with its battlemented walls did not look like the new Europe.

English taste was now aware of the new styles spreading across Europe. At King's College and Henry VII's chapels, wealthy patrons were ready to enhance a Gothic church with Renaissance furnishings, but they did so conscious that these were Italian or French. England's commercial success in the fifteenth century had bred an isolationist self-confidence that bordered on xenophobia. The Venetian ambassador to London wrote home at the turn of the sixteenth century that 'the English are great lovers of themselves and of everything belonging to them . . . There is no other world but England.' While French taste was respected, things Italian were considered vulgar. A doggerel verse held that 'The Englishman Italianate / Is the Devil incarnate.'

This ambivalence towards the continent contrasted with the outlook of the Scots. Scotland remained an independent kingdom and one in frequent conflict with England. It thus maintained good relations with England's perennial enemy, France. The Stewart (soon to be spelt Stuart) James V (r.1513–42) was eager to see his country modernized. In the 1530s his architect James Hamilton imported French masons to rebuild castles at Stirling and Falkland, the first with an overtly French Renaissance facade. Stirling ranks as the first such work anywhere in Britain.

No such style would have been chosen by the English king's most powerful adviser, Wolsey. As the papal representative, he saw himself as the monarch's equal, if not his superior. In 1519 he began what he intended to be the grandest palace in the land at Hampton Court. The style was traditional, with gatehouse tower, crenellated wings and enclosed courtyards, all in red brick. Italian and French terracotta adornments were applied to the facade. There were roundels of Roman worthies by an Italian sculptor, Giovanni da Maiano. Wolsey's Cabinet Room had a Renaissance frieze. But these were decoration, not architecture.

Other courtiers were soon exploiting the fifteenth-century fashion for gatehouses and carrying them to new heights. In 1523

Tudor Prodigies (1500–1616)

Lord Marney erected Layer Marney in Essex, taking to extreme the gatehouse as mansion. Its twin towers rose seven storeys, with large windows filling the linking wall. Marney died soon after and the intended adjacent mansion was never built. At the same time Sir William Compton began Compton Wynyates in Warwickshire, in part an elaboration of a previous house. It was uncompromisingly medieval, with an embattled tower attached. Lullingstone in Kent was a gateway tower with a richly crenellated roof. Hengrave in Suffolk was a hall house disguised as a symmetrical palace. Sir Richard Weston's Sutton Place in Surrey conceded the novelty of a symmetrical exterior with dressings of Renaissance terracotta.

As the 1520s moved into the 1530s, Henry's reign changed key. The advance of the Reformation across Europe was reflected in his break with Rome in divorcing Catherine of Aragon. The break traumatized the Anglican Church and the subsequent dissolution of the monasteries in 1536 was no less dramatic. Monastic houses had long stood underused and neglected. Their wealth was colossal and widely resented. It was said that if the abbot of Glastonbury were married to the abbess of Shaftesbury they would be richer than the king.

The dissolution left entire estates owned by the Church since the eleventh century reverting to the king for his disposal. They were effectively up for grabs. Some 840 monastic institutions and similar religious foundations were held or sold by the monarch or gifted to favourites. It was the greatest transfer of wealth since the Norman invasion. Fountains Abbey in Yorkshire went to Sir Richard Gresham, Lord Mayor of London. Rievaulx Abbey went to the Duke of Rutland, Bolton Abbey to the Clifford family. Other beneficiaries were the 'new men' of Henry's circle, Tudor courtiers, lawyers, officials and merchants.

These men found themselves with residences designed for a type of communal living out of keeping with the times. In the event, only some fifty monastic buildings were converted into private dwellings. Most effectively became quarries, from which local builders took dressed stone. A royal chaplain protested at the destruction of 'much fair housing and goodly building . . . whereby our country might appear so to be defaced as [if] it had been lately overrun with enemies in time of war'. Abbeys and churches, many as magnificent as cathedrals, passed into dereliction. But a new upper class was born, one that would soon be seeking its own buildings reflecting its status.

Given the flamboyance of his lifestyle, it was strange that Henry did not imitate Francis and commission a new royal palace. He initially contented himself with seizing Wolsey's Hampton Court and subjecting it to 'improvements' costing a staggering £67,000 (some £50 million today). It was not until 1538, nine years before his death, that he commissioned his answer to Fontainebleau. We have few sketches of the appearance of Nonsuch Palace in Surrey. We know only that the exterior bore echoes of Francis's Château de Chambord, a romantic composition round a hub of towers, turrets, cupolas and courtyards. The walls were apparently covered with decorative panels, created by an army of foreign craftsmen, many known to have worked on Fontainebleau. When Pepys visited Nonsuch a century later, he was amazed by the 'Italian adornments . . . walls incomparably beautified'. The palace was unfinished on Henry's death and demolished as derelict in 1683.

In 1547, Henry was succeeded by his infant son Edward VI (r. 1547–53), under the guidance of the cultured but autocratic Protector Somerset. Somerset lasted just two years in office, to be executed and replaced by John Dudley, Duke of Northumberland. These were not times conducive to grandiose buildings, but Somerset did produce one little-noted innovation. His ambitious steward, John Thynne, still in his twenties, was fascinated by the neoclassical revival emerging in Italy. This was distinct from the

Tudor Prodigies (1500–1616)

French Renaissance chateaux then appearing in the valley of the Loire. Thynne's interest lay in the strict traditionalism of Serlio, Brunelleschi and Bramante.

Their bible was Vitruvius' manual *De architectura*, now taken forward by a contemporary, Andrea Palladio (1508–80), whose four books on architecture also acquired quasi-biblical status. These architects designed in the Graeco-Roman style, involving a tripartite facade of a portico with pedimented windows, forward-thrusting wings and sometimes a dome. Palladio was later to exert a profound influence on English design as hero of the seventeenth- and eighteenth-century grand tour. His legacy is reflected in the continued use in Britain of 'first floor' for the second storey, in honour of his *piano nobile*.

Thynne was clearly a powerful influence on Somerset. He was accused by a contemporary of 'infesting his master's head with plattes and forms and many a subtle thing'. Thynne even persuaded him to erect a town house on the banks of the Thames at Aldwych. The house was a modest building of two storeys with a flat roof and parapets. Its central feature was a three-storey entrance bay above an arch, flanked by pilasters and pedimented windows. That Somerset saw it as eccentric is clear from the fact that he was at the same time building himself a palace in the medieval style upstream at Syon House.

The Duke of Northumberland might have executed Somerset but he shared his interest in classicism. In 1550 he despatched to Italy a member of his staff, a painter named John Shute, to 'confer with the doings of ye skilful maisters in architecture'. Shute brought back 'trikes and devises as well of sculture & painting as also of Architecture' and wrote a book based on Vitruvius and Serlio titled the *First and Chief Grounds of Architecture* (1563). This emphasized the importance of the five orders (Doric, Ionic and Corinthian and including Roman Tuscan and Composite) and the proportions and disciplines that went with them.

Shute is not known to have built anything, but he introduced an extensive readership to the classical language and style. He made architecture a suitable subject of middle-class discourse. More important, his study journey to Rome became the pilgrimage route of cultured gentlemen for some two centuries. Shute was joined in his championship of northern classicism by a Flemish writer, Hans Vredeman de Vries, whose first collection of drawings, borrowing heavily from Serlio, appeared in 1565. He thus initiated what was to be the most potent propagator of his craft's innovation: the architectural manual.

During the brief reign of the Catholic Mary I (1553–58) the Protestant Thynne retired to exile in Wiltshire. In 1541 he bought the dissolved Augustinian priory of Longleat for £53 (around £37,000 today) and began to rebuild it. Another member of Somerset's circle was a scholar and diplomat, Sir Thomas Smith, who went on to become ambassador to France and vice-chancellor of Cambridge University. In 1566 he was to build himself Hill Hall in Essex, a house of red brick with white pilasters and other dressings. Since Somerset's house has long gone, this stands as probably the oldest strictly classical building in Britain.

Those who object to 'ages' being named after monarchs must defer to Elizabeth I (r.1558–1603). Her re-establishment of the Protestant Reformation in England brought with it architecture's two surest allies, stability and prosperity. Another relevant feature of her rule was localism. She had little interest in an elaborate or costly London court. She raised few buildings, being content with those inherited from her father. More to the point, she wanted to keep her nobility on their country estates. They were expected to live, work and maintain justice at home, not cavort about the capital. Elizabeth even passed laws restricting the growth of London, at one point banning all building within three miles of its walls, though this proved less than effective.

Tudor Prodigies (1500–1616)

Meanwhile Elizabeth and her retinue spent their summers travelling England, visiting her courtiers at home and expecting to be entertained. They in turn became obsessed with her possible arrival. She was said to travel with as many as 600 packhorses, enough to cripple even the richest grandee. The result was ostentatious house-building such as England had never seen before. If an English medieval house was built from the inside out, an Elizabethan one was the opposite, from the outside in. Its design began with the spectacle it would present to an arriving monarch. To the ancient nobility, a castle might do, but to the new rich the challenge was awesome.

The appearance of a British building had long been the outcome of a conversation between its owner and a community of artisan masons. They knew what was wanted because it had always been so. Masons were members of a migratory culture entrenched in custom and practice going back to the Middle Ages. Their families became celebrated, as did their 'lodges' or local bases. The Parlers of Cologne and the Steinbachs of Strasbourg were known throughout Europe and highly sought after. Their secretive apprenticeships ran from mathematics and engineering to patterns and styles often memorized and drawn in the sand.

New ideas were now percolating from Italy and France, and owners also had ideas of their own. This was certainly true of Thynne and his new courtier house at Longleat. The building he had erected during Mary's reign was gutted by a fire in 1567 and only its great hall survived. A confirmed classicist, in 1572 he began a new structure under a team of masons led by a Frenchman, Alan Maynard. They included Robert Smythson (1536–1614), soon to be recognized as the leading architect of the age. The result was one of the first houses of what was later called the English Renaissance.

Of the new Longleat's classicism there was no doubt. The facades were a symmetrical sequence of advancing and receding bays round a central courtyard. Three storeys of windows were flanked by ascending Doric, Ionic and Corinthian pilasters, layered with strong linking entablatures. The ranges were crowned with a flat roof of parapets, statues and domes. The front door was strictly classical. That said, the proportions of the facade were strongly horizontal rather than vertical. While the house was no Loire chateau, neither was it a Palladian palazzo. There was no portico and no wings.

I first saw Longleat at dusk from the heights of the adjacent Cranborne Chase. A dying sun crept across the woods, setting the house's windows aflame. The menagerie of the latest Thynne (now Thynn), the Marquis of Bath, included lions prowling the parkland. Longleat was the embodiment of nature and architecture as one. It was a building classical in its clothing yet somehow unmistakably English. Longleat remains a defining building in the history of British architecture.

Queen Elizabeth favoured men of relatively humble background, such as William Cecil, Walter Raleigh, Christopher Hatton and Francis Walsingham. Most had prospered under her father and were now eager to confirm their new-found status. Cecil was a Lincolnshire man who became Elizabeth's chief counsellor. Ennobled as Lord Burghley in 1571, he began building his family seat in his home county three years later. Burghley House was to be Longleat galvanized. The facades and corner pavilions thrust forward and soared upward. The roofscape was a forest of towers, domes, elaborate chimneys and even a pyramid. Of the two gatehouses, one was a tower of the orders with a frontispiece of Doric, Ionic and Corinthian columns. Classical loggias or covered galleries were everywhere. There was a brashness to Burghley that was absent from Longleat, a Renaissance hotchpotch aching for a royal visit that never came.

A decade later classicism was more disciplined at Kirby Hall in Northamptonshire. Begun in 1570 by Sir Christopher Hatton,

Tudor Prodigies (1500–1616)

again in expectation of a royal visit, it was erected next to his existing house, Holdenby, but never used. The plan was medieval, that of forecourt, gateway, courtyard and great hall, with family and state rooms behind. Yet the exterior style was entirely classical. The front court was an Ionic delight, its giant pilasters rising from ground to roof. The decorative richness of Kirby can be traced directly to the pages of Serlio and Shute.

Smythson's next work after Longleat was Wollaton Hall outside Nottingham. Begun in 1580, it was square in plan with a high central belvedere and four corner towers, all rich in pilasters and a rhythm of swags known as strapwork. Wollaton was built for a local entrepreneur, Sir Francis Willoughby, yet again in hope of welcoming the monarch. Its visual impact from across the park remains impressive. The elevated tower room has Gothic tracery and domed turrets. To Mark Girouard, historian of these houses, visitors to Wollaton would have been 'amazed, excited but also appalled by the basilisk stare, the crash and glitter of the fantastic facade'. Elizabeth never came.

We now turn north to the most uncompromising celebrity of the age, Bess of Hardwick. She was by all accounts not an easy woman. Married four times, she was said by a contemporary to be 'of masculine understanding and conduct, proud, furious, selfish and unfeeling . . . but hideous, dry, parched, narrow-minded'. After founding the Cavendish dynasty with eight children at the family home of Chatsworth, she married a second time to the Earl of Shrewsbury and, when that marriage failed, moved to her former family home at Hardwick Old Hall on a Derbyshire hillside. There in 1590 she invited the now celebrated Smythson to build her a new house in the grounds.

Completed in 1597, Hardwick was the apotheosis of the show house. It was designed specifically for entertainment, rectangular in plan, with six towers rising from its roof. It sat on its hill, a beacon of warm limestone and shimmering glass, the windows growing larger with each floor until, as in a Perpendicular church, there was more glass than wall. It still retains much of its old glass, reflecting a light that shimmers in all directions.

The residential parts of the house on the lower two floors were modest in proportion, though with sumptuous rooms and fireplaces. A broad staircase, the first of the grand stairs that were to grace so many English country houses anticipating royal visitors, rose to the great chamber and long gallery on the top floor. The uppermost rooms were intended for the grandest of entertainments and are still lined with their original tapestries and paintings. These are so delicate that the rooms' principal function, to offer a view of the surrounding countryside, is rarely allowed. Blinds are everywhere.

Hardwick defies definition. Coming at the end of the Elizabethan period and by that era's principal architect, it is clearly 'Renaissance' in balance and detail. Its entrance is a loggia. An entablature strip divides the floors and the parapet carries copious strapwork. But there are no Palladian pilasters or pediments. It has a style of its own – or of Smythson's personal genius – into which we can read what we choose. Hardwick exudes an English dignity and calm, with a whisper of its patron's sadness. There is again no evidence that Elizabeth ever visited the house.

Where these buildings stand in the history of British style has divided historians. To some they seem neither one thing nor another, as if that makes them impermissible. (To a rigorous classicist such as the seventeenth century's Inigo Jones, Hardwick was 'impossibly vulgar'.) Later historians came to see them as 'prodigy houses', products of a golden age and representing England's unique contribution to Renaissance architecture. What they certainly were was exceptional. They were the creations of a minority of a minority, eager to establish their newly acquired credentials in the eyes of their monarch.

Tudor Prodigies (1500–1616)

Thus we should note that other houses of the sixteenth century made little or no reference to the prodigy style. While Smythson was building Hardwick, Little Moreton Hall, a moated manor in Cheshire, was a traditional black-and-white creation, its style that of fifteenth-century Ockwells and familiar in every town and village in the land. Here the eye is bombarded with gabled chequerboards and diagonals. On the top floor there is even a long gallery threading its way round the wings. Everything is restless and delightful.

This style, often termed 'Tudorbethan', was a continuation of English building in the vernacular. It can be enjoyed in the half-timbered frontage of the Lord Leycester Hospital in Warwick or in the market square of Lavenham in Suffolk. A new urban confidence was reflected in civic buildings such as Leicester's guildhall, home to one of England's first public libraries, or Much Wenlock's, which also served as its prison. It even survives in the facades that cling to life such as Staple Inn in London's High Holborn.

The most obviously Renaissance civic building of this period was imported virtually intact. This was Thomas Gresham's Royal Exchange in the City of London, begun in 1566. It was intended to establish Elizabethan London as a rival financial centre to Antwerp. Flemish builders were hired to replicate Antwerp's arcaded courtyard, with pilasters, gables and a clock tower. In the event, the war-torn Spanish empire ended Antwerp's supremacy without help from London.

We are left with a few eccentric oases of contrast. Nowhere did classicism express itself so explicitly as at Gonville Hall Cambridge. In 1555 its new master, John Caius, determined that scholars should attain wisdom by passing through three gates named Humility, Virtue and Honour. Each gate was dressed in appropriately classical references, as if Cambridge had been transported to a courtyard in Rome. Yet at neighbouring Queens' College the president's lodge was being built – or possibly remodelled – in black-and-white half-timbering, like a manor in the Cambridgeshire countryside.

No less eccentric is my favourite talisman of stylistic transition, Bishop Stephen Gardiner's chantry chapel in Winchester Cathedral. Dating from the mid-1550s, the chantry stands on its own in the retrochoir, apparently a last symbol of pre-Reformation Perpendicular splendour. Yet peer inside and we see a perfect classical interior, down to every detail round the altar. We can only wonder at the message intended by its designer. Meanwhile, house interiors were becoming festooned with classical allusions and romantic allegories, some exquisite, some primitive. None quite equals the town house of Plas Mawr (1575) in Conwy, north Wales. Its brightly coloured images are Renaissance in style if vernacular in execution. I am told the restorers had to debate the correct colouring of a classical angel's nipples.

The death of Elizabeth in 1603 and the dawn of the Stuart era saw no hiatus in British architecture. The new James I of England (r. 1603–25), also James VI of Scotland, was an unknown quantity. As he travelled south to take up the throne he was rumoured to be leading a rabble of northern barbarians, knighting everyone he met. His arrival in London blew a fresh wind through the English court. Westminster erupted in ceremonies and banquets. Drama boomed and Shakespeare's company was given royal status. The new king did not share his predecessor's aversion to London, quite the opposite. Elizabeth's Office of Works survived on an annual budget of £4,000 (£1 million today). In just three years James was to spend £73,000.

The king now guided the transformation of Westminster from royal enclave to aristocratic settlement. Courtiers took up London residences and acquired an early interest in fashion, notably in the most extravagant clothes. To be an aristocrat was to have an education, collect art and travel to France and Italy. Soon a young man might spend as long as two or three years in Florence and Rome, imbibing the Italian Renaissance. If he was particularly rich he would build himself a house on the Strand between Whitehall and the City, as did the Duke of Northumberland next to the king.

In the country the construction of prodigy houses continued apace, even if they were now dubbed Jacobean. Pride of place went to Hatfield in Hertfordshire, principal domain of the Cecils. This was begun in 1607 by Robert Cecil, the new Lord Salisbury, possibly to outshine his father's Burghley. Designed by Robert Lyminge (d.1628), it was firmly in the prodigy tradition. There is a record of Lyminge being asked to cancel six towers from the roof to save money. A measure of an architect's new status was that he refused, as it would be 'very deformed for the uniforme of the building which I will never agree to'.

Hatfield's north side is plain, echoing Longleat in its window bays. The south side is Jacobean, with a later Italianate loggia (possibly by Inigo Jones) under a triple-decker tower of the orders. Here the facade is extended by two generous brick-built wings, with windows smaller than on the north front. The Tudor fascination with glass was already passing. Lyminge went on to design the post-prodigy Blickling Hall in Norfolk in 1619, the most stylistically coherent of the Jacobean houses. Entrance front, tower and wings were all in deep red brick, as if to speak a new version of English classicism. The growing influence of the Netherlands was shown in often elaborate roof gables.

Grandest of Jacobean mansions was Audley End in Essex. Completed in 1614 for Thomas Howard at the then enormous cost of £200,000 (£30 million today), it was a mixture of styles, classical in plan but Elizabethan in fenestration. The great hall was now centre stage, with two entrances supposedly for the arrival of king and queen and with wings, now vanished, enclosing two courtyards. The screen in the great hall carries spectacularly grotesque human figures.

As under Elizabeth, much of the pleasure of these aristocratic houses lay in their idiosyncrasy, perhaps their most English characteristic. Thus Bolsover Castle in Derbyshire was begun in 1612 by Charles Cavendish, son of Bess of Hardwick, and designed by Robert Smythson's son John. It was in a style of Renaissance decoration labelled by Summerson 'artisan mannerism', in which classical motifs were exaggerated and distorted to give them often playful distinction. This followed an ongoing fascination with medieval chivalry, celebrated in Edmund Spenser's *The Faerie Queene* (1590). Cavendish and later his son William created at Bolsover an embattled castle with small rooms, narrow windows and ribbed vaults in the Gothic style. Chimneypieces mixed medieval and Serlio. Column capitals were classical and the first-floor balcony window had Renaissance dressings.

In disentangling the architecture of the prodigy era, we need to distinguish what might be termed English medieval/vernacular from classical plans and decoration. Classicism's pilasters, scrolls, plaques and friezes were not so much an invasion as a fashion, like antiques brought from the ruins of a distant land. Bolsover in 1634 was to serve as a stage set for Ben Jonson's court masque *Love's Welcome,* in the presence of Charles I and his queen, Henrietta Maria. A contemporary described the setting as 'divine, a pearl . . . the pendant of an ear'.

The purveyors of these 'antiques' gave English the word 'antics', seen as the activity of antiquarians. Often their motifs and devices clung to gateways, fireplaces, parapets and ceilings, like limpets on an alien creature. The fact that the work of Somerset's circle was so short-lived in the 1550s and was not taken up by the prodigy architects showed how far what became an Elizabethan Renaissance was from an Italian one. The prodigy tendency had emphatically won, at least among its elite of patrons, though that was only for the time being.

The strength of the vernacular tradition undoubtedly delayed the return of a stricter 'Roman style' to Britain. Girouard regarded it as 'responsible for nearly everything that is most interesting and alive about Elizabethan architecture'. He saw Smythson and his masons 'working out and improving their own Gothic tradition, rather than bungling ideas which they had borrowed from the continent'. As Shakespeare was pointing out, they saw England as a 'fortress built by nature for herself / Against infection and the hand of war'. They had no need to look to France or Italy in designing their new buildings.

8.
Inigo Jones to Christopher Wren (1616–1688)

A feature of the upward mobility of Jacobean London was that a young man from the back streets of Smithfield could attract the attention of a leading aristocrat. The drawing talent of Inigo Jones (1573–1652) secured the sponsorship of no less a figure than the Earl of Rutland for a visit to Italy to study art and design, staying there for what turned out to be a number of years. As a result, like Thynne and Shute before him, Jones's point of Renaissance reference was not that of northern Europe but the classical writings of Vitruvius and Palladio.

In Italy, Jones amassed a collection of Palladio's books and drawings, which survive with his annotations in Oxford's Worcester College library. Classical architecture to Jones was not about the surface decoration or what he dismissed as the 'composed ornament' of Elizabethan houses. As Palladio said, buildings should be 'proportionable according to the rules, masculine and unaffected'. Like any young man eager for heroes and villains, Jones took against the last generation's heroes, the classical Mannerists round Serlio and Michelangelo. The latter's buildings he considered suitable 'only for gardens'. He worshipped at one altar, that of Palladio.

Jones was a prodigious sketcher and also a student of stage design. He travelled home via Denmark, where he designed sets for the royal theatre. We hear of him back in England in 1605 at the age of thirty-two, designing theatrical performances for James I's wife Anne of Denmark. Here he is credited with inventing the proscenium arch and moveable scenery, continuing to work for the stage throughout his career. He was a rare architect who could switch between two dimensions and three.

We can see that Jones's architecture was looking back to the formal classicism of Thynne and the Somerset House circle of the mid-sixteenth century. Elizabethan buildings he held in open contempt. He described them as 'monstrous Babels of our Moderne Barbarisme'. Classicism should be true to itself. He even wrote for King James that Stonehenge was a Roman construction – indeed Doric in style – and the basis of Britain's architectural heritage from the days of the Roman Empire.

Commissions now appear to have flowed Jones's way, one for a classical portico for old St Paul's Cathedral and another for a commercial market building in the Strand, intended as Westminster's complement to the City's Royal Exchange. Both were in a Palladian style. By 1610, Jones was surveyor to the heir to the throne, Prince Henry, and in 1613 he became Surveyor-General of the King's Works. This put him effectively in charge of the Crown's landholdings, with a central influence on the court architecture of the day. For a man of humble origins and unconventional views it was a remarkable rise.

This does not appear to have mellowed Jones's personality. He may have been persuasive but he had a widespread reputation for domineering conversation, mimicking, singing, story-telling and derision. He began an alliance with the playwright Ben Jonson, deriving from Jones's interest in stage design, but they fell out in what became a bitter rivalry. Jonson was said to have remarked, 'When I want to express a word for the greatest villain in the world I call him an Inigo.'

Jones's first major building was, for England, so unusual it was widely considered a design for a theatrical backdrop. Begun in 1616, it was a villa built for James's Queen Anne on the Greenwich hillside behind what was then the medieval palace. The rectangular facade sits today symmetrical, plain and dazzling white. Two flights of stairs curve down from a front door, which I have always thought of as tears weeping for the state of British architecture. The interior includes England's first cantilevered staircase – that is, built out from the walls and not supported by a central column. Called the Tulip, it was copied by Jones from Italy. The composition could not have been less prodigy. Work on the house ceased with the queen's death in 1619 and it was finished for Henrietta Maria, queen of Charles I (r.1625–49) in 1635.

In 1619, Jones began what for over a century had been the dream of English monarchs: a proper royal palace in the manner of Paris's Louvre on the Thames at Whitehall. By way of preparation he built the Banqueting House, comprising a single chamber in a far more elaborate classicism than Greenwich. The exterior had attached columns and pilasters, heavy architraves and a frieze of swags. The inside was indeed palatial, with a throne and walls hung with tapestries. The ceiling painted by Rubens in 1636 was a eulogy of James I. The remainder of Jones's would-be palace was never built and the Banqueting House was left towering over the old Tudor enclave. Though altered, it stands in Whitehall today no longer an isolated intruder but surrounded by three centuries of classical buildings, all of which might claim it as their progenitor.

Jones continued to enjoy the favour of the Stuart court, designing a Chapel Royal for St James's Palace and completing his portico for old St Paul's Cathedral. He also gave 'advice and approbation' for the Earl of Pembroke's Wilton House in Wiltshire, designed by French landscaper and architect Isaac de Caus. The house's exterior was a model of classical decorum, but the interior included a double-cube hall, as rich in Renaissance ornament as any to be found in France or Italy. Jones's description of it well sums up the character of the English Renaissance:

'Outwardly every wise man carried a gravity, yet inwards has his imagination set on fire and sometimes licentiously flies out.'

An indication of Jones's influence is that when the Earl of Bedford in 1629 sought the king's permission to build on the dissolved Westminster convent garden, granted him by Henry VIII, the reply was only if Jones oversaw the design. Jones duly ordered that the buildings be set round a piazza in the manner of the Place Royale (now Place des Vosges) recently constructed in Paris. It should include a church filling the west side. When the earl protested against the cost of the church and demanded nothing more than a barn, Jones said he would have 'the handsomest barn' in England. St Paul's Covent Garden stands to this day, in a simple, indeed barn-like, Tuscan style.

In addition Jones designed a continuous terrace or 'row' of houses around two sides of the piazza, initiating a form that was to typify London house-building, rich and poor, for three hundred years. But Bedford neglected to guard the piazza itself. Covent Garden attracted suitably aristocratic clients, but the central area filled with what became, under the Commonwealth, the largest fruit and vegetable market in London. By then residents were protesting 'the great filth' and the 'noise, stench . . . and profligate and disorderly people' that thronged the place. Bedford was more interested in its rents, which he auctioned each year. The result was that Covent Garden as a smart suburb went swiftly into decline, compared with St James's Square to its west. Indeed, it did not recover its glamour until the twenty-first century. Short-term profit was a mistake Bedford's fellow London developers were careful to avoid.

Although the Queen's House and Banqueting House were not immediately imitated, Jones's Palladianism became the dominant influence on British architecture for the remainder of the Stuart period. He designed a house for the Prince of Wales at Newmarket in Suffolk and Chevening for Lord Dacre in Kent, now an official residence of the Foreign Secretary. London's Lincoln's Inn Fields saw town houses with pilastered facades, possibly designed or approved by Jones, two of which still stand on the west side.

Inigo Jones was cantankerous to the end. He was a firm royalist and was captured at the age of seventy during the Civil War siege of Basing House. Legend has him carried from the burning building in a blanket, stripped of his clothes. He died in Somerset House in 1652, eight years before the Restoration he championed. His legacy was important for what it represented as much as for what he built. He brought owner and builder together under a common doctrine, that of classical formality in place of the random diversity of the prodigy era. The stonemason, carpenter and plasterer spoke the same language as the grandee and his son returned from Italy.

Jones's influence was entrenched by the opening up of Europe in 1648 and the return of the grand tour after the end of the Thirty Years War in the Peace of Westphalia. Gone were Hardwick's walls of glass, Layer Marney's gatehouse and Burghley's turrets. The leading architect of the day, Roger Pratt, had begun Coleshill (then in Berkshire, now Oxfordshire), possibly from a Jones design, under Cromwell in 1651. It was characterized by an undemonstrative classicism. Its hipped roof with dormer windows above a symmetrical facade became the defining style of the seventeenth century. Such houses were to be defined as 'astylar' for lacking the columns usually associated with Palladianism.

The Civil War and the accompanying austerity of the Commonwealth saw a near cessation of new building. The war destroyed – or 'slighted' – many ancestral castles. Corfe and Kenilworth were reduced to ruins, as were some twenty bishops' palaces. The conflict was reflected in church-building. Very few new churches were erected across the span of the seventeenth century. Those that were tended to be by High Church conservatives expressing their aversion to the Henrician Reformation. High Gothic 'survival' was considered the style in which to do so.

One such conservative was Durham's Bishop John Cosin, who kept the light of the old religion burning with Gothic chancels at Brancepeth and Sedgefield in his diocese. Two other Gothic survivals were St John's Leeds (1632) and Staunton Harold in Leicestershire (1653). Classical churches were hardly more plentiful. Apart from Jones's in Covent Garden, there was Berwick church in Northumberland. Its coldly austere details were approved by Cromwell himself, at least to the extent of banning any tower. The church is a curious mix of Gothic and classical detailing – Venetian windows inside Gothic hoods – as if the masons were keen to avoid being labelled one or the other. Berwick is the only church that could be described as Roundhead.

Under the Restoration, Charles II (r.1660–85) was determined to restore the glory of his father's court. His personal ambition had been aroused by the palaces he had visited during his exile in France and the Low Countries. Louis XIV was beginning Versailles in the 1660s, while Spanish and Dutch monarchs were living in milder splendour. Charles had nothing but the antique quarters of Whitehall, Greenwich and St James's. He was extrovert and extravagant by nature. He wanted a palace, indeed more than one.

Pratt's most influential new work was still in the astylar tradition for a senior courtier, Lord Clarendon, on London's Piccadilly (1664). But the portico was not absent for long. Pratt's credo was catholic, that 'no man deserves the name of architect who has not been well versed both in those old [buildings] of Rome as likewise in the more modern of Italy and France'. In that tradition were Eltham Lodge in Kent (1664) by Hugh May and the portico added to the Vyne in Hampshire by Jones's pupil John Webb (1611–72). A portico, usually flanked by symmetrical wings, became the most imitated feature of the classical revival. A grander Palladianism was the twenty-three-bay block intended by Webb for a new royal palace for Charles II at Greenwich. It was supposedly to welcome foreign guests to London as they came up the Thames, though it never did. It stands to this day.

From this environment emerged the only man to rival Jones in the seventeenth-century pantheon, Christopher Wren (1632–1723). His upbringing could not have been more different from Jones's. A quiet youth whose father was a clergyman, he studied mathematics and science at Oxford, became a fellow of All Souls at twenty-one and Professor of Astronomy and co-founder of the new Royal Society at twenty-nine. As such, the polymath Wren took an interest variously in blood transfusion, the grinding of optical instruments and the measuring of temperature. He tried his hand at architecture only out of curiosity.

In 1663, Wren produced a design for Pembroke College Chapel in Cambridge and, a year later, for a new ceremonial hall in Oxford, the Sheldonian, inspired by the theatre of Marcellus in Rome. His career now advanced rapidly. The plague year of 1665 found him in Paris talking to the Italian baroque master Gian Lorenzo Bernini about his plans for the Louvre. He recalled that 'the old reserved Italian gave me but a few minutes' view'. He complained that in Paris the French women 'do make here the language and fashions, meddle with politics and philosophy, so they sway also architecture'. To Wren that was unsatisfactory, since architecture 'ought to have the attribute of the eternal, and therefore [be] the only thing incapable of new fashions'.

On returning from Paris in 1666, Wren was in time to watch the City of London burn to the ground. To the diarist John Evelyn, 'London was, but is no more.' Evelyn immediately set to and had a proposal for a new city on the king's desk within ten days, but he found Wren had beaten him by forty-eight hours. Within another week, plans by a young architect and associate of Wren, Robert Hooke, and others were also presented, but it was

Inigo Jones to Christopher Wren (1616–1688)

Wren who won the royal ear. His plan was influenced by Vitruvius, with a grid of straight avenues radiating from St Paul's and with two *ronds points* at the Royal Exchange and the Strand. Along them would be neatly arranged palaces, churches, obelisks and wharves. It was a geometrical planner's city, as of one papal mind, rather than the restoration of the pre-fire, organically evolved settlement.

Evelyn's plan was equally modernist. He proposed an urban grid, with 'tiresome trades' moved east and 'fragrant and odoriferous flowers' taking their place. He wanted the city to burn wood not coal. To Evelyn a city 'which commands the proud ocean to the Indies' should not 'wrap her stately head in clouds of fuliginous and filthy vapour'. He also wanted a green belt round the suburbs, another remarkably modern vision. Other architects variously wanted a 'garden city' spread over the Thames valley and a London acquired by the government and 'started again'. It is intriguing how the architectural mind veers towards authoritarianism.

Charles favoured Wren but heard the cries of the City's aldermen that property owners were fast returning from their suburban refuges and squatting on their sites. They needed to get back to business and could not be stopped. The king duly changed his tune and said he was 'solicitous for the rebuilding of this famous city with as much expedition as possible'.

A rebuilding act was passed in 1667, ordering only the widening of streets and offering compensation for any consequent loss of any land. It required all new buildings to be of brick and stone rather than wood. Dimensions were categorized as of four grades, from modest terrace to urban mansion. Of the top grade only one survives, the handsome Old Deanery tucked away close to the west end of St Paul's. This was probably the most detailed planning control in London's history.

London recovered fast. The pressure of population had been eased by the plague deaths of the previous year. Some 9,000 houses were built in just four years, roughly on the medieval street plan, replacing 13,000 old ones. Many citizens did not return, seeking new homes instead in the suburbs of Westminster, Holborn, Shoreditch and Wapping. Land-rich London was on its way to having the lowest population density of any city in Europe. The new regulations were ruthlessly applied, with anyone disobeying the law 'taken to the place of the offence . . . and whipped until his body be bloody'. Given the subsequent laxity of London planning, it seems a sensible discipline.

In 1669, Wren became Surveyor of the King's Works. His priority was the rebuilding of St Paul's Cathedral and over fifty of the hundred churches destroyed in the fire. Both tasks were to produce architectural wonders. Wren's initial plan for St Paul's was for a centrally domed church, but this was rejected by the chapter as looking too Catholic. It was replaced by a cruciform church with a nave and west front with a portico and two towers.

From outside, the main vessel of St Paul's appeared designed, like Jones's Banqueting House, as if to fit into the surrounding streets. The dome and west towers seemed to float over it, as if to dominate the City rooftops when seen from a distance. In his paintings Canaletto apparently disapproved of the towers, reducing them almost to pinnacles and leaving the dome supreme. Until the arrival of Big Ben's tower this dome became London's signature landmark.

The interior of the cathedral bordered on the austere. Wren referred to it with that all-purpose time-honoured phrase 'in the good Roman manner'. Some critics found the contrast with the old medieval nave shocking. One said it was, 'almost as if it was a change of religion'. The inside of the dome was a ceiling, built within a brick cone that supported the outer dome and the lantern. In the nave the Corinthian order showed few of the pyrotechnics of Italian baroque. God's house was that of an English gentleman at peace with the world. Heaven lurked discreetly

Inigo Jones to Christopher Wren (1616–1688)

in the background while Hell was nowhere to be seen. Only the exquisite choir stalls by Grinling Gibbons lent a touch of vitality.

I recall being taken as a small boy by one of the cathedral staff to inspect the as yet unrepaired bomb damage. It was an unforgettable adventure, clambering along planks and ladders past gaping holes into the cavern of the nave interior. We had not so much as a single hard hat. I was awe-struck by what seemed a torn and battered stage set. That it had survived the war seemed miraculous.

Wren's approach to the City's churches could not have been more different. There had been virtually no church building since the Gothic era and therefore little precedent for what a classical church should look like. The new ones were often replacing two or three churches in a street, but on mostly tiny polygonal plots. A number are thought to have been by his assistant, Robert Hooke.

The challenge clearly appealed to the mathematician in Wren, with a different geometry for each location. Most had naves and aisles but some had no room for both. St Stephen Walbrook was thought to be a rehearsal for the first plan for St Paul's. The cramming of sites meant there was rarely space for ostentatious exteriors. Wren pointed out that Protestantism had no need of chancels, only pulpits. 'Our churches are to be fitted out for auditories.'

Where the City churches needed to make a mark they did so with their steeples. Whatever Wren's reputation may have suffered in the rejection of his plan for a new London was compensated by his steeples. They were his signature of a transition from classical to a new baroque. St Mary-le-Bow is a series of Roman temples piled on top of each other. St Magnus Martyr is inspired by a baroque church in Antwerp. St Vedast Foster Lane might be by a young Nicholas Hawksmoor. St Bride's Fleet Street, perhaps the most celebrated, is the largest. Its four octagonal stages beneath an obelisk became the model for English wedding cakes from the moment of its completion in 1703. By the end of the century Wren's steeples had turned the London skyline into a forest of vertical exhilaration. That skyline was an architectural wonder of urban Europe. It survived into the twentieth century but sadly is no more.

Less progress was made with the king's palaces. Greenwich had been in the hands of John Webb but was incomplete. Later, in 1692, Wren expanded it into a naval hospital, its painted hall by James Thornhill glorifying the monarchy of William and Mary (r.1689–94). At Winchester a Wren palace was begun but not used and later became a barracks. At Hampton Court, new ranges, again by Wren, were converted in 1685 for William and Mary, but work ground to a halt on their deaths. As for the long-delayed palace at Whitehall, this was finally abandoned. Its location on what was then a desperately polluted River Thames was considered unhealthy. The monarch was left with just St James's and Kensington as London palaces. There was to be no British Louvre, let alone a Versailles.

Wren also turned his attention to Cambridge, with a new library for Trinity College, and to Christ Church Oxford, where, as if to display his diversity, he designed a gatehouse in the Gothic style. Finally, at the topping out of St Paul's in 1723, Wren's son, also Christopher, hauled him to the top of the lantern in a basket to survey what he declared to be 'my finest work'. On his tomb below is inscribed the famous epitaph 'If you seek a monument, look around you.' No architect could wish for better.

The rebuilding of the streets of the City of London after the Great Fire marked a new departure. As we have seen, designers had to adhere to the pre-existing medieval pattern. Regulations stipulated the dimensions and materials of new buildings, though not their appearance. Jones had drafted plans for Covent Garden and Lincoln's Inn Fields, but those days were over. A new breed of aristocratic developer now appeared on the scene. He owned the city's most precious commodity, land, and was chiefly concerned with maintaining its value for profitable housing over time.

That market was for an urban middle class eager to flee the crowded streets of the old City of London. On the pattern of Bedford's – and Inigo Jones's – now-established Covent Garden, this demand was to be met by squares and terraces of dignified brick houses built to a uniform plan of straight streets, curving only where they met the boundaries of what would once have been fields and gardens. Houses had handsome front doors opening onto a square or main streets. Tucked behind would be a maze of mews, stables, stores and cheaper properties, shielded by gates from the associated square. The necessities of city life were thus catered for but concealed. Each development was a sort of community, an urban village.

After the Restoration the first developer on this scale was Henry Jermyn, Earl of St Albans. He obtained leases on the old St James's hospital land west of Whitehall, it is believed through the influence of Charles I's widow, Henrietta Maria, to whom he had grown close in Paris during the Commonwealth. The result, begun in 1662, was St James's Square, the first of west London's formal squares. Freeholds were allowed by the king provided they went to the most aristocratic owners. Initially the square housed seven dukes and seven earls. Wren built for them a friendly, country-style church, St James's, to the north on Jermyn Street.

St James's Square was a novelty. Each house was individually designed as a classical town house. Properties that in Paris or Vienna would be detached 'hotels' behind gates and walls were here huddled next to each other, sharing party walls. They might be five or more bays wide and lavish inside, but they had little security or privacy, and had to share an often chaotic area of mews and stables behind. Foreigners were shocked. But since most of the houses were second homes, occupied only for the London spring season, proximity was seen as tolerable, even sociable.

The satirist Jonathan Swift was an ardent publicist for the new residences. He recorded his delight at visiting the Earl of Ormonde, who owned three adjacent plots in the square. Swift said he could do business with the earl on the ground floor, gossip with his wife on the first floor, flirt with his daughter on the second floor and attempt to seduce the maid on the third. He was impressed that the maid considered herself too grand to consent. The south side of the square was left as the rear of houses on Pall Mall and is today a bland facade of new buildings.

Where Jermyn led, a boom followed. The Earl of Southampton began to develop land in front of his Bloomsbury house north of Bedford's Covent Garden. In 1670 the Earl of Leicester built over his Leicester fields, eventually creating a square in his name. In 1681 came Soho Square, at first a fashionable neighbourhood but soon colonized and crowded by French Huguenot refugees. The land was divided among lesser developers and builders, who gave their names to Frith, Gerrard, Wardour, Monmouth and Panton streets. Each terrace saw a frantic scramble to secure smart residents, fearful of a lurch downmarket.

Even the grandest mansions were not safe from building mania. In 1675, just sixteen years after its completion, Pratt's Clarendon House on Piccadilly was sold to speculators and demolished. The purchasing consortium lost money but immortalized themselves in the streets that replaced it, they being the Duke of Albemarle, Lord Dover and Sir Thomas Bond. Adjacent was land of the Duke of Grafton and Lord Berkeley. As each new development rose, it was immersed in brick kilns, potteries and labourers' camps. A frequent complaint – to continue throughout London's growth – was from residents who thought they were moving to a smart address and found they were sharing it with a building site.

London's squares were raw speculative ventures and not all worked as planned. In 1685 a developer, Thomas Young, bought land in what he thought was the promising suburb of Kensington and began erecting substantial town houses round a new Kensington Square. He was hopelessly ambitious. The arrival of William and Mary at what became Kensington Palace in 1689 partially rescued the project but Young was finally jailed for debt. Building proceeded slowly, as is indicated by the diversity of its Georgian architecture.

The fact that the early squares were erected as and when the market allowed negated efforts to unify their architecture. There was to be none of the coherence of Jones's Covent Garden until late in the eighteenth century. Wherever a development needed a touch of distinction, something to 'distance' itself from its neighbour, the builder might slap on a pilaster, pediment or porch. Schomberg House in Pall Mall is a surviving example of this, still standing as if brought up to town for a season and accidentally left behind.

This growth of Restoration London dominated seventeenth-century Britain. The restraint on population sought by the Tudors relaxed. Within two decades of the Great Fire, the capital was being reconstructed with brick facades, surrounded by suburbs of terraces and squares. These were of a spaciousness wholly new in urban development, which elsewhere in Europe remained concerned primarily with security, driving the rich into gated palaces and the poor into tenements. London meanwhile was supplanting the Dutch and challenging the French as a premier trading nation. It was benefiting from an influx of religious refugees from the continent, notably France's Protestant Huguenots.

The nearest to a development on the scale of west London was proposed for Edinburgh as early as 1680. The author was the king's brother the Duke of York, the future James II (r.1685–88), who served briefly as high commissioner to Scotland. Taking his cue from London, he saw that the medieval city on the hill was overcrowded and polluted. He duly planned what eventually became Edinburgh's New Town on a slope to the city's north. Before he could start it he was summoned back to London, later to take up the crown and then lose it. The New Town had to wait for the best part of a century. The port of Bristol was the only other city to take up London's baton. Its decorous Queen's Square was begun in 1708 and completed in fifteen years.

9.
Burlington versus Baroque (1688–1750)

Wren was not a radical. He took forward Jones's Palladian message and sought to fashion it to the ambitions of his monarch, Charles II. Hints of the direction in which Wren might otherwise have gone can be gleaned from the originality of his City of London churches. But Britain had nothing to compare with the Roman baroque of Bernini's Sant'Andrea al Quirinale (1658) or Francesco Borromini's San Carlo alle Quattro Fontane (1665). Wren's supreme talent was in honouring the dictates of classical order and proportion while supplying an essentially English platform for the cravings of the king.

The question now was over Wren's legacy. Already in the 1680s a pupil of his, William Talman (1650–1719), had refaced two ranges of the Duke of Devonshire's Chatsworth in Derbyshire. One claimed inspiration from Bernini's Louvre and the other from Louis Le Vau's chateau, Vaux-le-Vicomte. The baroque chapel at Chatsworth could rival any in seventeenth-century Rome. Talman's masterpiece was the east front of Dyrham Park (1704) near Bath, though it hardly merits the term baroque. His reputation for rudeness to clients – fatal in an architect – secured him little work and his career did not prosper.

Wren was more fortunate when in 1679 he employed an eighteen-year-old clerk from Nottingham named Nicholas Hawksmoor (1661–1736). This unassuming young man had studied the classical masters but lacked the resources to visit Italy. In Wren's office he made an instant mark, soon assisting on St Paul's, the veterans' hospital at Chelsea and the palace at Winchester. He may also have supervised Wren's work at Hampton Court and Kensington Palace. At the palace after the accession of Queen Anne in 1702, Hawksmoor designed a grand orangery in a Wren style.

At the same time a markedly different personality arrived on the scene. John Vanbrugh (1664–1726) was a marine captain of Flemish origin who had been imprisoned in France for four years as a spy, for a while in the Bastille. Well connected in Whig circles and said to be of 'colossal geniality and great good humour', he came to attention in London as a writer of risqué plays, including the popular, and still performed, *Provoked Wife*. When Restoration comedy went out of fashion at the end of the 1690s he switched his attention to architecture. In 1699 he succeeded in 'out-charming' the unfortunate Talman in securing a commission from the Earl of Carlisle to design what amounted to a palace, Castle Howard, in Yorkshire. The earl seemed unconcerned that Vanbrugh had neither the qualifications nor the experience to be an architect.

Vanbrugh clearly needed help. Back in Wren's office, the dogged Hawksmoor had at last won a commission of his own, to build Easton Neston in Northamptonshire (1702). It was a mansion in a tentative baroque style with large pilasters flanking prodigious windows on all sides. Vanbrugh at some point contacted him over Castle Howard and the relationship jelled. The project proceeded with the two men in tandem. Though of widely differing backgrounds and personalities, they contrived to work together and apportioning the contribution of each to the final project has defied historians ever since.

In his essay on the Vanbrugh/Hawksmoor authorship of Castle Howard, Summerson decided that either Vanbrugh was 'an incompetent poseur dependent on Hawksmoor's brilliance', or Hawksmoor was 'a mere clerk of works' to Vanbrugh's genius.

Burlington versus Baroque (1688–1750)

Or perhaps, he suggested, Hawksmoor warmed to Vanbrugh's 'splendid unorthodoxy, his love of movement and gay, humane temperament', while Vanbrugh 'leapt at Hawksmoor's passion for serene rhythms and dour Roman grandeur'. Either way the relationship was 'a fertile marriage of equally creative minds'.

The building that arose on the Yorkshire hillside is one of England's greatest houses. In configuring the dome, in the balance of ranges, the rhythm of pilasters and the decoration of parapets, Castle Howard embodied what passed for English baroque after the age of Wren. Seen from a distance, the warm stone turns to gold, glowing amid the hills. The interior is every inch a match. The central hall rises to the full height of the dome, its marble columns concealing unusual flying staircases. It made a fitting set for the television production of *Brideshead Revisited*, if more than a little over the top.

Vanbrugh was now launched in a new career. When in 1704 Queen Anne needed an architect to reward the Duke of Marlborough with a palace after the Battle of Blenheim, she engineered him the commission. Vanbrugh again turned to Hawksmoor for help and the result was a work of extreme ostentation, possibly the most un-English building in England. Blenheim expressed military triumph rather than domestic comfort. Its two storeys with porticos and towers on every corner bristle with ornament. Indeed, it was always intended to be a celebratory memorial as much as a residence. Inside, the visitor wanders through grand chambers as through the galleries of Versailles or the Hermitage. I once went there for a student dance, and we all thought we should be marching in step.

Before Blenheim's completion, Vanbrugh had fallen out with the Duchess of Marlborough and been banned from the site. The palace staggered into the sky like a fantasy castle out of its time. On a visit in 1727, Voltaire declared Blenheim 'a great mass of stone with neither charm nor taste'. Alexander Pope complained:

'Thanks, Sir, cried I, 'tis very fine, / But where d'ye sleep or where d'ye dine? / I find, by all you have been telling, / That 'tis a house but not a dwelling.' Blenheim proved a strange blind alley in the story of British architecture.

Vanbrugh became Comptroller of the Royal Works for ten years and produced a number of buildings with at least a hint of baroque. His Seaton Delaval Hall (1718) in Northumberland had a muscular elegance of rising towers and advancing and receding planes. He built the similar Kings Weston House (1712) outside Bristol, and a place for himself in Greenwich in the form of a sham castle. All attracted what became the familiar criticism of English baroque, that it was too heavy. Horace Walpole, who had found Castle Howard 'sublime', said that otherwise Vanbrugh, 'with his ponderous and unmeaning masses, overwhelmed architecture in mere masonry'.

Hawksmoor's achievements were less eye-opening, but he was to emerge as the more original architect. In 1717 he fashioned a quadrangle for All Souls College Oxford in a wayward Gothic, as required by its conservative fellows. In 1721 he redesigned the west front of Westminster Abbey in a Gothic style with twin towers, although here he could not resist a baroque gesture, crowning the clock faces with broken classical pediments. Few people notice this bizarre feature of Britain's best-known church facade.

The most radical of Hawksmoor's works were for the 1711 commissioning of fifty new churches. Funded by a tax on coal, these were intended to reinvigorate the Church of England after the lethargic seventeenth century. Hawksmoor contributed six buildings that were a sort of climax to the modest English baroque tradition. They took the form almost of abstract sculptures. Each was an exercise in stacking boxes of diminishing size and then penetrating them with pediments, arches and niches. Thus St Mary Woolnoth in the City of London had a pair of pavilions balanced on top of a rusticated, almost military entrance arch. Christ Church Spitalfields sent a sequence of arches bursting upwards to meet an obelisk on top. St George's Bloomsbury had a grand Corinthian portico backed by a tower culminating in a lion, a unicorn, a pyramid and George I sitting uncomfortably on top of it. Walpole called it a 'masterpiece of absurdity'.

A lesser contributor to England's modest baroque was Thomas Archer, who designed the Queen Anne churches of St Paul's Deptford and St John's Smith Square. The latter, on a square plan, allegedly resulted from Queen Anne being asked how it should look. She kicked over her footstool and said, 'Like that!' The church emerged as a dramatic composition with four corner towers. Archer went on to design a cathedral for Birmingham and a house at Chettle in Dorset, its thrusting bays and giant pilasters a startling composition to find in the soft English countryside.

One area in which English baroque felt able to let rip was the decoration of interiors. Many secular buildings saw ceilings painted by Antonio Verrio, Louis Laguerre and the ubiquitous Thornhill. Thornhill's illusionist style gave depth and drama to halls and staircases. He worked at St Paul's, Greenwich Hospital, Hampton Court, Chatsworth and Blenheim. He designed with Verrio one of the most sumptuous baroque interiors in England, the hall at Moor Park in Hertfordshire, now a golf club. A surprising mural by Thornhill appeared in the Vernon family's Hanbury Hall in Worcestershire. Here in a quiet William and Mary country house the family were expected to ascend to bed beneath a massive mural of the life of Achilles.

The death of Queen Anne in 1714 was followed by that of Wren in 1723, Vanbrugh in 1726 and Hawksmoor in 1736. It might have been expected that their tentative steps in the direction of an English baroque would have stimulated more adventurous successors. It was not to be. Just as English Gothic ran out of creative steam in the early 1500s, so English baroque did in the 1720s. A fashion for all things Dutch had preceded and accompanied the invasion of William of Orange in 1688. The Restoration style had matured through 'William and Mary' to 'Queen Anne'. Facades were redbrick and classical in detail, with modest pediments and pilasters, topped by hipped roofs with prominent chimneys. The style was displayed at Uppark (1690) in Sussex and Dyrham (1692) outside Bath.

The leading contender for Wren's crown was James Gibbs (1682–1754), a Tory, a Catholic and a Scotsman, those three attributes placing him at odds with the Hanoverian establishment. He produced two London masterpieces, one for the 1711 commission at St Mary-le-Strand (1714) and the other for St Martin-in-the-Fields (1722). St Mary's west tower was composed of tiers of baroque pavilions, its interior a delight of naturalistic plasterwork. St Martin's became a model copied worldwide for marrying two usually quite separate classical features: a tower and a portico.

Gibbs went on to design the Senate House in Cambridge and the Radcliffe Camera in Oxford, neither quite meriting the description baroque. Working mostly for Tory patrons, he built Wimpole in Cambridgeshire for the Earl of Oxford, Cannons in Middlesex for the Duke of Chandos and Ditchley in Oxfordshire for the Earl of Lichfield. What was unquestionably baroque was his beautiful Octagon Room added in 1720 to Orleans House in Twickenham.

With the arrival of George I (r.1714–27) and the Hanoverians, British politics embarked on what became the 'great divide' between the outgoing Stuart Tories and the incoming Hanoverian Whigs. This was reflected, albeit tentatively, in matters of style. Despite Vanbrugh's Whig associations, England's flirtations with baroque were seen as Tory. Hanoverian classicism went in a quite different direction, reverting to the strict Palladian style of Inigo Jones of a century before and with an almost identical dogmatism.

Burlington versus Baroque (1688–1750)

The driving force this time was a Whig aristocrat, the Earl of Burlington (1694–1753), who by 1719 had completed two grand tours of Italy. Like Jones he specifically studied Palladio and the buildings of classical Rome, but rejected the baroque. Like Jones too, he returned to England convinced that the architects of his native country had strayed into heretical and vulgar ways and needed to return to the path of truth. Burlington brought with him from Italy 878 packing cases of classical treasures.

The Hanoverian classical revival was signalled by a barrage of publications. Between 1715 and 1720 new editions of Palladio's tetralogy appeared in London, edited by the Italian architect Giacomo Leoni. Another volume, entitled *Vitruvius Britannicus, or the British Architect*, appeared at the same time, the work of Colen Campbell (1676–1729), a sternly orthodox Scot. It surveyed those English buildings that met with Campbell's approval, culminating in his own creation, the impeccably classical Wanstead House, north-east of London. No buildings by the Tory Gibbs were listed, though Vanbrugh was included. Campbell was taken up by Burlington, who in turn had formed a close association in Rome with the painter/architect William Kent (1685–1748). Unlike later architects, the group tended to work as partners, making individual houses hard to attribute.

This trio exerted an about-turn in British architecture as radical as when Inigo Jones rejected the prodigy Elizabethans. They dismissed the work of Wren's followers, though they were deferential to Wren himself. They made little pretence of originality and were determined to adorn Georgian England according to the canons of Roman architecture as dictated by Vitruvius. Gibbs was removed from rebuilding Burlington's house in Piccadilly – core of the present Royal Academy – and replaced by Campbell. The new movement was all-consuming. It founded a Society of Antiquaries in 1717 and of Dilettantes in 1734, both devoted to the task of recapturing the correct and uncorrupted spirit of the classical past. The Dilettantes were to study classical remains 'in the more inaccessible Roman provinces, under Turkish rule and dangerously unsuitable to travellers'.

In 1723 Burlington began a villa for himself in Chiswick, inspired by Palladio's villas and other Roman remains. It is an immaculate reproduction – modernists would describe it as pastiche – consisting of a suite of rooms for the display of Burlington's collection of antiquities. The rooms were sumptuous in comparison with the chaste exterior. The house also revived the perceived form of a Roman garden. Designed by Kent, it departed from the tight, formalized patios of the Restoration – much influenced by the Netherlands – while retaining their geometrical layout. A *patte d'oie* or goosefoot of paths splayed out from the house, its straight lines culminating in architectural features such as pavilions, temples and obelisks. Pools of water and groves of trees hinted at later excursions in the picturesque. Similar gardens now blossomed at Viscount Cobham's house of Stowe in Buckinghamshire, where Kent, Vanbrugh, Gibbs and others laid out a version of the Elysian Fields of the Villa Borghese in Rome. Others appeared at Stourhead, West Wycombe and Rousham.

While the French aristocracy's focus at this time was on Paris and Versailles, England's retained an essentially provincial character. Wealthy young men returning from the grand tour competed in the Augustan splendour of their country estates. In 1734 the Burlingtonian Henry Flitcroft was summoned to redesign and greatly expand the mansion of Wentworth Woodhouse in Yorkshire after the manner of Wanstead. In the same year Kent, with input from Burlington, designed Holkham Hall in Norfolk, specifically to display its owner Lord Leicester's grand-tour acquisitions. Today it stretches out against its hillside as beautifully composed as any house in England.

Through Burlington's influence, Kent was appointed to the

Office of Works and left plans for the Horse Guards Parade in Whitehall in 1750. Others fell into line. They included George Dance, architect to the City of London and designer of its new Mansion House. Francis Smith of Warwick (1672–1738) and John Carr (1723–1807) promoted the Palladian message from their respective bases in the Midlands and Yorkshire, making provincial England as architecturally vigorous as was London. To Smith we owe Stoneleigh, Chicheley and the majestic Palladian ruin of Sutton Scarsdale near Hardwick. Carr's output of great houses was phenomenal, including Harewood, Aske, Lytham, York's palatial Fairfax House and Constable Burton (1768). This last might be a villa from the Veneto lurking on a windy Yorkshire plane. Carr's work embraced Buxton Crescent, York courthouse and bridges galore.

The Burlingtonians had their lay supporters. To Horace Walpole they were granting architecture 'her rights, true principles and correct taste'. There were 'men of genius to execute her rules and patrons to countenance their labours . . . to establish the throne of architecture in Britain while it languishes in Rome and struggles in vain in Paris'. Alexander Pope wrote of Leoni and his Palladian compendiums, 'You show us Rome was glorious, not profuse, / And pompous buildings once were things of use.' They would gather at Burlington's villa at Chiswick and glory in all things Italian, while the bust of Inigo Jones oversaw their celebrations.

Others sounded a more sceptical note. Gibbs remained productive until his death in 1754 and published his own rejoinder to Campbell, *A Book of Architecture*, which became a bestseller. A more searing critic was the artist and satirist William Hogarth. To him England's baroque architects had been the true Britons, depicted with bulldogs and roast beef. He regarded the Burlington set as effete, frog-eating Frenchies. This critique took the form of satirical prints, one of which, 'The Man of Taste', depicted Pope whitewashing Burlington's front gate, above which Kent is portrayed alongside

Raphael and Michelangelo. A bucket of paint falls on the (anti-Burlington) Duke of Chandos's carriage below. The print, whose authorship by Hogarth is contested, was considered so offensive it was suppressed.

Aligned with Hogarth was Batty Langley (1696–1751), a popular gardener and author of a building manual. He eagerly championed medieval revivalism (which he called 'native Saxon') and deplored the 'imported' styles of the Burlingtonians. Langley published a series of pattern books covering all manner of styles and devices in the 1730s and 40s. His books, if not his medieval advocacy, became popular among vernacular builders throughout the Georgian period, in Britain and then extensively in America.

A consequence of this erudite conflict was that to the Georgians architecture mattered. The grand tour, the outpouring of books and prints and a degree of rivalry between the principal figures highlighted the question of how a building should look. Debate was no longer confined to provincial palaces and noble London squares. Britain was urbanizing fast. Classicism took hold of town houses and civic halls, covered markets and shopping streets. As the historian Simon Thurley has pointed out, the outcome was that architectural debate became a national one. Craftsmen across the land could produce 'proportional, rational and text-based' classical buildings that were 'fashionable and handsome without complex training'. Style was almost becoming democratic.

A result was that over the course of the eighteenth century English towns gradually turned from Tudor to Georgian. In 1728 Burlington personally designed assembly rooms for York with the most regal of Corinthian arcades. York Castle Prison was rebuilt to a Palladian design. City fathers everywhere were invited to decide whether they were Doric, Ionic or Corinthian. Edinburgh's long-planned New Town finally began construction, its houses more luxuriously proportioned than their equivalents in cramped Mayfair or Marylebone. One town that broke ranks was Tory Worcester, whose guildhall of 1723 was an outlier. In a jovial Wrennish baroque it sported a statue of Charles I prominent on its facade.

Nowhere so embodied the classical revival as John Wood's Bath. If Burlington was a high priest of classicism, Wood was a fanatic. He considered himself descended from Druids and Romans, and was happy to claim an obscure link with Stonehenge. His Bath was a city replete with circuses, crescents, forums and gymnasiums. All were built in a golden Cotswold stone that could turn the town ablaze in the sunlight. Greek orders were displayed everywhere, curling round hillside contours and rising like tiers in a colosseum. Crucial to Bath's architecture was its modified classlessness. The town had no function as a civic entity but was simply a leisure resort. Its houses differed in size but there were no princely palaces or grand town houses.

This Bath survives elegant and largely intact. Its circuses and crescents, like London's squares, were widely imitated. The simple dignity of its terraces entered the language of British urban design and never left it until the twentieth century. The residential neighbourhoods of English towns – poor as well as rich – were typically composed of rows of identical houses, their floors of descending proportions, with shallow tiled roofs and plain windows. The building materials were brick or stone. Early casement windows were replaced in the eighteenth century by sashes, as successive building acts updated that of 1667, largely to minimize the risk of fire. Only in Scotland were poorer quarters largely composed of tenement buildings round courtyards rather than terraces.

In London the waywardness of the market left less opportunity than in Bath for stylistic coherence. Terraces tended to progress at the speed of demand. Today we can tell a confident development, with streets numbered odd on one side, even on the other. Only where each side was extended in fits and starts do numbers rise consecutively. Few London squares displayed any architectural unity. Berkeley (1700s) and Grosvenor (1720s) had none of the formalism of Jones's Covent Garden. An overall design was achieved later at Bedford (1740s) and Fitzroy (1750s). A distinctive feature was found at the Earl of Scarbrough's Hanover Square (1717). Designed to offer a welcome to the new Hanoverians, its facades inserted a stone apron beneath each window after the German fashion. Examples of this survive opposite St George's church.

The result of the regulation and stylistic restraint of Georgian development was that early eighteenth-century houses concentrated any decoration on doorways. This is seen most vividly in Queen Anne's Gate, Westminster (c.1704) where elaborately sculpted pilasters and hoods are crowded with pediments and pendants. These were later banned as a fire risk, and decoration confined to the mildest plasterwork.

The Georgian street thus evolved into what the Victorians were to dismiss as an insufferable dullness and twentieth-century estate agents as the peak of urban decorum. Jones's ascetic classicism had taken a full century to assert its influence, in large part through the Burlingtonians. By the mid-eighteenth century it had won the day. The British city was 'planned' as never before, or since.

10.

The Golden Age (1750–1810)

Every history claims a golden age. That of British architecture is variously said to stretch from the Restoration to the coronation of Victoria or, more narrowly, from the Burlington ascendancy to the 1820s Regency. Over this period, most of wealthier landed families built themselves new country houses, either extending ancestral halls or castles or building afresh, almost all in the classical style. Unlike much of Europe, Britain at this time enjoyed sustained peace and security, suffering no invasion and minimal civil conflict. Agriculture was enclosing land and specializing, leading to a steady migration from country to town and a surging demand for urban housing. The technology of processing cloth, iron, coal and manufactures was revolutionized. Overseas trade boomed under the aegis of a burgeoning British Empire.

Meanwhile, architecture still laboured under a neoclassical orthodoxy. At the start of the eighteenth century, Hawksmoor could freely mix classical with Gothic on facades in Oxford and Westminster. By mid-century that would not do. The veneration of classical Greece and Rome was fanatical and to disagree was heretical. Such dogmatism, eccentric in itself, was of a sort once confined to the Church and court. It now extended to a fast-expanding middle class. It could almost be said that, for the first and perhaps only time, a large constituency of Britons managed to speak architecture – and yet disagree about it. As the century progressed, younger architects rallied to the Burlingtonian flag. James Paine designed New Wardour Castle in Wiltshire and Robert Taylor Heveningham Hall in

Suffolk, handsome houses but with little of the personality of a Castle Howard or Blenheim.

By mid-century, with Burlington dead, leadership of his tendency had passed to the stiff figure of William Chambers (1723–96). He had spent dutiful years as a young man in Rome, visited Sweden and – his one break from custom – journeyed as far as China. In 1759 he published *A Treatise on Civil Architecture*, in which he codified the orders and their use by sixteenth- and seventeenth-century Italian masters. As Comptroller of the King's Works, he spent most of his time upgrading buildings for the royal family and court. The visit to China resulted in a fascination with Chinoiserie, hence the pagoda now standing in Kew gardens.

Chambers's most prominent building was the official replacement for the old Somerset House on the Strand, appropriately on the site of the Protector Somerset's first classical building. It was to be London's first purpose-built office block, headquarters for the Royal Navy and a number of government offices and arts organizations. These included the new Royal Academy, founded in 1768. Somerset House, begun in 1775, comprised four ranges set round an extensive courtyard by the Thames. Here and with Paris's Louvre in mind it appeared to float on a platform above quaysides built for naval supplies. Today, hidden from the Thames by ill-sited trees, it fronts nothing more exciting than an embankment road.

As Chambers's building was being planned on the Thames, another immediately upstream was to prove the first sign of a breaking of ranks. The leading Scottish architect of the day was William Adam, designer of one of Scotland's grandest houses, Hopetoun in South Queensferry, while his sons Robert and John designed Dumfries House in Ayrshire. The first was a palace in the style of Vanbrugh, the other in a more demure Palladian. William Adam and Roger Morris had in 1746 designed Inveraray

The Golden Age (1750–1810)

Castle for the Dukes of Argyll at the enormous cost of £250,000 (£48 million today). This was an extravagant four-square building, essentially an upgrading of a medieval fortified mansion. It was the first substantial Gothic revival building in Britain and, it is claimed, the first in Europe. Given that the sixteenth-century Stuarts had introduced Renaissance architecture to Britain, this confirmed Scotland in the van of British taste.

Robert Adam (1728–92) worked for his father and then spent three years in Italy, from where he visited the newly excavated palace of the Roman emperor Diocletian in Split. It made an immediate impact on him. The Croatian city was full of decorative innovation, yet it was incontrovertibly Roman. The Burlingtonians could hardly declare it heretical. The designs and motifs Adam brought home were captivating in their rococo delicacy, and he determined to put them to marketable use. He was a classicist but able to apply a personal decorative flair to the basic rulebook. An Adam building almost dances before the eye in comparison with the four-square Palladianism from which it parted company. In 1758, ten years after his father's death, Robert Adam set up a practice in London with his brothers, James and John.

The trio's most substantial speculation was in 1769 immediately adjacent to Somerset House on the Thames. In honour of their partnership they called it the Adelphi, Greek for brothers. Conventional terraces of houses were set on a platform overlooking the river. What was new was the decoration of facades with friezes and of pilasters with filigree ornament. The main block faced the river while the streets behind were each composed of mostly four-bay, four-storey houses, each with its own front door and railings. The variation was hardly radical, but it was novel – and controversial.

Robert Adam's background in Scottish architecture clearly freed him from English convention. His delight in surface decoration, borrowed from Diocletian, was wholly absent from Chambers's

Somerset House next door. Indeed, the two offered a delightful contrast in Georgian taste. The Adelphi did not immediately sell and had to be rescued financially by disposing of the houses through a lottery. It survived until the main block was tragically demolished in the 1930s. The side pavilions remain, giving some idea of the development's novelty in bringing a lighter-hearted spirit to a Georgian street.

Adam was one of the most productive architects of the Georgian age. Though eager to give his architecture 'movement', he always claimed to be true to 'the good old Roman form'. He was adamant that he 'had not trod in the paths of others, nor derived from their labours', of which he could be highly critical. In a book advertising his works in 1773, he declared his aim was 'to seize the beautiful spirit of antiquity and to transfuse it with novelty and variety'. As for his rivals, followers of the now departed Burlington, he dismissed them as 'ponderous' and even 'disgustful'. As we shall increasingly see, British architects did not take kindly to each other.

Where Adam stole his grandest march was in his interiors. Those at Kedleston in Derbyshire, Saltram in Devon, Osterley in West London and Home House in Portman Square were wholly innovative. Benefiting from new excavations at Pompeii and Herculaneum, walls cascaded with scrolls, leaves, flowers and classical characters, making free use of the newly fashionable chinoiserie. Adam depended on a regiment of plasterers and 'artificers'. The drawings of his designers were replicated by skilled craftsmen across what became acres of walls and ceilings. Prime among these was the uncle-and-nephew partnership of the two Joseph Roses. Their names crop up in virtually every house Adam designed. Time has dulled much of their colour into pastel shades, but where restored, as at Osterley, their interiors are dazzling in their brilliance.

The failure of the Adelphi project and a downturn in the

property market in the 1770s saw Adam's English practice collapse. He drew in his horns and retreated to his father's old firm in Scotland. There he refreshed a tradition that had remained largely free of English dogmatism. The baronial castle held its appeal as a symbol of domestic nobility and security. Adam reintroduced himself to this market with one of his most impressive works, Culzean Castle (c.1777) on the Ayrshire coast. Its classical facades framed by battlemented towers on a rock looking out to sea are one of the sights of Scotland. Variations on this theme saw Adam produce ten more Scottish castles, their appearance more picturesque than military. At the same time in the north of England, the Percys were rehabilitating Alnwick. Like many northern owners, they retained a battlemented exterior and let Gothic rip inside.

Style is a creature of fashion, and fashion craves novelty. Thus it was with Gothic. To the historian Howard Colvin, Gothic had survived the Reformation and lived on in the vernacular tradition of local builders. He catalogued churches of the Georgian period that were still using Gothic across the Cotswolds and into the Midlands and the north throughout the eighteenth century. Secular Gothic soon caught up. At Stowe, Gibbs designed a Gothic temple in 1741. Gothic too were William Halfpenny's Stout's Hill (1743) and Frampton Court Orangery (1752) in Gloucestershire. In Scotland the term extended well beyond its 'baronial' ubiquity to anything castellated or even ruined. At Hagley Hall in Worcestershire, Sir George Lyttelton ordered the architect Sanderson Miller to build an entire 'ruined' castle in his grounds. Miller went on to build a similar ruin at Wimpole and contribute a complete Gothic interior to Arbury in Warwickshire. Begun in 1750, it even boasted a ceiling based on Vertue's Henry VII Chapel at Westminster. Miller became celebrated as 'the Great Master of Gothick', the final 'k' being a widespread affectation.

Burlington's most devoted supporter had long been the dilettante Horace Walpole. In 1749, Walpole acquired a cottage in Twickenham and proceeded to join the trend to diversity. He converted his Strawberry Hill into a castellated Gothic house, to honour the 'gloomth' of his antique collection. Walpole had often criticized Gothic in the past for its 'unrestrained licentiousness'. Now he adopted it as an exercise in romanticism, roaming free of the rigid dictates of Palladianism, a characteristic that Gothic was to retain during the later battles over style. He saw his venture as a folly, in which he would be guided by a 'committee of taste'.

This committee was composed of ten architects, each of whom was expected to contribute a room or a furnishing. Every known Gothic device was to be adapted to create a disorderly, enchanting dream. 'The design of the chimneypiece,' Walpole wrote, 'is taken from the tomb of Edward the Confessor improved by Mr Adam.' Strawberry Hill became so popular a riverside attraction that Walpole insisted on timed tickets and limited visiting groups to four.

By the 1770s, Adam's chief commercial rival was close to him in spirit. From the age of nineteen, James Wyatt (1746–1813) had spent a full seven years in Rome, where, among other tasks, he measured the dome interior of St Peter's while lying on his back in a cradle. He returned to London to join his entrepreneur brother Samuel, beginning with the Pantheon (1772) in London's Oxford Street. Intended as an entertainment space, it was marketed as an 'indoor Ranelagh Gardens', referring to the outdoor venue in Chelsea. The Pantheon was the largest interior in England, galleried and beneath a dome vaguely based on the Pantheon in Rome.

To guard his business interests, Wyatt supported Chambers and the Burlingtonians against Adam. He explained to George III (r.1760–1820) that Chambers produced 'the last great architecture' before 'public taste was corrupted by the Adamses and he [Wyatt] felt obliged to comply with it'. Wyatt, like Vanbrugh, demonstrated the power of charm in an architect. He was said to have refused vast sums from Catherine the Great of Russia but used the offer to induce a club of British noblemen to pay him £1,200 just to stay available to work in England. There is hardly a castle, college or military headquarters on which Wyatt did not leave a mark. Ashridge House, Belvoir Castle, Castle Coole, Gaddesden Place, Heaton Hall and Broadway Tower all reflect an architect of imagination and breadth. While Wyatt might claim to be close to Chambers, his classicism was as uninhibited and 'rococo' as Adam's. The Adam brothers complained that Wyatt shamelessly plagiarized their designs.

In 1796, Wyatt took over from Chambers as Comptroller of the King's Works, though the Napoleonic Wars stifled most official building. His extrovert temperament had by now made him a celebrity architect, but one with a reputation for loose living and heavy drinking. He would send underlings to client meetings and offer an outline plan to be passed to assistants and builders to execute. Through all this, Wyatt proved adept at keeping up with each turn in Georgian taste.

In this spirit, Wyatt in 1797 took the Gothic fashion literally to new heights. He designed a house at Fonthill in Wiltshire for the aesthete William Beckford, claimed to be the richest man in England thanks to his family's West Indies plantations. Fonthill was an extravagant vanity project, requiring 500 labourers and rising to a 300ft tower. This tower twice collapsed and was eventually demolished, but Wyatt's popularity was undimmed. He was also engaged to restore numerous cathedrals, many after centuries of neglect. His casual removal of contents and screens and his smashing of medieval windows earned him the nickname 'The Destroyer'. He drastically scraped the walls of Durham and Salisbury and probably caused more damage to cathedral contents than any seventeenth-century iconoclast.

★

As Adam blazed his trail in the 1760s and 70s, and Wyatt after him, a new stylistic revival was approaching over the horizon. Though still under Ottoman rule, Greece was opening its doors to historians and archaeologists, offering a different ancient culture from the long supremacy of Rome. Books by two architects working in Athens, James Stuart and Nicholas Revett, caused much excitement. 'Athenian' Stuart was soon in demand for Greek porticos and follies. Given Rome's cultural debt to Greece, argument between the two tastes, Greece versus Rome, seemed absurd. But argument there was. To the Greeks the buildings of the Acropolis were dogma, while Palladio was the heretic. The Society of Dilettanti attempted to cover both bases with the slogan 'Greek taste and Roman spirit'.

By now the market for architecture was changing. Those in the Burlington tradition continued to dominate big projects. Henry Holland (1745–1806) was a leading favourite among Whig grandees. He designed their club, Brooks's, in St James's, and in 1783 was chosen to build Carlton House as a residence for the Prince of Wales overlooking St James's Park. There were now fewer calls for new houses and more for 'improving' existing ones, especially their interiors and surroundings.

The year 1763 had seen the end of the Seven Years War and the Peace of Paris. A chief beneficiary of the peace was Britain's fast-expanding empire in the Americas and India. This opened up new trading routes and cultural stimuli. One such was indicated in 1788 by George Dance's refashioned entrance for the medieval Guildhall in the City of London. Its style was later described as 'Hindustani Gothic'. It did not catch on but it was imitated by a Colonel Cockerell, returning with a fortune from Bengal in 1805. His brother, the architect Samuel Pepys Cockerell, built him a Cotswold mansion, Sezincote, in a Mughal style. An early guidebook describes the resulting house as a celebration of the empire in 'green onion-shaped domes, umbrella-shaped chatris, Mughal

The Golden Age (1750–1810)

gardens and serpent fountains . . . while Surya temples and Nandi bulls guard the estate'. The empire had truly come home to roost.

At the same time there were calls for the ever closer regulation of the rapidly growing cities. Ever since the Great Fire of London, British governments had considered it their duty to control development. The Rebuilding Act of 1667 had prescribed street widths and housing materials. Further acts in 1707, 1709 and 1774 make twentieth-century planning controls seem libertarian. They stipulated that terrace houses be of one of four 'rates' or sizes on a given street. They banned exposed wood on eaves and window surrounds. Windows had to be recessed a precise distance. Lower-floor 'areas' were required to give light to servants' basements. Every house should enjoy rear privacy and yet show its front door to the street.

The 1774 Act was the work of two Palladians, the City of London's George Dance and Robert Taylor. The impact on urban design across the nation was mixed. Benjamin Disraeli later called a typical 1774-Act development, Gower Street in Bloomsbury, 'flat, dull, spiritless . . . like a large family of plain children'. The unassuming dignity of the eighteenth-century English town house was nowhere better illustrated than in the home of the prime minister himself, initially Sir Robert Walpole. No. 10 Downing Street was distinguishable from its neighbours only by a number on the door, considered by foreigners a typical British understatement.

For all this rigour – later relaxed by the Victorians – these Georgian town houses were to rank among the most popular of urban dwellings. There is nowhere a billionaire would rather live than behind the smart, anonymous facade of a Mayfair first-rater. In particular the houses presented themselves immaculately to the street. Their railings, area, shallow front steps, dignified windows and inoffensive doorways offered the perfect combination of privacy and good neighbourliness.

*

One area in which stylistic diversity did take hold, and from the start of the Georgian period, was the formal garden. Kent and Burlington had studied those of ancient Rome and replicated them at Chiswick and Stowe. The slopes of Tuscany and the Veneto were transported to the glades of the Home Counties. The royal gardens of Hanoverian Kew now sprouted an Alhambra, a House of Confucius, a mosque and Chambers's pagoda. Places of popular assembly followed suit. London's Vauxhall and Ranelagh Gardens offered diversion to all classes of citizen, albeit for the then high entry fee of between a shilling and two and sixpence. The craving for exotic novelty rose to Disneyland proportions. Vauxhall Gardens boasted a Chinese pavilion, a Turkish tent and a Gothic piazza. Ranelagh opened in 1742 with a giant rotunda, a Chinese house and, at one point, Mozart performing and Canaletto painting.

The final task of the Georgians was the marriage not just of a house to its garden but the much wider relationship with its landscape setting. Throughout the second half of the century, the ubiquitous figure of Lancelot 'Capability' Brown (1716–83) could be found in almost every corner of the land, practising his concept of managed landscape. Some 170 designed parks have been attributed to him. While few have survived untouched, their influence on successive movements 'back to nature' has rarely dimmed. Brown declared that his question was never 'What do I want to see?' It was 'What does nature want to see?'

Brown began his career as an under-gardener to Kent at Stowe. He went on to plan landscapes at Burghley, Harewood, Bowood, Blenheim and Highclere. The grounds of Chatsworth in Derbyshire were transformed from a formal layout of avenues and trees in the Dutch style to peakland that appeared to spring naturally from the surrounding valley. Brown also designed buildings, notably Croome Court in Worcestershire, but always as subordinate to his landscapes. The old guard hit back. Chambers complained of the 'new manner', of Brown's gardens as 'differing very little from common fields, so closely is vulgar nature copied in most of them'. But Brown became a celebrity. If he visited an owner to suggest changes to his estate, neighbours would plead to be invited to dinner. He was proud to be described as a designer who, 'so closely did . . . copy nature that his works will be mistaken for it'. Today he would be a 'rewilder'.

Brown's message was eagerly taken up by the rural artist and writer William Gilpin, champion of the romantic view of landscape known as the picturesque in the 1790s and 1800s. During the stop to European travel during the Napoleonic Wars he championed the 'wildness and rugged mountain scenery' of Britain. In place of the Italian grand tour he demanded Britons study their own landscape, with a preference for the Wye Valley and the Lake District. Gilpin's theories of the picturesque were satirized by Thomas Rowlandson (who dubbed him Dr Syntax). But they became popular, appearing in their most extreme form in the writings of Uvedale Price. A Herefordshire landowner, Price diverged from Brown in preferring his nature untended by man and truly wild – though he found such wildness needed careful fabrication.

Brown's most devoted disciple was Humphry Repton (1752–1818), whose landscape proposals were delivered as watercolours in beautifully bound Red Books. His style was more mannered than Brown's. While the romantic leaning tended to express itself in words and paintings, Repton saw landscape as architectural. His agents were armies of labourers with picks and shovels, heightening the drama of a house's setting by glimpsing it from curving approach roads, with carefully sited spires, outbuildings and *cottages ornés*. His sketches placed people and activity in the foreground, with the house in the middle ground against a backdrop of wildness and nature.

A well-preserved version of this work is Sheringham Park (1812) in Norfolk, a modest white house set across a small valley with behind it a steep wooded hill. Behind lies an infinity of sea. Repton disliked straight lines and right angles. Sheringham's entrance drive thus doubled the distance from the local village, cutting into the side of a slope. The eventual view of the house, said its Red Book, 'would burst at once on the sight like some enchanted palace of a fairy tale'. Repton called Sheringham 'my most favourite and darling child'. To its owner, Abbot Upcher, it was 'a gem of inestimable beauty'.

Brown and Repton put to practical use the abstractions of picturesque romanticism at the climax of the golden age. They clothed the country house in Turner's vision of Tintern Abbey and Wordsworth's dancing daffodils. They brought a new depth to the style of rural England and usurped the primacy of London in the architectural narrative.

11.

Nash and the Italianate (1810–1825)

By the first decade of the nineteenth century the stylistic diversity that had enlivened the last decades of the eighteenth had run its course. In essence it was an argument among a group of aesthetes over whether to insist on Palladio's adherence to Vitruvius or give freer rein to the language of classicism. That this should matter was absurd, as was its periodic degeneration into abuse. The Palladians were finally overwhelmed by the ingenuities of Adam and Wyatt and by a scatter of Goths and Greeks, both baronial and effete. All was then overlaid by the charmed landscapes of Capability Brown and Repton. But events in France in the 1790s produced a widespread cessation of new buildings – other than 100 Martello towers round the coast of England. The personalities of the golden age had mostly departed and by the dawn of the Regency in 1820 a new middle class clientele was beginning to make itself felt in architecture.

Two men now moved to centre stage. John Nash and John Soane were both rooted in the classical tradition and both were prepared to adapt it to the mood of the day. Beyond that the two could not have been less alike, in personality or professional behaviour. Nash was driven by hyperactivity and commercial opportunism, Soane by stolid intellectual conviction. Indeed, as with Chambers and Adam, we might wonder if style was just a product of personality.

Nash (1752–1835) was a Londoner of Welsh pedigree who had worked for a decade as a speculative builder. He went bankrupt in 1783 and retired to Wales, where he designed modest houses in Carmarthenshire. In 1796 he returned to work with Repton, designing houses to complement his landscapes and clearly sharing Repton's intuition for architecture in a rural setting.

Nash became a champion of the asymmetrical or 'rambling' facade. He liked crenellated parapets and medieval or Tudor features. While closer to Chambers than to Adam in his classicism, Nash would turn to any style to suit his market. This was perhaps best indicated in the use of the word Italianate to indicate a freer and more decorative interpretation of the classical revival. Thus Nash built Cronkhill in Shropshire, said to be the first properly Italianate English house, but most of his buildings, such as Ravensworth in Durham and Caerhays in Cornwall, were in his favourite castellated Gothic. His one complaint, he said, was that he could run up two classical windows for the price of one Gothic.

Nash was odd in appearance. He described himself as a 'thick, squat dwarf with the face of a monkey'. Yet his ambition knew no bounds. His career shot from obscurity to prominence in 1806 when he took under his wing the twenty-five-year-old Ann Pennethorne. She was mother of five children, reputedly by George, Prince of Wales, who was desperate to find them a respectable home. Nash, who was possibly homosexual, occupied first a house with Ann in Dover Street and then built himself a house next to the prince's Carlton House at the foot of Regent Street. He thus acquired a new family, a government post and the personal confidence of the royal heir. His house also had a common space with a house he built next door for John Edwards, his lawyer and lifelong friend. Edwards already had a son, whom he called Nash, and the boy went on to inherit Nash's estate.

Nash succeeded Holland as the prince's favourite architect and became effective head of the government's Commission of Woods and Forests, forerunner of the Crown Estate. In 1815 he refashioned

Nash and the Italianate (1810–1825)

the now Prince Regent's seaside villa built by Holland in Brighton. Nash transformed it into a Mughal palace, encrusted with Arab, Indian and Chinese designs, characterized at the time as Hindoo and now as Indo-Saracenic. Walking through the pavilion's gallery of oriental decorations and objects we find it hard to believe this is England.

In London, Nash's primary task was to realize the prince's obsession with recreating Napoleonic Paris. Like Wren, as royal architect, this required him to accommodate the fantasies of a spendthrift royal within the confines of the Exchequer. The prince might want a new London but London was not his property or that of the government. Any plan had to be adjusted to the constraints of private ownership and realistic planning.

Nash's great achievement was to succeed where Wren had failed. The prince had envisaged a 'royal way', a *via triumphalis*, running from Carlton House in St James's north across Mayfair and Marylebone to a new estate on the former royal hunting ground facing Primrose Hill. Since it was impossible to smash through the new Mayfair estates, Nash proposed what amounted to a winding Champs-Élysées, swerving past the estates and demolishing only slums. His metaphor was that of a tree, with its roots in St James's, its trunk as Regent Street and its foliage Regent's Park. The boulevard would also serve as a buffer between the elegant Jermyn, Burlington and Portland estates and less smart Soho to the east. It would mark, said Nash bluntly, a 'complete separation between the streets and squares occupied by the nobility and gentry and the narrower streets and meaner houses occupied by mechanics and trading classes'.

At the route's southern end would be the forecourt to the prince's Carlton House, where now is Waterloo Place. At the northern end would be a Bath-style circus giving onto a park of villas set among water and trees. Nash's idea was that 'no villa should see another but each should appear to possess the whole of the park'. It would be a true *rus in urbe*, a fusion of architecture and landscape in the Repton manner. A new town to service it would be built to the east round Cumberland market.

Nash's plan had no official status. It was published in 1812, the year after the future George IV (r.1820–30) had become Prince Regent. Nash was in effect his own developer, architect, engineer, estate agent and financial adviser. Not surprisingly, he was better suited to some of these roles than others. He worried little for the design of individual buildings, which he left to subcontracted builders. His task was to execute the overall vision, to bring it to pass against any odds. Above all, he had to keep the prince and his Treasury paymasters on board.

The plan went into swift operation, involving the extensive acquisition and demolition of dozens of back streets and slums on the Soho fringes. The route progressed from Waterloo Place past Pall Mall, where to the east Nash proposed a piazza in what later became Trafalgar Square. It then ran up Lower Regent Street to Piccadilly Circus. There the route swung round a handsome quadrant into Regent Street, where more kinks were required to avoid Hanover and Cavendish Squares. On a final swerve to the west, Nash designed All Souls church in Langham Place, intended to look as if it were facing both south and west.

The whole enterprise was neoclassical town planning at its most ingenious and pragmatic. The facades were mostly of the cheapest brick covered in Nash's signature white stucco, concealing a multitude of slapdash sins. Nash ran increasingly short of backers as he neared the park. The final circus became the present crescent and then two sides of a square. Sites still did not sell and parliament baulked at further loans. In 1820 the prince took the throne, gained a kingdom and lost heart.

Nash was now on his own and in trouble. Throughout the 1820s, Regent Street was a river of mud and scaffolding. As for the park villas, the sites for forty of them failed to sell and the number was reduced to eight. At this point Nash was rescued. A wealthy builder, James Burton, developer of the Duke of Bedford's Bloomsbury estate, took over a large number of Nash's Regent Street leases in return for Nash taking on Burton's son Decimus as a pupil. In a last gesture of desperation, Nash decided to abandon any more Regent's Park villas and instead surround the park with ordinary terraces behind facades built to imitate classical palaces.

This final gamble was breathtaking. Regent's Park saw no ordinary terraces. It was encased in a drum roll of arches, porticos, pavilions and domes such as might be seen in St Petersburg or on the banks of the Seine. They were mostly put in the hands of Burton Jr, who proved a talented architect but who had a mind of his own. Constant disputes with Nash ensued. The quality of the building work was mostly dreadful, some of the houses being just two rooms deep. It is now thought Decimus designed most of the grand terraces, while the Burton family lived in The Holme, a villa overlooking the central lake.

Either way the 'Nash terraces' were built and eventually let, to become symbols of Regency grandiloquence. They were given royal titles to help with marketing, such as Chester, Cumberland, York, Sussex, Hanover and Ulster. These were interspersed with lodges and villas. Nash pleaded, wheedled and short-changed his way to London's most coherent set-piece design. Speculative capitalism was harnessed to the cause of aesthetic town planning, with a panache as yet equalled only in Bath.

The fastidious Summerson called Regent's Park 'a sham, flagrant, absurd, an architectural frolic', though he later admitted that, when seen through the mists of time, the terraces can equally be 'dream palaces full of romantic ideas . . . making Greenwich tame and Hampton Court provincial'. As I mention in the introduction, to me in my childhood their stucco facades, creamy white in a mostly black city, were as in a fairy tale. After the Second World War the local Marylebone council tried to demolish them, provoking one of London's earliest conservation battles. They were saved, but York Gate and Park Crescent were so poorly built they had to be reconstructed.

Nash's grand plan survived but was much abused. In 1820 the newly ascended king felt that, as a European monarch, he should have a more distinguished residence than Carlton House. He wanted a Versailles or a Hofburg, but had to make do with Buckingham House down the road, which Nash was charged with rebuilding. To pay for this, Carlton House was demolished and replaced by the stately Carlton House Terrace, designed by Nash but sometimes attributed to Burton. The old forecourt of Waterloo Place saw Nash's United Services Club (1826), now the Institute of Directors, built opposite Burton's Athenaeum Club (1824). When Burton came to alter Nash's club in 1858, he moved its doorway round into Pall Mall so as not to detract from his own work opposite. Old battles never died.

Soon the pressures of ambition took their toll on Nash's projects. His conversion of Buckingham House into a palace involved a three-sided courtyard surrounding what became Marble Arch. Nash was savaged by the Treasury for overspending, even fraud. He was accused of 'inexcusable irregularity and great negligence' and denied the knighthood he expected and deserved. Meanwhile, Regent Street steadily deteriorated as its pavements were colonized by prostitutes. It was gradually demolished and rebuilt, beginning as early as 1848. Eventually not one Nash building beyond Waterloo Place (apart from the church) survived along its route. He died in disgrace, but is one of the outstanding personalities of British architecture.

Nash's contemporary John Soane (1753–1837) was a studious young man, the son of a Reading builder. He found work in the City office of George Dance and then went dutifully to Italy to

Nash and the Italianate (1810–1825)

study. He was clearly talented but lacked the essential quality for architectural success: self-promotion. He deplored Nash, knowing 'few persons more anxious of fame and who would make more sacrifices at the altar of public approbation'. But while Nash worked without cease, Soane needed his patron Dance in 1788 to secure the post of architect to the Bank of England. He was to spend thirty years rebuilding it in the heart of the City.

The bank's sequence of secure vaulted chambers with windowless walls meant that any daylight had to come from shallow top-lit domes. Each was considered a masterpiece. The Dividend Office in particular displayed the spatial volume of a great church, illustrations of it suggesting a replica of Rome's Pantheon. The ageing Chambers dismissed it as 'in a barbarous style of which . . . the peculiarities are borrowed from the example of the Dark Ages'.

Soane's approach to any project was the opposite of Nash's: it would be meticulously designed, yet with a stylistic radicalism new to the classical tradition. He fashioned interiors for Wimpole in Cambridgeshire and Aynhoe in Northamptonshire, but none of his London churches, St Peter's Walworth, St John Bethnal Green and Holy Trinity Marylebone, was particularly distinguished. His Dulwich picture gallery and mausoleum were in a Georgian style that was almost modernist in its austerity.

The best-known surviving works by Soane were the houses he built for himself. Pitzhanger House in Ealing was Adamish, with a frontage borrowed from the Arch of Constantine in Rome. Columns in front of the house supported nothing but a row of statues, to the horror of traditional classicists. Soane's town house in Lincoln's Inn Fields carried a pattern of Greek motifs on panels and arches. It now contains the Soane Museum, the one gallery in Britain dedicated to architecture. Rooms of classical pictures and drawings lead on to caves, passages, mirrors, alcoves and strange pools of light. To wander them is to join Soane on a miniature grand tour.

There was an air of sadness to Soane's life. His career was distinguished. He became professor of architecture at the Royal Academy and he ended with a knighthood but he never recovered from the death of his wife and estrangement from his two rebellious sons. The demolition of his Bank of England in the 1920s was tragic, regarded even at the time as an architectural crime. That said, in his first academy lecture Soane took leave of his senses. He openly attacked the work of his patron George Dance and his former pupil Robert Smirke. This led to such recrimination that a rule was introduced that no lecturer could attack a living architect. Soane objected to the curb on his freedom of speech but was forced to acquiesce. It said much for the state of the profession that such a rule was thought necessary.

The truth was that architecture seemed unable to avoid controversy. Under the Hanoverians, it had acquired political connotations, that of baroque with Toryism, Palladian with Whiggism. In church circles, Gothic had long been the language of High Church Anglicanism, classical of Protestant gentility. Across Europe revolutionary movements had identified with the imagery of classical mythology. The paintings of Jacques-Louis David depicted democracy and republicanism against a backdrop of Doric columns and Athenian temples. Democratic Greece was eagerly espoused by Americans. The Washington Capitol, begun in 1793 by the English architect Benjamin Latrobe, was majestically classical, as was the White House. Almost every state built itself a classical capitol. Hence Gothic must equal tradition.

The peace following the Congress of Vienna in 1815 reopened Europe to British travel and also to a building surge. Two years later a scholar, Thomas Rickman, produced a systematic analysis

17. Perpendicular Climactic: King's Chapel, Cambridge, 1509

18. Llananno church screen, fifteenth century

19. The musicians of St Mary's, Beverley, after 1520

20. The tower mansion of Layer Marney, 1523

21. Tudor prodigy: Bess's Hardwick, completed in 1597

22. & 23. Hampton Court English, with Renaissance roundel, late 1510s

24. Italy for the Stuarts: Queen's House, Greenwich, completed in 1635

25. 'Handsomest barn': St Paul's, Covent Garden, 1630s

26. If you require a monument: Wren's London skyline, *c.*1745

27. City of dignity: St James's Square

28. Yorkshire paragon: Castle Howard, 1699

29. The architecture of triumph: Blenheim Palace, 1704 onwards

30. London Baroque: Christ Church, Spitalfields, completed 1729

31. Queen Anne's stool: Smith Square Hall (formerly St John's), completed 1728

32. Bath's geometric majesty: the Royal Crescent, *c.*1775

33. Nature's architecture: Sheringham, *c.*1812

34. A new Rome: Osterley entrance hall, 1760s

of medieval Gothic. John Aubrey had done likewise in the seventeenth century but failed to put names to the various periods. Rickman did this, distinguishing Norman, Early English, Decorated and Perpendicular. Although the names have been challenged they have stuck, though Early Gothic is often preferred to Early English. More than that, Rickman gave Gothic a new academic respectability. It now saw a fully fledged revival and entered into open competition with a classicism that had reigned supreme in British architecture since the seventeenth century.

The Church was first to enter the fray. At issue was the 1818 'Waterloo' Church Building Act, a rerun of the new Queen Anne churches of a century before. The Act was named in celebration of Napoleon's final defeat and aimed at correcting the Church's neglect both of northern industrial towns and of the new suburbs. It was also to fight the rise of Methodism and Catholicism and advance 'religious and moral teaching as a bulwark against revolution'. The Act was funded with £1 million, though it carried a requirement to accommodate 'the greatest number of persons for the smallest possible expense'. The three commissioners to judge the applicants were none other than Nash, Soane and Soane's pupil Smirke.

Unlike the Queen Anne churches of the previous century, which were all versions of classical, the Waterloo churches left open the question of style. So far the churches in most Georgian suburbs, if they had churches at all, conformed to the classicism of their streets, as had Nash with his All Souls Langham Place. By the 1820s Gothic was returning to fashion and this was its first trial. Soane produced a collage illustrating what the commission had in mind. In the middle was a classical church designed by Soane himself with a baroque tower. This was flanked on one side by a Romanesque church and on the other by an elaborate Gothic one. Other classical buildings dotted the hillside behind. Of all the illustrations, just one was Gothic.

The first application to the commission was for an aggressively Gothic St Luke's in Chelsea. It was awarded a grant. This was followed by 214 others, including some by the three commissioners themselves. The message from public opinion was emphatic. No fewer than 174 Gothic churches received grants against a bare handful of classical. The pointed arch was back with a vengeance.

While that might apply to churches, it did not do so for houses. Gothic had been chosen for a few country piles, notably by Wyatt and Nash, in response to a nostalgia for abbeys and castles. But the eighteenth century had seen the new urban Britain settle firmly into a Georgian pattern from which it showed no desire to deviate. Georgian was now firmly Italianate, with heavy rooflines, deeply rusticated ground floors and basements and pillared entrance porches. The whole was then smothered in thick creamy stucco. It was Nash's version of classicism and it went viral nationwide.

One town where it was immediately on display was Brighton. The Prince Regent's Royal Pavilion stimulated a seaside boom, exploiting a new enthusiasm for the curative properties of sea bathing. In 1815 Amon Wilds, father and son, and their partner Charles Busby arrived to create a sort of Bath-on-Sea. This was primarily a holiday town that sought to be distinctive, even light-hearted. The result was some two miles of stucco squares, crescents and terraces along the seafront. The Wilds knew their market. They even designed their own classical 'order', of so-called Ammonite capitals. Though otherwise classical, they abandoned the orders in favour of shell capitals, so adding a maritime touch. Brunswick Square of 1823 also had rolling waves of bow windows so residents could glimpse the sea.

Brighton was widely imitated during the Napoleonic Wars. Torquay began to develop its hotels in the 1830s. Traditional spas such as Harrogate promoted health vacationing with

Nash and the Italianate (1810–1825)

Regency villas and terraces. Its chalybeate and sulphur springs had been discovered as early as 1571. It now became the Bath of the north, with its Royal Spa Hotel opening in the 1820s. Cheltenham had exploited a visit to the town by George III in 1788 with spacious terraces and parks for walking and entertainment. Joseph Pitt's estate of Pittville on the edge of the town, built in the 1820s, made Georgian London look overcrowded. Tree-lined avenues had as their focus the colonnaded Pump Room (1825). It was adorned with statues of medicinal celebrities, Hygieia, Asclepius and Hippocrates.

No one was to be more adept at exploiting the Italianate suburb than the London developer Thomas Cubitt. In the 1820s he stepped forward to follow Nash into the speculative housing market. Unlike Nash he was bound by no royal ties and committed only to profiting from a postwar demand for suburban housing in salubrious locations. He employed his own labourers, was rigorous in his building quality and concerned for good roads and sewerage.

Initially, Cubitt's activities were concentrated on the Grosvenor estate immediately west of Westminster. The area was initially all called Pimlico, but was later divided with Belgravia. Here Cubitt secured parliamentary permission in 1826 to start building on Grosvenor's behalf. He adhered to the leasehold principle that the London landlords had imported from their country estates. This held first that the freeholds would remain with the family, and secondly that its value was best maintained through long repairing leases, typically sixty or ninety-nine years. These anticipated that generations of tenants would share an interest with the landlord in sustaining the value of the property and its neighbourhood. It was as if London were still a rural estate.

Cubitt created buildings of quality and grandeur. Careful estate management ensured the richest and most reliable tenants. Even mews and side streets were in a style consistent with the main terraces, as any walk round the back streets of Belgravia will attest. Most mews still have their own pub, originally installed for the labourers' refreshment. Cubitt's ninety-nine-year Belgravia leases were to remain at the peak of residential fashion – and value – for over two centuries. Their residents loved Cubitt. One wrote in the 1820s, 'A fairer wreath than Wren's, should crown thy brow, / *He* raised a dome – a town unrivalled *thou*'.

The Belgravia formula set the tone for suburban development for at least the first half of the nineteenth century. It was followed on the Bishop of London's Tyburnia estate in Bayswater, the Sloane/Cadogan estate in Chelsea and a tidal wave of developments round the perimeter of the metropolis. Only at the fringes where the market was weak did the leasehold system fail, as it did spectacularly on the Ladbroke estate in North Kensington. Here, as the ninety-nine-year leases ended, many properties were sold off to slum landlords and went into multi-occupancy. Otherwise the outskirts of urban England sprouted with Italianate elaborations of the eighteenth century's Georgian terrace. The rich Veneerings of Dickens's *Our Mutual Friend* dubbed them 'Stucconia'.

A markedly different story had been unfolding in Scotland since the previous century. The idea of the planned suburb, so successful in London, saw a sort of apotheosis with the completion of the New Town in Edinburgh. Its Charlotte Square was finally built in 1820 with a unique sense of grandeur. Its roads and pavements were generous and the district had a suaveness that overcame the tedium attributed to much Georgian townscape. It was within easy walking distance of the old town centre.

Outside Edinburgh, Scotland's switch from peasant farming to sheep rearing had depopulated large areas of the Highlands. The 'clearances' moved some 70,000 Highlanders either abroad, mainly to America, or to Scotland's towns and cities. Housing them went on to produce some of the worst overcrowding in

Nash and the Italianate (1810–1825)

Britain, particularly in Glasgow, later to be aggravated by inflows of famine-racked migrants from Ireland. An exception in the 1780s was David Dale and Richard Arkwright's New Lanark on Clydebank, pioneering a new era of workers' housing. Its giant tenements serving the mill estates expanded until it was the largest such complex in the world. At the dawn of the nineteenth century Glasgow's population was the fastest growing in Britain.

Scotland's country houses had long developed a definitive style of their own. Northern Gothic was moving not towards the picturesque of Strawberry Hill but to an ever more individualistic version of Scots baronial. A group of architects round James Gillespie Graham (1776–1855) and William Henry Playfair (1790–1857) were in demand from a landowning class grown rich on the new economy of the Highlands. Graham served as virtual house architect to the Macdonald clan and contributed to their ancestral seat at Armadale on Skye. He designed Glasgow's Gothic St Andrew's Cathedral with its Decorated tracery, and also the faux-medieval Duns Castle in Berwickshire. Graham's talents were not confined to Scotland. He laid out Hamilton Square in Birkenhead (1825), one of the most handsome and least celebrated Georgian squares in England.

Most impressive of Scotland's innovators was the Earl of Breadalbane and Holland, a branch of the Argyll Campbells. In 1806 he sought to rival his Inveraray cousins by commissioning the brothers Archibald and James Elliot to build a monumental house at Taymouth in Perthshire. It was – and still is – a vast embattled structure of towers and rambling wings, sternly baronial on the outside but the interiors a riot of Gothic decoration. Later work was contributed by Graham and Pugin and included fan ceilings in high Perpendicular by an Italian plasterer, Francis Bernasconi. Campbell at one point owned half a million acres of land round about.

Wales was quite different. Unlike much of Scotland, it was not poor. Its economy consisted of upland sheep and lowland dairy farming enhanced by shipping, weaving, clothing manufacture and the mining of coal, metals and slate. The result was that the principality did not suffer the mass outward migrations that occurred in Scotland and Ireland. Welsh colonies were established in the Americas but they were small ones. The Welsh language thus survived throughout the nineteenth century and into the twentieth largely because its population remained stable and Welsh speakers, notably preachers, teachers and farmers, stayed put.

From the turn of the nineteenth century the growing industrial prosperity of Glamorgan saw the rapid expansion of Cardiff, Swansea and Newport. The workers' housing was not necessarily of the poor standard found in many northern industrial towns. My father's mining family in the Merthyr valley lived in a company-built terrace with its own front door, back yard and view over the valley. My father recalled his shock at the overcrowding of the mill town tenements of South Yorkshire which he later visited. Merthyr's Crawshay ironmasters did not flee to some distant palace but built themselves a castle at Cyfarthfa (1824) that looked proudly out over the foundries of the ironworks below their estate.

In one area Wales was exceptional: the architecture of ecclesiastical Dissent. Wales had taken only tentatively to Reformation, but it was averse to the Church of England and thus receptive to Welsh-speaking Nonconformity. Presbyterians, Baptists, Congregationalists, Quakers and various strains of Methodist found a ready welcome throughout the principality – sects that needed and could afford chapels. Welsh towns enjoyed diverse sources of employment, leading to disparate religious identities – and the much-cited Welsh 'chapel I won't go to'.

Chapels originated in 'meeting houses', outbuildings and

barns. Reputedly the oldest in Wales, Maesyronnen (1697), near Hay-on-Wye, began life as a cow-house. By the time of the Regency, chapel builders were importing English styles, with the sole requirement that they avoid the Gothic revival associated with Anglicanism. To Anthony Jones, biographer of the Welsh chapel, this meant classical by default. 'Builders were under the spell of the old enchantment, that of the ancient world.' Reputedly the first in the classical style was Peniel Chapel (1810) in Gwynedd's Tremadog, its portico inspired directly by Inigo Jones's St Paul's Covent Garden. It could hardly be less Gothic – less English.

12.
The Battle of the Styles (1825–1850)

Sayre's Law states that academic disputes are so bitter because the stakes are so low. One had broken out in Cambridge in 1804 over how the new Downing College should look. It was the outcome of fifty years of dispute over the legacy of the builder of Downing Street, a source for Dickens's case of *Jarndyce* v. *Jarndyce* in *Bleak House*. The dispute escalated from an issue of architectural style to an argument over the purpose of a university, interpreted as introvert Gothic versus extrovert classical. No sooner had both George III and a high-court judge expressed a preference for classical than the dispute shifted to Greek classical versus Roman. It was as if academics could not tolerate agreement.

Collectors at the time were travelling to Greece and returning with statues, drawings and in 1805 a set of carvings from the Athens Parthenon. Argument inevitably ensued. What was a proper style? Downing College's current architect, James Wyatt, was considered a 'lax Roman' and was summarily sacked. The darling of the Greek revival, William Wilkins, was appointed in his place. Nothing was resolved. Visitors complained that Wilkins's Downing ranges were just 'all porticos'. A leading Greek scholar, C. R. Cockerell (1788–1863), described the ranges as 'like a string of sausages'. Cockerell had himself spent his grand tour in Greece, not Italy, and declared that no institution of intellectual repute should use any other style.

Battle now turned to Trinity College's New Court. Here the college was rich and proud of its past. Wilkins offered a choice of both classical and what he called 'my monastic style', or Gothic.

The Battle of the Styles (1825–1850)

Battle followed and eventually Trinity chose Gothic. This led the university to employ Cockerell for the Grecian university library (1829) and another Grecian, George Basevi, for the Fitzwilliam Museum in 1834. In his account of the dispute, the historian David Watkin suggests the university authorities defined themselves as 'expanding into a new world view' (which meant classical) while the colleges were more monastic (hence Gothic).

Oxford took things more calmly. Its Ashmolean and Taylorian museum and library buildings of 1839 were among Cockerell's most distinguished classical works. In London the Greeks also enjoyed a series of triumphs. The new British Museum in Bloomsbury chose Greek by Smirke for its new building. A stern Ionic colonnade shielded its entire southern facade, fitting home for Parthenon marbles sold to it by Lord Elgin in 1816. Wilkins went on to design University College London in 1827 and the National Gallery in Trafalgar Square in 1833, though the latter was attacked as a weak climax to the square.

Over domestic architecture there was almost no argument. Unlike scholars, house buyers knew what they wanted. New homes for a rising middle class in the years following the Napoleonic Wars had been supplied by a coalition of landowners, developers and leaseholders. The result was miles of disciplined brick, stucco or, where available, stone in terraces that were variants of the now familiar Italianate. Cubitt was everywhere.

The same went for more commercial buildings. Among my most treasured books is the 1840 edition of Tallis's *London Street Views*. This is a gazetteer of the main thoroughfares of the metropolis as they appeared at the end of the Regency period, as built since the Great Fire under various building acts. Tallis illustrated, named and numbered every building, residential and commercial, in every main thoroughfare. Facades from the City to Holborn, Fleet Street, Regent Street and Mayfair presented possibly Europe's only post-medieval city on this scale in handsome, mostly Georgian uniformity. The pattern would have been much the same throughout the country, though less spacious where medieval quarters survived. Where previously stood rows of wooden Tudor gables there were now lines of stone parapets.

Outside towns and on freehold sites a wilder market took hold. Here owners and small-time builders made their own choices. Just as Batty Langley had offered a variety of styles in the mid-Georgian period, so a new encyclopaedist, John Claudius Loudon, primarily a garden designer, did likewise in the 1830s and 40s. His *Encyclopaedia of Cottage, Farm, and Villa Architecture and Furniture* was published in 1833 and ran to a thousand pages and at least six editions. The illustrated manual is a voluminous record of British building style as it emerged from the Regency, rich in the picturesque eclecticism of Nash and his contemporaries.

Loudon offered his readers classical, Gothic, Tudor, castellated, Italianate, even 'Old English'. He did not advocate or condemn, he merely recorded. A client could point to a page in Loudon and hand it to his builder. A contemporary critic credited him with heralding 'the transition from the serene graces of the Georgian period to the chaotic romanticism of the Victorians'. To put it another way, Loudon liberated popular taste from the dogmas of the eighteenth century. He explicitly wanted to bring to the general public the privilege of choice once enjoyed by the aristocracy. His books were as influential as any formal architect in conditioning mid-nineteenth-century taste.

Those whose role it was to commission public buildings were in a different position. As has ever been the case, they were choosing not where they would live but what their friends and acquaintances would think of them. We saw in the last chapter how Rickman and the Waterloo church commissioners in 1818 had put Gothic back on the map. But Gothic was now taking on a variety of guises, ecclesiastical, academic, military, vernacular and picturesque. A post-Napoleonic surge of nationalism was in full swing across

The Battle of the Styles (1825–1850)

Europe. In Britain it recalled the days of Elizabeth I and beyond. But Britain was now a United Kingdom, of England, Wales and Scotland since 1707 and Ireland since 1801. What did it mean to be British and might Britain desire an architecture of its own?

In Scotland the work of 'Athenian' Stuart in the 1750s had long popularized the Greek style north of the border. Scholars such as David Hume and Adam Smith had presented Enlightenment Edinburgh as among the intellectual capitals of Europe. It was the 'Athens of the North'. In 1822 the newly crowned George IV paid a first visit to Scotland in a ceremony staged by the country's leading writer, Sir Walter Scott. It was a lavish affair of parades, banquets, presentations and balls.

Scott decided on a dramatic redefinition of what it meant to be Scottish. Gone was the Georgian formalism that had accompanied the 1707 union, the pretence that Scottish and English would forthwith be one culture. Highland clans, tartans and music had been outlawed by the English government after the 1745 Jacobite rebellion as symbols of the barbarian north. Scott did the opposite. He transformed and celebrated them as symbols of national identity. At ceremonies to greet the king, everyone was ordered to wear Highland dress. A new Scotland was on display.

As for Scottish architecture, that too had its moment in the sun. The Greek revival, hesitant in Athenian Stuart's time, was now 're-revived' with tenacity. In 1822, Playfair built the sternly Greek Royal Scottish Academy, a flurry of grandiose porticos, pediments and Greek statuary. The New Town's expansion towards Calton Hill stimulated the idea of rebuilding the hill as an Acropolis. A start was even made on a Parthenon, which still stands unfinished. Thomas Hamilton's High School, perched on the same hillside, is the purest product of the revival, looking as if shipped intact from Athens.

Back in England, Liverpool's Rodney Street and Hope Street, designed by John Foster in the 1800s, had established that city's classical reputation. They were not on Edinburgh's scale, but they shared its Georgian graciousness. The city's St George's Hall was a different matter; begun by the twenty-seven-year-old Harvey Lonsdale Elmes in 1841, it was the apotheosis of the Greek revival. Elmes was heavily influenced by the Berlin museum built in 1838 by the German Karl Friedrich Schinkel, an architect whose strict classicism was to dominate the rise of the Beaux Arts style across Germany and France.

In Newcastle profits from the coaling ships crowding the Tyne waterfront financed the stately terraces of Grainger Town, designed by John Dobson for its developer Richard Grainger in the 1830s. It is the most handsome of Britain's late-Georgian townscapes, benefiting like Bath from a sloping site and a readiness to bend its thoroughfares to take advantage of the contours. Gently curving Grey Street is urban classical at its most immaculate, climbing to a theatrical portico and monument.

Gothic was not idle in its response. As already noted, Howard Colvin charted the revival of Gothic as rooted in a long-standing vernacular tradition that saw it as the embodiment of architectural patriotism. Thus parish church building was persistently hostile to the classical revival, regarding it, according to Colvin, as 'a parasitic growth imposed on English architecture by aristocratic pressure, an exotic product of the Grand Tour rather than a natural expression of English taste'. Sooner or later, he said, advocates of a truly English Gothic promised to 'burst forth once more, like fresh green sprouts which owe their existence to the life still lingering in some venerable forest oak'.

This is indeed what happened. For churches, Gothic's success in the 1818 commission resolved nothing. In Belgravia, the parishioners of one of its successful applicants, the plutocratic St Peter's Eaton Square, requested in 1824 that it be Gothic. The Grosvenor estate refused as it was unthinkable in an Italianate stucco estate. The architect Henry Hakewill was told to

The Battle of the Styles (1825–1850)

design a building in the Greek style, crowned with a tower like that of St Martin-in-the-Fields.

Local residents were unhappy, and when the completed church was gutted by fire in 1836 large crowds came to watch in delight. The unapologetic Grosvenors ordered St Peter's to be rebuilt as it was before, leading the press to declare it 'the ugliest church in London'. Such are the vagaries of style that when the church was finally listed for preservation in 1991, *The Times* could write that it 'ranked among the most beautiful churches in London'.

A more prominent conflict arose in 1824 over a secular building of national significance. This was a competition for a major extension to the upper ward of Windsor Castle. It was won by James Wyatt's nephew, Jeffry Wyatt (later Wyatville), beating Nash, Smirke and Soane, no less. A new south front was intended to dominate the length of Windsor Great Park in the manner of Versailles. What Wyatville supplied was the exact opposite, a feeble collegiate Gothic range, more a tenement than a royal palace, as it appears today. The adjacent Norman keep looks more regal.

The Windsor decision was highly controversial, unleashing a national debate on what was widely seen as a decline in the nation's architectural taste. Nash's rebuilding of Buckingham Palace was discredited as extravagant. His Regent's Park was bankrupt. Wyatville's mock medieval Windsor was ridiculed. Smirke's British Museum and Wilkins's National Gallery were criticized as lifeless Greek copies. In 1828 a parliamentary committee was asked to investigate 'the quality of [public] buildings that was exercising the public conscience'. The premise appeared to be that public buildings should be in a consistent and appropriate style. But no one could agree on what that meant. Battle was joined.

With the Waterloo churches and Windsor Castle now under its belt, the Gothic lobby saw a surge in popularity. In October 1834, just two years after parliament had passed the Great Reform

Act, the old Palace of Westminster was gutted by fire. The conflagration was colossal, drawing crowds not seen, it was said, since the Great Fire of London. Only the twelfth-century Westminster Hall, a cloister and the chapel undercroft survived. The symbolism – the sweeping away of an old politics and the advent of a new – was not lost on public opinion. The opportunity should surely be taken to express in architecture the dawning of a new era.

Commissioners appointed to decide on the new building duly announced that 'London should have at least one structure worthy of being placed beside the noble monuments of St Petersburg and Paris.' Debate consumed the political as well as the architectural establishment. It was taken up by newspapers and journals, factions formed, reputations rose and fell. But when Smirke, a Greek revivalist who was current head of the Office of Works, was asked to prepare a temporary chamber in which the Commons might meet, a furious argument ensued.

A group of Tories supporting Smirke was formed at Decimus Burton's Athenaeum, adamant that the new parliament should be classical. In the words of the *Westminster Review*, this would be 'more expressive of the character of the institutions of a free people'. Classical was the architecture of liberty and would be more economical and of 'bold and pleasing outline and just proportions'. In comparison, Gothic was all 'petty details . . . quickly begrimed in London soot'. It had 'no true principles and no real hold on the enlightened intellect'. Such a parliament would be 'an architectural romance'.

To others the very suggestion that Smirke might construct the new building was outrageous. It looked like an inside job. The *Spectator* magazine called it an instance of 'jobbing, precipitancy and secrecy', and insisted there be a competition. It happened that Sir Robert Peel was briefly prime minister in 1834 and he agreed with the critics. Though a Tory, he was an opponent of

The Battle of the Styles (1825–1850)

the Athenaeum group. He felt so strongly that he secured the services of an anti-classicist, Sir Edward Cust, to chair a new commission and invite bids for a competition.

The first decision of Cust's commission was flatly to rule out classical. It stipulated that 'only the Gothic or Elizabethan styles were appropriate for a great national monument' and nothing else would be considered. The commission of 'hand-picked men of taste' declared that Gothic was among 'the original and time-worn buttresses of our constitution . . . from a time when classic architecture was unknown in this country'. Gothic was 'derived from our ancestors . . . old English . . . better suited to the German character of the British nation . . . rooted in the botanical works of nature'. Classical was alien, unreliable, the style of continental revolutionaries.

The battle was not just of styles but also of ideologies, reflecting deep-seated biases in Britain's political mood. The nation was still on a patriotic high. In 1830–32 it had witnessed – and avoided – the revolutionary upheavals taking place across Europe. The nation was passing through one of its periodic bouts of isolationism, and a 'European' style such as classical was not welcome. The Gothic traditionalists were averse to mimicking the Greek assemblies, associated with democracy, being erected by revolutionaries in Europe and America. The classicists protested in turn that a modern British parliament need hardly retreat to the vernacular nationalism of the Middle Ages.

This stress on history led to another insistence, on showing respect for buildings surviving from old Westminster, notably Westminster Hall and the Henry VII Chapel in the abbey next door. A much-noted article in the *Quarterly Review* stressed that the new should respect and enhance the old. In a view rarely heard today, it declared such fusion of new and old was 'one of the principal elements of beauty'. The opposite, 'the discordance of adjacent buildings, is a source of positive pain to the beholder'.

Parliament's historian, M. H. Port, described the debate as that of 'a profession in a state of war: Greeks v. Goths'. The competition for a new parliament received no fewer than ninety-seven entries. It was eventually won by the forty-year-old Charles Barry (1795–1860). This was remarkable since Barry, already a successful architect, had worked almost exclusively in the classical style. His grand tour had embraced not just France and Italy but Greece, Egypt, Palestine, Lebanon, Syria and Turkey. He had visited and sketched a range of buildings from Pompeii to Philae, Jerusalem to Palmyra, Delos to Hagia Sophia. He was particularly taken by the urban palazzi of Florence and Rome.

By the age of twenty-three, Barry had been determined enough to secure six of the 1818 commission churches, all of them Gothic, including the prominent St Peter's Brighton in 1824. Barry's son later recalled that his father was so ashamed of these works that he 'wished he could destroy' every one of them. From then on, Barry became the rising star of the classical tradition. He designed the Manchester Art Gallery in a Greek revival style and the Travellers Club in Pall Mall as an Italianate palazzo. There followed the Greek Royal College of Surgeons in Lincoln's Inn Fields (1835) and the Reform Club (1837) in Pall Mall, based on the Palazzo Farnese in Rome. How he was going to manage the most prominent commission in the land in a style to which he was now so hostile was a mystery.

The qualification that Barry brought to the task was simple: experience. He accepted the challenge, but to meet the rules of the competition he had to clothe what he designed as a classical building in Gothic garb. Of the classicism there was no doubt. His parliament was symmetrical, with lords to the south, commons to the north round a central octagon. The model, it was said, was none other than Inigo Jones's old plan for a Whitehall palace downriver – or possibly even the Louvre.

Barry needed a Gothic disguise and for this he recruited a

The Battle of the Styles (1825–1850)

brilliant twenty-three-year-old, Augustus Welby Pugin (1812–52). Of Pugin's proclivities there could be no doubt. He had been brought up by his parents as a strict Scots Presbyterian and had fiercely reacted against it. His biographer Rosemary Hill told of his 'unmitigated disgust at the cold and sterile forms of the Scottish church'. He duly 'rushed into the arms of a church [Roman Catholicism] which, pompous by its ceremonies, was attractive to his imaginative mind'.

Pugin was a passionate Gothicist. He had witnessed the Palace of Westminster fire in 1834 and 'rejoiced' to see classical buildings by Soane and Wyatt 'consigned to oblivion as they . . . shivered to a thousand pieces and fell like a pack of cards'. Meanwhile he gloried that medieval Westminster Hall survived the fire solid as a rock. Pugin was among those shocked to hear that 'the execrable Smirke' might be the architect called on for the rebuilding.

That Barry's plan for parliament was not Gothic was perfectly apparent to Pugin. He explained that all he had done was prepare drawings and designs to give a superficial dressing to its exterior and interior. After his and Barry's victory he walked away and promptly disappeared into private practice. Between 1836 and 1843 he published a series of books that did for Gothic what the Burlington circle had done for classicism a century before. He offered a textbook reinterpretation of the medieval style, including a return to what he saw as its theological fundamentals. In *Contrasts*, a semi-satirical study of architectural style, Pugin called for 'a return to the faith and social structures of the Middle Ages'. Gothic, he affirmed, was 'not a style but a principle'. It was something far more significant, a desirable, moral way of life.

Pugin deplored the fact that 'every architect has a theory of his own, a beau ideal he has himself created, a disguise . . . generally the result of his latest travels'. One man 'sees the Alhambra, another the Parthenon, a third is all lotus cups from the banks of the Nile and a fourth all dome and basilica from Rome'. The result was that style had become 'a carnival of architecture', one in which gentlemen 'not satisfied with perpetrating one character appear in two or three costumes in the same evening'. It was a good description of Barry.

A building's appearance, Pugin declared, should embody the beliefs and manners of its day. For modern architecture to mimic the works of classical pagans was both a parody of their integrity and an abuse of Christianity. To posit a link between a Greek temple and Christian practice was a travesty. 'The history of architecture is the history of the world . . . Vitruvius would spew if he beheld the works of those who glory in calling him master.' Pugin dismissed the architects of the Regency with particular contempt. Nash was 'Mr Wash, plasterer, who jobs out day work on moderate terms'. His colleague and rival, the fashionable Decimus Burton, marketed himself as 'a talent of no consequence, premium required'. Exchanges between Pugin and Burton were to be vituperative.

To Watkin, Pugin was a man who saw in Gothic 'the unchanging truths of the Catholic church . . . since architecture could be true or false, morally good or bad'. In the interest of honesty, 'it therefore ought to reveal its structure and function and make use of natural materials'. This notion of functional purity and simplicity as the essence of style was potent throughout the Victorian period. It underpinned the Arts and Crafts movement and went on to fuel much of twentieth-century modernism. Superficial decoration was a form of sin, which led Pugin to deplore much that was decorative in late Gothicism.

Where Regency architecture had offered its customers a shopping list of styles, Pugin offered them a Ten Commandments. Where classicists had suggested an educative grand tour of Italy, Pugin proposed a tour of old England. Though a Catholic, his identification of architecture with liturgical and spiritual rectitude appealed to High Church Anglicans. He became a hero to

The Battle of the Styles (1825–1850)

trainee university clerics, in the Oxford Movement and the Cambridge Camden Society, later the Ecclesiological Society. These two High Church groups were committed to returning the established Church to the rituals, if not the governance, of Rome and with an appropriate architecture. The movement was termed Ecclesiology and kept the Gothic flame burning over church architecture for the rest of the nineteenth century.

Pugin's private commissions were largely from those who shared his ideas. The grandest was from an ardent Catholic, the Earl of Shrewsbury, who in 1837 engaged him on three Staffordshire projects: Alton Towers and Castle and a new church at Cheadle. The tower was a Gothic extravaganza that in its now ruined state has become the Legend of the Towers for the adjacent amusement park. Cheadle church was the purest expression of Gothic design. With the earl's unlimited resources, Pugin toured England, Belgium and France, seeking the finest stone, glass, tiles and woodwork. The church burst with colour, painting, rood carving, window tracery and a 200ft tower. It remains spectacular to this day.

In 1845, Pugin returned to Westminster, where the foundations for Barry's parliament were at last ready to receive their superstructure. Pugin hurled himself into the task. He worked day and night on the building's outer skin and interior furnishings. Though he was to dismiss the project as 'Tudor details on a classic body', the sheer amount of space he had to cover was enormous. Hill recorded that hardly a seat, table, wallpaper, carpet, window or piece of cutlery in Westminster did not show evidence of his hand. He designed the clock tower of Big Ben, though he did not live to see it built. Exhausted by work, and suffering from increasing mental illness, he was eventually committed to Bethlem Hospital, and died in Ramsgate at the age of forty in 1852. Despite Barry's authorship, the Palace of Westminster is regularly attributed to Pugin, if only because what the public sees of it is principally by him.

Barry combined Westminster with an extraordinary output. He never reverted to Gothic and most of his projects were 'improvements' in whatever style was required. Thus Duncombe in Yorkshire (1843) was baroque, Dunrobin in Sutherland (1835) Scots baronial, Highclere in Hampshire (1842) Elizabethan and Cliveden (1851) splendidly Italianate on its bluff over the Thames. He also found time to lay out Trafalgar Square in 1840, erect the Treasury building in Whitehall (now the Cabinet Office) and design Halifax's eccentric town hall in a 'North Italian Cinquecento' style. Four of Barry's sons became architects and two of his grandsons. He embodied the type of Victorian later called superhuman. But Westminster dominated his career. It took twenty-six years to complete at the very end of his life, and it finally exhausted him.

Just four years after the destruction of the Palace of Westminster, the old Royal Exchange in the City also went up in flames. Again the question arose as to what style should be its replacement. There was little argument. This was the City, not Westminster, and classical won. A little-known City figure, William Tite, erected a giant Corinthian portico facing the Mansion House, concealing an inner court copied from Rome's Farnese Palace. There was not a whiff of Gothic. For good measure the ubiquitous Cockerell responded with a new Grecian front to Soane's Bank of England next door.

The most dramatic architectural innovation of the 1830s was required by the railway. As a means of transport, it was initially seen as dirty and dangerous. Queen Victoria (r.1837–1901) for many years refused to use a train, even to get to Windsor. The ownership of the first intercity railway, opened in 1830 between Liverpool and Manchester, felt obliged to reassure its nervous passengers by disguising its Manchester terminus as a Georgian town house. There were different entrance doors for different classes of passenger. Inside they would wait in segregated rooms

The Battle of the Styles (1825–1850)

to be ushered upstairs to elevated lines as if to their bedrooms. When Isambard Kingdom Brunel constructed his Great Western railway, he similarly designed its Bristol Temple Meads terminus in a homely Tudor style. The shed roof was supported on hammerbeam brackets above Perpendicular colonnades. It was architecture as reassuring psychology.

Eight years later, when Robert Stephenson came to open his London-to-Birmingham line, the mood of the railway had changed completely. As it charged towards a new industrial empire it demanded symbols of greatness. At Euston passengers were greeted with grand Doric arches designed by Philip Hardwick, as if announcing a military triumph. Cuttings were banked so spectators could admire the trains. Tunnel entrances were castellated or dressed with Greek orders.

Hardwick's Royal Hotel for the Great Western at Paddington (1851) was the largest such accommodation of its day, with the appearance of a Loire chateau. Brunel treated it as the frontage to the station itself, though he hired another Wyatt, Matthew Digby, to Gothicize the ribs of his train shed as in a cathedral transept. Stoke-on-Trent station had the appearance of a Jacobean stately home. Shrewsbury station (1849) was so embarrassed to have smashed down the walls of the medieval town that it portrayed itself in Elizabethan Gothic. As for train sheds, those at Newcastle and York were wonders of the age, their curved wrought-iron frames cradling clouds of steam and smoke rising from the engines below.

The nineteenth century's battle of the styles was a mess, intellectually if not aesthetically. The issues in dispute never resolved themselves, and carried little meaning for the general public. Those responsible for commissioning national projects could build a British Museum and a National Gallery in the classical style, yet they could denounce a parliament in the same style as un-British. The monarch's palace could be classical in London but in Windsor it had 'to embody the native English style'. When Brunel wanted to speak safety and reliability, he turned to Tudor. When the Bank of England wanted to speak the same, in its London or Liverpool offices it turned to Greek. A church must be Gothic but a London club Italian.

As we can see, style in architecture was a matter of choice bordering on whim. It came down to who was doing the choosing. Patrons commissioning public buildings were influenced by personal contacts and by an increasingly self-important profession. In 1833, Britain's architects formed themselves into an institute and four years later received a royal charter. Yet they were never quite able to resolve a dichotomy. Were they essentially subcontractors to the building industry? Or were they truly artists with a view to beauty or, at least in Pugin's case, philosophers? If they could not decide, it was unlikely that the public would do so for them.

13.
Palaces of Prosperity and Faith (1850–1870)

British architecture was seldom so variegated as in the middle years of Queen Victoria's reign. On the one hand was domestic building, where the overwhelming preference was still classical/Georgian/Italianate. But it was an increasingly restless Italianate, as if anticipating something new. There was a shift towards decorative variety in facades, notably in materials such as brick and terracotta in place of stucco. Chimneys, roofs and gables developed lives of their own.

A different direction was taken in public buildings. Here a street might go in many directions, classical Greek or Roman, Gothic ecclesiastical or medieval, Tudor and/or Elizabethan. The mix became a joke. Charles Kingsley's popular 1863 novel *The Water-Babies* satirized a country house (based on Bramshill in Hampshire) as having been built 'at ninety different times, in nineteen different styles, and look[ing] as if somebody had built a whole street of houses of every imaginable shape, and then stirred them together with a spoon'.

In the 1840s came a proposal from Victoria's husband, Prince Albert, for a Great Exhibition of British – and some foreign – achievements, to be held in 1851 in Hyde Park. He wanted to stage it in a great hall but the question of its style was left open. An initial competition produced 257 entries, none of which was considered suitable. Then a garden designer, Joseph Paxton, stepped forward with a 'crystal palace' that was immediately applauded. He had already built a similar conservatory at Chatsworth in 1837, and a Palm House had been erected at Kew in 1848. But neither was on the scale of the Hyde Park project. Paxton mobilized two industries, of wrought iron and plate glass, to erect the greatest expanse of windows ever known.

The Crystal Palace was industrial architecture brought to London. Paxton was assisted by the railway engineer Charles Fox under the direction of Brunel. These titans of the railway knew the meaning of project management. From proposal to opening, the palace was erected in just nine months. To some historians it was Britain's first truly modern building, its form dictated solely by function and materials. The ailing Pugin dismissed it as 'crystal humbug', though that did not stop him contributing to the medieval court display. When the exhibition closed, the palace was relocated to Sydenham in south London, where it continued to attract crowds until its destruction by fire in 1936.

South of the site in Kensington, land was set aside for a district of museums devoted to the empire, science, natural history, arts and crafts, built from the exhibition's profits. There would later also be the Royal Albert Hall in memory of the prince. Each of these institutions was built in a style of its own, bequeathing London an extraordinary jumble of Victorian architecture. When Queen Victoria opened the Albert Hall in 1871 she was so overcome by emotion she could only say 'it reminds me of the British constitution'.

From the 1840s onwards the industrial revolution, whose buildings had long been purely utilitarian, came to architectural life. Towns and cities saw civic and commercial buildings of unprecedented splendour. Their style was overwhelmingly, though not exclusively, classical. Typical was the town hall of Leeds (1853), by Cuthbert Brodrick, looking as if designed by Wren on a flying visit, no expense spared. It combined the offices of mayor, council, courts and public rooms and embodied the confidence and pride of a new municipal Yorkshire. The same city's Corn Exchange

Palaces of Prosperity and Faith (1850–1870)

(1860), also by Brodrick, was hardly less ostentatious. There could be no more bravura expression of industrial self-confidence than in architecture.

The response of Leeds's adjacent rival Bradford was in the hands of the partnership of Lockwood and Mawson. Their style was more eclectic and restrained than Brodrick's, moving from Italianate to Gothic as the mood – or suitability – took them. Bradford's town hall was early Gothic, its St George's Hall was classical and its Wool Exchange Venetian Gothic. Birmingham's town hall (1834) by Joseph Hansom was a classical temple so immaculate it would sit happily on a Greek acropolis. Rochdale's by W. H. Crossland is a magnificent Gothic creation with a tower by Alfred Waterhouse.

The great cities of the north were consciously taking on the mantle of sixteenth-century Italy, and particularly Florence. The princes of Manchester's Deansgate were eager to see themselves as in the tradition of the Medici. Manchester's Free Trade Hall (1853) by Edward Walters was a recreation of a Florentine palazzo, as were its surrounding businesses and banks. Yet fifteen years later the same city's town hall (1868) broke ranks. A monumental Gothic work by Waterhouse arose in Albert Square. Almost a parody of Westminster, with a tower emulating that of Big Ben, this embodiment of civic pride cost a million pounds (£125 million today).

Commerce followed suit. Earlier factories, docks and mills had been almost architecture-free, if often magnificently so. The mills of Manchester's Ancoats or Liverpool's Stanley docks were little more than huge walls punctured by openings. Now palazzo followed palazzo, marching across north-country towns, depicting British commerce in line of descent from the great business houses of continental Europe.

Some enlightened mill owners were quick off the mark. Bradford's Titus Salt in 1851 moved his 4,000 workers four miles from the town's pollution and squalor to a settlement at Saltaire in the Aire Valley. Round a giant mill building he created an estate of terraces that was to be a model for the philanthropic housing movement. Twenty years later, Bradford saw another clothing giant, Samuel Lister, rebuild his Manningham silk mill as reputedly the largest in the world. The Italianate structure borrowed its chimney, much elaborated, from St Mark's Square in Venice. It today presents its retrofitters with a mammoth challenge to become a block of flats.

Glasgow's native architect, Alexander 'Greek' Thomson (1817–75), showed how flexible the Greek – and by extension Egyptian – style could be. He designed everything from Glasgow's churches to its banks, offices, shops and warehouses, from his Grosvenor Buildings (1859) to his Egyptian Halls (1871). Style was simply for show, a marketing device. For an escape from urban congestion nothing matched William Bliss's Tweed Mill (1872), which was set in the Cotswolds outside Chipping Norton. The eccentric Bliss wanted to produce his wool cloth as near as possible to the sheep that grew it. The mill was in the style of a Georgian country house, with a tall Tuscan chimney to carry the smoke away across the hills. It still sits, albeit as flats, glorious in its valley like a building lost on its way to somewhere else.

While Italianate was keeping its grip on secular architecture, Gothic was holding on to churches. The Church of England saw a rise in evangelical fervour, with a return to church building of an intensity not seen since before the Reformation. The classicism of Nash and Soane was now past. St Peter's Eaton Square might have been rebuilt in a classical style, but by 1844 round the corner at St Michael's Chester Square parishioners insisted on Gothic. Italianate suburbs now grew used to seeing the jarring outline of a Gothic steeple looming over their stately stucco facades.

The agent to the Grosvenor estate, Thomas Cundy, eventually

abandoned the estate's insistence on classical and personally designed at least eight so-called 'Cundy churches' in a production-line Gothic in the 1840s and 50s. For decades their soot-blackened walls contrasted with their stucco surroundings – Dickens called them 'churches of Saint Ghastly Grim' – though most have since been cleaned to their Kentish ragstone beige. The message was Pugin's and it was clear: godliness demanded Gothic to counteract the sinfulness of a pagan classical world.

This boom in church building and restoration was led in large part by one man, George Gilbert Scott (1811–78). Another giant of the Victorian age, he shared with Pugin and the Anglo-Catholics a conviction in the religious superiority of Gothic and a belief that this required respect for the style's medieval roots. Unlike Pugin, Scott was devout but not an ideologue. He admitted that 'if we had a distinctive architecture . . . worthy of the greatness of our age, I should follow it. We have not.' Scott remained broad-minded in his revivalism. He regarded Gothic as a style with a multitude of uses, dismissing 'the absurd supposition that Gothic architecture is exclusively and intrinsically ecclesiastical'.

Scott made his early name as a designer of workhouses, a demand for which arose from the 1834 Poor Law requiring 'indoor relief' for the unemployed. He completed some forty of them. His first church was St Giles Camberwell in 1844, lauded by the Ecclesiological Society as incomparable 'in its purity of style and orthodoxy of arrangement'. He moved on to a career dominated by church architecture. He became the restorer of almost all of Britain's then distressed cathedrals, working on eighteen of the twenty-six, including many sorely damaged by Wyatt a century before.

Thus Scott's Gothic screen at Ely was a wholly original attempt to envisage how its precursor might have looked. He salvaged Westminster Abbey's chapter house from a rotting store and the west front of Lichfield Cathedral from total erosion. His masterpiece was the screen at Hereford Cathedral, regarded as one of the finest works of Gothic revival. Yet such is fashion that it was thrown out by the cathedral in 1967, fortunately rescued to be exhibited in the V&A.

We find it hard to imagine how Scott worked. A record of some 850 buildings were attributed to his office, including dozens in Scotland and across the empire, from Bombay to New Zealand. He had a reputation similar to Barry's for overwork. He would supposedly arrive at a station and then telegraph his office to ask why he was there. He was not wholly a restorer. Scott's early All Souls Halifax (1855) towers over the town and is an original work of Victorian Gothic revival. Other churches by him rise over Doncaster, Hanwell in Middlesex, Hawkhurst in Kent and London's St Mary Abbots, Kensington.

Not everyone approved of Scott's work. His most vocal critic was Pugin's successor as prophet of Gothic purity, John Ruskin (1819–1900). In his *Seven Lamps of Architecture* (1849) he widened Pugin's vision of architectural morality to embrace the complete range of aesthetics. In the dogmatic *Stones of Venice* (1851) Ruskin blessed those Venetian buildings he considered true to the Gothic tradition as against those of the heretical Palladian revival. There is no better way of sensing the battle of the styles than to go round Venice with Ruskin's enjoyably prejudiced book in hand. On Scott he was merciless, declaring that a visit from him would result in 'the most total destruction that a building can suffer'.

This was unfair, and Scott bitterly rejected the attacks. Large parts of the Church of England estate at the time were close to dereliction and restoration was the only alternative to ruin. Scott's defenders have established that he was largely true to his word. The recovery from neglect and the passage of time of England's medieval churches, both episcopal and parochial, was largely due to George Gilbert Scott.

Palaces of Prosperity and Faith (1850–1870)

For all that, this architect's two most celebrated buildings were not churches but secular institutions. Both involved him in a resurgent battle of the styles. In 1858 a competition was held for a new Foreign and India Office in Whitehall. Scott submitted an initially Gothic proposal and the Tory Lord Derby as prime minister accepted it. Almost as if a fight were compulsory, the Liberal opposition leader, Lord Palmerston, took up the cudgels to stop it. To him, Scott was 'going back to the barbarism of the Dark Ages for a building which ought to belong to the times in which we live'. He said this in the new parliamentary chambers whose Gothic style had been chosen specifically for its Britishness.

Before the contracts could be let, Palmerston won an election and became prime minister. He reversed Derby's decision, remarking that the 'Battle of the Gothic and Palladian' over the Foreign Office recalled 'the Battle of the Books, the Battle of the Big and Little Indians and the Battle of the Greens and Blues in Constantinople'. Like politicians before and since, Palmerston felt entitled to order the public realm to his own taste.

Scott was duly summoned and told he could keep the commission but only if he designed a new building in 'the ordinary Italian style'. Palmerston suggested Scott work in collaboration with the India Office's architect, Matthew Digby Wyatt. The argument continued for some two years, culminating in a debate in parliament in July 1861 that filled forty-two columns of Hansard. It must rank as a high point of public discussion of architecture. It is heartrending to see the attention the Victorian public and their MPs paid to architectural quality compared with today. The debate finished with a vote in which a majority of MPs supported an Italian design.

Scott was shattered, but he accepted the commission and went to Paris to inspect the new Louvre in its Renaissance revival style. Palmerston was delighted with the eventual outcome, feeling he had a Foreign Office fit for an imperial power. To this day the foreign secretary's offices are adorned with paintings, murals and furnishings recalling the high points of Britain's historic glory. They make nearby 10 Downing Street seem like a pokey attic.

Partly as a result of this prominence, Scott was chosen to design a new hotel for the Midland Railway at St Pancras. Railways needed parliamentary legislation to acquire routes, and the Midland's rival, the Great Northern, had for years blocked permission for it to gain a foothold in central London. In 1863 the Midland finally won access and a pathway to St Pancras immediately next to the Northern's 1851 terminus at King's Cross. Eager to get its own back it selected an extravagant proposal by Scott that wildly overshot its budget but made its point. The towering structure was regarded as humiliating the adjacent King's Cross and its diminutive Great Northern Hotel.

Scott's extravagant towers and galleries, the sweeping entrance ramp and soaring hotel staircase were not, as rumour had it, a rehash of his design for the Foreign Office. They merely showed that a secular Gothic building could have grandeur and presence. But St Pancras was never free of controversy. Scott wrote that it had been 'spoken of by one of the revilers of my profession with abject contempt'. And yet it had been 'often spoken of as the finest building in London'. He felt it was if anything 'too good for its purpose'. A comment on the history of style is that when, in the 1960s, battle was joined to save Scott's work, modernists opposed it as 'pastiche' while saluting King's Cross next door as true to purpose and 'honest'. Mercifully, both buildings have survived. The best epitaph was that of the historian Dan Cruickshank, that at St Pancras Scott 'gave the modern world the pedigree of history'.

Victorian church building now became intense. Between 1835 and 1875 it was recorded that 3,765 new Anglican churches were built in England and Wales, while 7,000 medieval ones were restored. But by 1850 a change set in. A new generation of church architects emerged, less interested than Scott in the correct revival of ancient structures and more in their own freedom to design in the Gothic style. They cared less for truth to the thirteenth century than for the medieval tradition as inspiration.

The late Victorians were among the most original talents to strut the architectural stage. To them, Gothic, unlike classical, was not a textbook of rules to be obeyed. It was an invitation to show dexterity, a theme on which the creative imagination could be allowed to play. Scott's successors included William Butterfield, Alfred Waterhouse, George Frederick Bodley, John Loughborough Pearson and George Edmund Street. The studio of Street in particular became an architectural forcing house throughout the period. Gothic was merely their language, the start of a journey. Their churches took the form, said Watkin, of 'an extraordinary sculptural violence, vigorous muscularity and strident polychromy'. They no longer felt any need to pretend – as Scott did – to be medieval.

Thus while Scott's All Souls Halifax of 1855 could have passed for a medieval work, the same could not be said of William Butterfield's All Saints in London's Margaret Street (1849). Butterfield might be an ecclesiologist but he was also a radical. At All Saints he squeezed a mass of polychrome brickwork onto a cramped site, its interior rich in furnishings, tiles and murals. Butterfield was rare in appreciating the role that colour had played in the Gothic style. He went on to design a reputed one hundred churches in every corner of Britain and the empire, including in India and Australia. This left time only for secular buildings such as Rugby School and Keble College Oxford (both begun in 1868), exercises in a wild redbrick Gothic that typified all that twentieth-century taste was to dislike in Victorian architecture.

A stylistic key was now being turned in the architectural lock. Brick was replacing stone as a favoured building material. Iron and steel were coming into use. Oriel Chambers (1864) in Liverpool's city centre, by the architect Peter Ellis, was a first experiment in using a metal frame to hold glass as curtain walling. The facade was a series of vertical shafts, Gothic in appearance, dividing an entire wall of projecting windows, one of the most remarkable buildings of its date anywhere in Europe. It was matched by John Honeyman's steel and glass Ca' d'Oro (1872) in Glasgow, as dramatic a work as its Venetian namesake.

Church naves rose ever higher and steeples and campaniles rose over them. Masters of the new Gothic included Pearson, whose cathedral-like St Augustine Kilburn (1870) was followed by the Victorian era's only new cathedral, that at Truro in 1880. Both were variants on Perpendicular that was virtually Anglicanism's house style. Each church by Bodley, a pupil of Scott's, was an essay in diversity, from the sternly medieval All Saints in Cambridge to the almost Tudor Holy Angels at Hoar Cross in Staffordshire. Bodley became the connoisseur's revivalist, a master of space and light. He ended his career designing America's national cathedral in Washington DC (1907).

No less dramatic were Gothic ventures into secular architecture. Waterhouse, like Scott, was adamant that the style should not be seen as exclusively ecclesiastical. His Natural History Museum in South Kensington (1872) defied definition. Ostensibly Romanesque, it was both Gothic and Italianate, covered in decorations from nature. Capitals and brackets of owls, bats and gargoyles jostled with all manner of creatures real and mythical. The building was coated in terracotta, thought resistant to London's soot and grime. Inside, animals and birds peered at the viewer from every inch. It remains one of London's most enjoyable buildings.

The wildest of revivalists was William Burges (1827–81), an eccentric genius who dressed in medieval gowns and specialized in wealthy clients with distinctive tastes. He designed one of the period's loveliest small churches, the shrine to a twenty-three-year-old relative of the local Marquess of Ripon, murdered by Greek brigands in 1870. It stands alone in Studley Royal Park in Yorkshire, an exotic array of Gothic tracery, painting and statuary. The opium-addicted Burges came to treat his clients as mere extras to his work. At Knightshayes in Devon he told the owner, Heathcoat Amory, that the house was 'mine' and Amory merely a lucky occupant. He was fired.

In Wales, Burges found a more indulgent patron, the young Marquess of Bute. He was reputedly the richest man in Britain as owner of much of Glamorgan's coal. In Cardiff, Burges built for him two architectural fantasies, Cardiff Castle (1868) and Castell Coch (1875). Each was a pictorial and sculptural encyclopaedia of the Middle Ages, every inch of their interiors being coated in historical and mythical characters. Such links with the past assuaged the fear that many Victorians felt towards the mechanization of their society. Burges presented an architecture that sought escape from industrialization and mass production. It was architecture as emotional release, reminding a fast-changing world of its roots in the past. A similar reminder is sought in today's world of digitization and artificial intelligence.

Under the walls of Burges's castles another mixing point of styles was emerging in virtually every Welsh town and village. Since the turn of the century, classicism had ruled the roost in the architecture of the chapel. Now it had matured. In 1872 the 'cathedral of Welsh Nonconformity' arose in Morriston outside Swansea, designed by a popular architect, John Humphrey, and intended as the biggest chapel in Wales. It cost its congregation £10,000 (almost £1 million today), a sum that took forty years to pay off. Its steeple soars over the Swansea valley to this day. Architects became Welsh celebrities. One of them, William Jones, reputedly built 200 chapels.

Welsh chapels were perhaps the nearest Britain came to a popular public architecture. There was no lord of the manor or diocese to pay the bill. Chapels were funded by small communities over years of borrowing and fundraising. By the end of the nineteenth century, the principality boasted 4,700 new chapels. Initially the aversion to Anglican Gothicism remained, but by the 1870s versions of Gothic revival began to appear, often for English-speaking congregations to distinguish them from Welsh-speaking neighbours. Wales's use of style as a proxy for cultural conflict could not have been more explicit.

Perhaps the most significant architect of this generation remained Street (1824–81). A pupil of Scott, an ecclesiologist and master of early Gothic, he spent most of his life working on churches. In this he studied and borrowed freely from abroad, notably in his Italian-style St James the Less in Pimlico. The climax of his career came in 1868 when his Gothic design was chosen for the Law Courts in the Strand. This was when Palmerston was condemning Gothic as of the 'Dark Ages' and beneath the dignity of the British state. It now miraculously embodied the full majesty of the law. Street could not prevent it looking like a cathedral. Litigants still emerge daily to be photographed with it behind them, as if they have just attended mass.

Street's principal claim to fame was his output of apprentices. His studio's grounding in the writings of Pugin and Ruskin treated the Gothic revival not as an antiquarian pursuit but as the opposite, a liberation, a looking forward. It inspired William Morris and a cohort of young architects who were to become the backbone of the Arts and Crafts movement. Through his studio passed Richard Norman Shaw, Philip Webb, Edward Godwin, J. D. Sedding and others. Street was the fountainhead for what was to be the last great age of British design.

14.

Sweetness and Light (1870–1900)

Britain in the 1870s was at a turning point. The mid-century's economic surge was over. The rise in the trading power of America and Russia and the newly unified state of Germany was rebalancing a western economy over which Britain had long been dominant. Agriculture entered a long recession. In architecture the battle of the styles was all but exhausted. How a building looked depended on what seemed most appropriate, typically classical for civic buildings, Gothic for faith and eclectic for houses and commercial buildings.

For the ideologues who had argued over style since the days of Pugin, the new prophet, Ruskin, was raising an ever more shrill voice against the machine age. This became a move for 'back to nature' and 'truth to materials', couched in a search for a new vernacular, a new English truth. In the field of art, the Pre-Raphaelite Brotherhood (c.1848–54) had stripped medievalism of its piety. The ambition of Holman Hunt, John Millais and Dante Gabriel Rossetti was to return art to the simplicity of the fifteenth century, before its corruption by Raphael and Michelangelo.

The brotherhood did not last long and its artists went their separate ways. Some joined forces with the young William Morris (1834–96) to form what became an artistic climax to the Victorian period. Morris had been trained in Street's studios. In 1861 he set up an architecture and design practice with another Street apprentice, Philip Webb (1831–1915), and the Pre-Raphaelites Edward Burne-Jones and Ford Madox Brown. They took their lead from

Ruskin in rejecting machine-led design and calling for a return to traditional craftsmanship, to handworking with natural materials and in traditional styles. Its motto was Ruskin's dictate that 'Fine art is that in which the hand, the head and the heart of man go together.'

Morris was a man of phenomenal energy. What emerged from his initiative came to be known as the Arts and Crafts movement. Its ideology was dubbed by the poet and cultural philosopher Matthew Arnold 'sweetness and light'. Morris was determined the movement should practise what it preached. His company, Morris and Co., crafted interiors, wall coverings, furniture, fabrics, cutlery and jewellery. Under his tutelage – and commercial enterprise – the firm came to dominate British design in the 1870s and 80s. It influenced the formerly Puginian decorating company, Crace and Co., responsible for the interiors of Buckingham Palace and many country houses, as well as Staffordshire potters, Minton's ceramics and William De Morgan's tiles.

Under Morris the movement was attracted to early socialism. For a while the group went to live together in an austere Tudor/ Gothic Red House (1860), built for them in eponymous brick by Webb in Bexleyheath in Kent. The experiment in cohabitation was predictably short-lived, but Morris did not give up. He and his associates founded and nurtured organizations such as the Art Workers' Guild, the School of Handicraft and the School of Art Needlework. They supported the new Liberty store in Regent Street, where its rear extension was later hand-crafted in Tudor timbering – still visible today.

In 1877, Morris founded the Society for the Protection of Ancient Buildings, in part to protest at what he saw (with Ruskin) as Scott's excessively destructive church restorations. This also reflected a self-confident Victorian belief that Britain's global success lay in its respect for its past, for relics that should be guarded and understood. It was in precisely this spirit that Scott – despite

Sweetness and Light (1870–1900)

Ruskin's critique – had sought to restore Gothic churches and cathedrals, and that Morris had acquired a second home, Kelmscott Manor, by the Thames in Oxfordshire. Antiquarianism was no longer an elite pursuit but a deep-rooted ideology.

A feature of Morris's movement was that architects should now see themselves as artists personally inspired. They had their professional body, the Royal Institute of British Architects, which in 1882 introduced a formal examination for admission, though the profession remained open to any practitioner. From 1893 they had their own magazine, *Studio*, to be followed by the *Architecture Review*, whose publicizing of innovation and modernity in all its guises continued throughout the twentieth century. Architects were now to see themselves emphatically as artists – some might say as beyond stylistic contradiction.

For all Morris's activity, the Arts and Crafts movement produced little sense of direction. It claimed to be searching for a 'national style' to unite architecture's various traditions, but no sign of such unity emerged. In his history of the 'sweetness and light' period, Mark Girouard saw Arts and Crafts as partly a Ruskinian reaction against the advance of industry and partly a response to the 'muscular' architecture of the High Victorians. To Girouard these young people, often the wealthy beneficiaries of Victorian prosperity, felt they could afford to relax. 'Their views grew less dogmatic, their manners smoother, their morals easier.' They called themselves 'aesthetes'.

The 1870s were in Britain a time of political reform on a par with the 1830s. They saw a wider democratic franchise, new schools, philanthropic housing and a greater concern for public health. Cities were filling with theatres, restaurants and libraries. If Arts and Crafts had an early hero it was another Street disciple and friend of Burges, Edward Godwin (1833–86). A passionate aesthete – and lover of the actress Ellen Terry – he in 1877 designed a house in Chelsea's Tite Street for his friend the artist James

McNeill Whistler. Though classical in detail, its sparseness of form and sweeping roofs were highly original. There followed other houses by Godwin in the Tite Street artists' colony, most in a Dutch Renaissance style.

Godwin opened his own studio at Liberty, where he created theatrical sets and costumes. He plunged into constant artistic controversy, often in defence of Whistler. His aesthetic circle, which included the young Oscar Wilde, was an easy target for critics. Agnostic and detached, they professed themselves intensely committed, even if they did not know to what. Godwin's type was satirized as an 'ultra-poetical super-aesthetical . . . intense young man', sporting his 'greenery-yallery, / Grosvenor Gallery' in Gilbert and Sullivan's 1881 opera *Patience*.

The narrative of style often coheres round one person. In the 1870s this person was Richard Norman Shaw (1831–1912). Shaw was employed in the office of the Scottish architect William Burn in the 1840s. He moved to London to work under Street before setting up his own practice in 1862. Shaw developed a style of domestic building that contrasted with and emphatically replaced Victorian Italianate. As such, he ranked with the great stylistic innovators. He was rooted in a love of English vernacular of the sixteenth and seventeenth centuries, with red brick, mansard roofs and high chimneys. He disliked symmetrical facades and hated stucco. He was drawn to Morris, though not to his politics. As for Morris's ally Webb, Shaw called him 'a very able man indeed, but with a strong liking for the ugly'.

Shaw's first major work was Cragside (1869), built outside Newcastle for the arms magnate Lord Armstrong. At a time when classical and Gothic were still in contention, the house ignored both. It was in effect a gigantic cottage of medieval half-timbering, a pile of exaggerated gables, tall chimneys and sweeping views, an exercise in picturesque revival. Shaw repeated the style the following year at Grim's Dyke near Harrow. Visiting it from France, the Gothicist Eugène Viollet-le-Duc described it as 'conveying the attractive suggestion that the house has grown over the centuries'.

The essence of Shaw's early career was eclecticism. His New Zealand Chambers in the City (1871) was revolutionary, a study in Jacobean Renaissance, marking a move towards red brick and Dutch gables. At Lowther Lodge in Kensington (1873), now housing the Royal Geographical Society, Shaw initiated the 'Queen Anne' revival that was to be his signature. His artists' houses in Melbury Road, Holland Park, and his own in Hampstead's Ellerdale Road were widely copied, most vigorously by J. J. Stevenson in Hans Town and elsewhere on the Cadogan estate in Chelsea. If there was a signature in this architecture it was individualism. It strove to make every house, even in a continuous terrace, slightly different in design.

Shaw was fascinated by terracotta, polychrome and banded brickwork, eager always to interrupt the rhythmic Italianate of the streets in which he was asked to build. This is nowhere more evident than in his glaring redbrick intrusions into the creamy facades of Kensington's Queen's Gate. Under his hand seventeenth-century Cheyne Walk in Chelsea was steadily replaced with Dutch gables, Elizabethan windows and soaring chimneys, notably at Swan House. Shaw's influence on the Cadogan estate was awarded a style of its own by the cartoonist Osbert Lancaster: 'Pont Street Dutch'. This period culminated in Shaw's Dutch-style Alliance Assurance offices (1881) at the foot of St James's Street. It signalled that a new style was free at last of the classical/Gothic dichotomy – though it did not stop Shaw later reverting to classical.

If Shaw appeared to concentrate on London it was because London's property market was expanding fast and the sprawling low-density metropolis was being compared unfavourably to Haussmann's elegant and lofty boulevards of Paris. With this in mind, Shaw designed London's first tower block. The luxury apartments of Albert Hall Mansions (1879) dwarfed the adjacent Royal

Albert Hall. The building's foyers and corridors were lavishly appointed and its seven-storey facade had variegated windows, balconies and oversized gables. All this was designed to allay the stigma attached to 'living in flats'. The concept was much imitated, including in muted form by the first LCC council flats, spaciously appointed behind what is now the Tate Gallery (1897) and at Boundary Road in Bethnal Green.

Yet it was the housing of the poor that was in many ways showing the way forward for an urban living that was intolerably polluted and overcrowded. In the lead was the philanthropic movement activated by Octavia Hill and George Peabody in the 1860s. To them the condition of urban working-class living was the greatest blot on nineteenth-century Britain. Their answer had been to erect tidy and well-serviced blocks of flats in former slum areas and, by firm management, to prevent them from sliding back into squalor.

Equally significant were the many industrial settlements initiated by concerned industrialists since the days of New Lanark in the 1780s and the socialist Robert Owen. After Titus Salt's Saltaire in the 1870s (see Chapter 12) came Lever's Port Sunlight in the 1880s and Cadbury's Bournville outside Birmingham in the 1890s. The last two were Arts and Crafts inspired. Port Sunlight was the most extravagant of industry-sponsored model villages, a rich display of neo-Tudor, Dutch revival and Queen Anne set in a lavish parkland on the banks of the Mersey. The Birmingham suburb of Bournville was built round the Cadbury factory relocated there in 1879. Also mostly neo-Tudor, it indicated the dominant style of housing at the time and became an exemplar for the garden cities movement of the 1900s.

Shaw's flirtation with a similar development was his design for Bedford Park in west London. This was begun in 1875 on the initiative of an 'aesthetic' landowner and friend of Morris, Jonathan Carr, eager to create Morris's vision of 'little communities among gardens and fields'. Carr even had Godwin draw up the first designs. There was no pretence that this was for working-class housing, only a search for an acceptable pattern for a new suburb.

Carr soon switched to Shaw, and the style's debt to his affection for Queen Anne was emphasized in the naming of its streets: Queen Anne's Grove, Marlborough Crescent, Blenheim Road and Woodstock Road. The mix of smart and inexpensive houses, villas as well as terraces, was aimed in part at artists. No street was intended to be uniform, nor was any of them named a 'street'. Some houses had names, not numbers, such as Pleasaunce and Ye Denne, often with as many as six sizes of windows. Bedford Park's informal road layout – and its plethora of Morris interiors – was widely publicized. A newspaper report of 1883 praised its streets' 'cunning carelessness, to curve in such a wise as never to leave the eye staring at nothing'. It was an admirable intention now sadly ignored.

The estate included a full range of community services, appropriate for 'middle-class people of modest means'. There was an 'old-fashioned' (co-operative) shop, an old-fashioned inn called the Tabard, a club and even an art college. There were soon two schools, one High Church, one Low. Even the church was nominally Queen Anne, though Shaw conceded to convention by making the interior a demure Perpendicular Gothic. The suburb was summed up in a doggerel verse: 'Thus was a village builded / for all who are aesthete / Whose precious souls it fill did / with utter joy complete. / For floors were stained and polished / and every hearth was tiled / and Philistines abolished / by Culture's gracious child.' To Girouard, Bedford Park was the essence of the age. 'Light gushed out of it; its sweetness was almost overpowering.'

As Shaw matured he became more diverse, but always with an eye on the past. By the 1880s his Queen Anne style had grown to be both domestic and almost absurdly grand. In 1887, outside Blandford Forum in Dorset, he built a mansion for Lord Portman that might have passed as a Stuart palace, and was dubbed by

Edwin Lutyens 'Wrenaissance'. It is now Bryanston School. His New Scotland Yard (1887) for the Metropolitan Police on the Embankment had magnificent protruding corner windows and vivid bandings of brick and stone.

Shaw was in many ways the most attractive and the most original British architect. He had sat at the feet of the radicals, of Ruskin and Morris, and had learned from them but did not imitate them. He accepted the licence Morris offered, to look back over the history of English architecture and see what suited him best. He found an abundance of sympathetic clients whose taste he could flatter with gables, roofs and windows, with facades and decorations. His Bedford Park showed an aversion to monotony and an instinct for informality. His affection for the English village reflected the picturesque tradition of the early nineteenth century. If ever an architect was happy in his creations it was Shaw, and his influence on popular British architecture throughout the twentieth century is seldom fully recognized.

Another of this 'Queen Anne' group was Basil Champneys (1842–1935), who produced at Newnham College Cambridge a vivid enclave of sweetness and light. The earlier women's college at Girton had been built by Waterhouse two miles out of town, its fortress gatehouse and Gothic windows conveying what was thought would keep its inmates safe from harm or temptation. Newnham was a deliberate contrast, relaxed, private, yet 'at home', with swirling gables and oriel windows. Each room had an open fire and Morris wallpaper. Virginia Woolf wrote *A Room of One's Own* after visiting Newnham, describing 'gardens laid before me in the spring twilight, wild and open . . . the windows of the building curved like ships' windows among generous waves'.

Most extraordinary from this period is a group of houses on the Alexander estate in South Kensington. Harrington and Collingham Gardens were built by the partnership of Sir Ernest George and the Peto brothers in 1882, and they made even Shaw seem mundane. A series of redbrick and terracotta facades are, as the *Survey of London* says, 'at first sight a jumble of vernacular motifs from every country of northern Europe'. Each is a variant, if not a parody, on a Shaw theme: Dutch Renaissance, French chateau, Antwerp town house, Queen Anne revival. The house in which W. S. Gilbert (of Gilbert and Sullivan) lived, 39 Harrington Gardens, has half its height embraced by a giant stepped gable. The windows are surrounded by naturalistic carvings, the eaves reckless, the porches bizarre. Harrington Gardens is the extremity of late-Victorian individualism. I know of no street like it anywhere in the world.

Queen Anne's most prominent showing was in the new Board schools built for the introduction of compulsory schooling in the 1870s. The chief architect of the London Board of Education, E. R. Robson, worked at first with fellow progressives such as Stevenson and Champneys in the Shaw style. They produced airy classrooms, high windows, steep gables and tall chimneys. The schools were intended by Robson to dominate their surroundings, to compete with church steeples to mark the arrival of the new faith of education. The architect, said Robson, should take 'every opportunity of proclaiming his intentions'. These buildings can still be seen dotting the Victorian skyline across almost all of inner London. Robson was to build 500 schools in thirty-three years.

Even the Gothic tradition in church design was not immune to sweetness and light. Architects such as Bodley and Pearson continued working into the 1880s and beyond. The most original was J. D. Sedding, yet another graduate of the Street office. An ardent Arts and Crafts architect, his most mature work was Holy Trinity Sloane Street (1888). Though essentially Perpendicular Gothic with giant east and west windows, its fittings made it an Arts and Crafts treasury. They included railings, screens, lecterns, an organ case and stalls by Sedding's followers, as well as windows by Morris and Burne-Jones. To anyone who supposes European art nouveau had no base in Britain, I say visit Holy Trinity.

At the end of the century the Catholic Church staged what might be considered a curtain call on the stylistic disputes of the nineteenth century. The argument was yet again over how a cathedral should look. Should the new Roman Catholic cathedral for Westminster be Gothic or classical, given the notional rivalry with Westminster Abbey down the road? The compromise reached in 1895 was Byzantine, in a proposal by J. F. Bentley.

The cathedral's rich marble panelling rose as far as the first floor and was then left to await later mosaic, leaving the interior apparently unfinished beneath a vast space of undressed brick. The nave was surrounded by individual chapels brilliantly lit and in a rich variety of styles. The St Andrew's Chapel of 1912 was furnished by Ernest Gimson and Sidney Barnsley and is a gem of Arts and Crafts. The building was hailed by Shaw as 'the finest church that has been built in centuries'.

The last two decades of the nineteenth century were devoid of orthodoxy. Architects sensed the end of an age. Their status as artists was undimmed, their eyes and imagination open to all and every style. The ageing Burges complained at an RIBA meeting in 1881 that the aesthetes were 'deserters from the Gothic school'. But most of his colleagues – Bodley, Sedding, Shaw, Stevenson and Champneys – had grown up during the Gothic revival and had heard enough argument. In the late-Victorian rush to build theatres, libraries, institutes and department stores, they had done what the Arts and Crafts movement had told them. They had sought and many had found a new eclecticism that clearly suited the mood of the time.

By the turn of the twentieth century, sweetness and light was like a comet that had passed across the sky. It had produced a more satisfying domestic architecture probably than any other period. Yet the spirit of discovery that had inspired it began to dim. As the historian of the Edwardian age, Alastair Service, concluded, the search for a modern vernacular 'rooted in national or local traditions and recognizably British . . . had failed'. *British Architect* magazine could welcome the new century with a plea for 'yet greater architectural progress and – who knows? – perhaps even a new national style!' There was as yet no sign of it.

The year 1897 saw the founding by Edward Hudson of *Country Life* magazine. Its ambition was not, as popularly supposed, to celebrate the English country house but to bring the pleasures of the countryside to the attention of city dwellers. The first building featured was, significantly, Baddesley Clinton, a moated manor in the Midlands and embodiment of everything preached by the Arts and Crafts movement. The magazine was soon being referred to in parliament as 'the keeper of the architectural conscience of the nation'.

What *Country Life* came to represent – its masthead today still firmly Arts and Crafts – was not a new national style but more a respect for old ones. Along with its fellow champion of the countryside the National Trust, founded in 1895, *Country Life* saw its task as to prevent the destruction of the best in Britain's historic buildings, to set an example for architects yet to come. It was carrying forward the work of Morris, the ruralists and the antiquarians.

The architectural battles that were to be fought in the new century would not be so much between styles – though that continued – as between the past/present and a vision of the future. Whereas architects had traditionally seen themselves as creating structures on virgin soil, they would now have to share that soil with its previous occupants. This would mean competition and require compromise. For many architects, and for the communities they claimed to serve, that was not always a happy experience.

15.

Fit for Empire (1900–1920)

As the new century arrived, the aesthetic movement was in retreat. The Pre-Raphaelites were long gone. Morris was dead. Waterhouse, Bodley and Shaw were the grand old men of their profession. Even Shaw had moved on from Queen Anne to immerse himself in neoclassicism. The heavy windows and beefy columns of his Piccadilly Hotel (1905) are unequivocally baroque. Meanwhile French influence, so long kept at bay across the Channel, made a brief foray into British design.

This movement arose from the 1800s neoclassicism of Paris's École des Beaux-Arts. From 1830 it was to influence architecture across much of Europe and an America eager to retain cultural ties with its European past. Half of America's state capitols, universities and railway termini were to be designed in a Beaux Arts style. Its appeal to the grandeur of power seemed limitless. Its lack of warmth or the intimacy of individualism seemed to enthral twentieth-century autocrats and modernists alike.

In Britain the Beaux Arts had been ignored, at least since the Greek revival of the 1830s. This ended with the international success of the Paris Exhibition of 1900. Imitations of its Grand and Petit Palais were to spring up everywhere. Britain's Prince of Wales, soon to be Edward VII (r.1901–10), had long admired France and was to play a part in the signing of the Anglo-French entente of 1904. The result was that Britain saw something rare in its history, a bout of Francophilia. The new Ritz Hotel (1903) was emphatically French. Designed by the Anglo-French partnership of Arthur Davis and Charles Mewès, it was the first non-industrial building to be constructed on a steel frame. The same pair went on to produce the RAC Club in Pall Mall (1908), supposedly modelled on the Hôtel de la Marine in Paris's Place de la Concorde.

Elsewhere, civic and institutional buildings were not so much French as British imperial. The ageing Queen Victoria had complained that there was little of the empire about the streets of her capital. She noted how poorly they compared to the grand avenues of Paris, Berlin and Vienna. The times called for what was termed the Grand Manner, which meant yet another classical revival. The question was whether, as before, this meant a straight-laced Palladianism or whether Britain might at last see what previous revivals had largely ignored: a departure from neoclassicism into baroque and its variants.

A foretaste was given by an extraordinary work of 1888 by a former Arts and Crafts enthusiast, John Belcher (1841–1913), for the Institute of Chartered Accountants in the City. It was almost a baroque cartoon, heavy with rustication and elaborate windows, restless with pilasters and relief panels. The front doorway was not so much baroque as all-in wrestling. Belcher was an architect of panache and shamelessly attributed much of his building style to Michelangelo. The sculptor Hamo Thorneycroft supplied a frieze of the arts and sciences that is sadly too high up to read.

Belcher and his partner John Joass went on to design town halls, institutional headquarters and department stores. Their extrovert bombast was ideally suited to a revitalized municipal government that followed reforms to local democracy in the 1880s. New civic buildings rose over towns as varied as Bath, Wakefield, Stafford, Battersea, Belfast, Lambeth, Harrogate and Stockport. Colchester's town hall was a baroque extravaganza by the now ubiquitous Belcher. East Ham's was hardly less grand. The year 1897 was famous as the 'year of competitions'. The winners sometimes followed Liverpool and Edinburgh in an austere

Greek revival. Others followed Leeds in its homage to Christopher Wren.

Outstanding was the port town of Cardiff, as yet graced only with Burges's castles for the Marquess of Bute. In 1897 a charismatic young Cockney, Edwin Rickards, teamed with James Stewart and an engineer, H. V. Lanchester, to win the competition for a new civic centre and law courts. The city was eager to show off as the capital of Glamorgan's 'coal rush', and Rickards's fascination with German baroque produced a hall that would do credit to a German principality. No local authority in Britain had a more handsome civic enclave, certainly not the LCC's tedious County Hall (1911) by Ralph Knott. Rickards went on to design a baroque headquarters for Deptford (1906) in south London and challenge Hawksmoor's west front of Westminster Abbey with his Methodist Central Hall (1902).

At the same time, Liverpool asserted its full magnificence in the Three Graces on its waterfront. They comprised the Port of Liverpool building (1904), the Royal Liver building (1908) and the Cunard building (1914). The outer two were in a wild baroque, sandwiching the Cunard building's restrained Italianate. They gave the historic port as rich a backdrop as any in Europe, gazing down not just on the older Albert Docks but on what was by then a gracious Victorian city centre. The composition was defaced in 2011 when the council erected the aggressively horizontal gash of the Museum of Liverpool in front of it on the quayside.

Bravura architecture was now everywhere. Almost all British town centres still display a prominent institutional building constructed in the early twentieth century – though most people will declare it Victorian. The palm should go to Frank Matcham (1854–1920), who designed ninety theatres and redesigned another eighty in London and the provinces, including his cathedral, the London Coliseum. All were in the most florid classical style, as if the gods of drama had ordered their creator to go over the

Fit for Empire (1900–1920)

top. A tedious play in a Matcham theatre can always be relieved by studying its interior.

In London's Whitehall two magnificent buildings now arose adjacent to Scott's Foreign Office. They were John Brydon's government offices (1900) overlooking Parliament Square and William Young's palatial War Office (1906). The latter was explicitly designed to complement Inigo Jones's Banqueting House opposite. Four centuries of British classicism can thus be viewed from outside the Horse Guards in Whitehall. Jones's seventeenth-century masterpiece faces Kent's reticent eighteenth-century Horse Guards, while opposite the trumpet blast of Young's War Office (now a luxury hotel) bursts with military self-importance. Finally facing it is diminuendo, Vincent Harris's Ministry of Defence headquarters, a frigid pile of 'stripped Georgian' bureaucracy built in 1916.

As for Victoria's desire for a ceremonial thoroughfare, plans were indeed laid for a London 'Champs-Élysées'. It would be the first such project since Nash's by then mostly demolished Regent Street. The chosen location was another ancient slum, Clare Market, at the east end of the Strand. Here a new avenue would drive north from the Thames at Aldwych to the British Museum in Bloomsbury. Funding delayed the project, and in 1901 the Queen died, so what was to be Queensway became Kingsway, opened by Edward VII in 1905. With its ponderous beginning at Aldwych, the avenue was a commercial failure and had to be occupied with government offices. It is an example of how an architecture that cares only for buildings and not streets will starve itself of life. Adjacent Covent Garden, conserved not destroyed, is now bursting with vitality while Kingsway lies dead.

A more successful avenue was designed by the master of Edwardian classicism, Aston Webb, as a processional route through St James's Park from Trafalgar Square to Buckingham Palace. To the palace Webb supplied a new Palladian facade as backdrop for a memorial to the late Queen. Her statue, accompanied by figures depicting imperial virtues, was so ridiculed that the satirist Saki invented a villain who blackmailed the government by threatening to build copies of it everywhere. The Mall was intended to become the start of a triumphal way to St Paul's, crossing the new Kingsway, hence the location of 'imperial' Canada, South Africa, Rhodesia, India and Australia embassies along that route.

The leader of the Grand Manner – though he called it the 'High Game' – was another graduate of the Arts and Crafts tradition, Edwin Lutyens (1869–1944). One of fourteen children in a poor household, Lutyens was first apprenticed to George and Peto – of Harrington Gardens – but after six months at the age of twenty he set up on his own, designing houses in the tradition of Norman Shaw. One of his first houses was for his friend the gardener Gertrude Jekyll, for whom he built Munstead Wood (1896) in Surrey. It was wholly unclassical and heavily influenced by Shaw, with massive chimneys, sweeping roofs and quaint windows.

Lutyens was exceptional among architects in being a humourist. To his biographer Christopher Hussey he was 'genial, whimsical, facetious . . . habitually schoolboyish'. To Vita Sackville-West he was 'an irresponsible, imaginative jester of genius'. He married the daughter of a Viceroy of India and would win clients by sketching houses for them on table napkins at dinner parties. His career went from strength to strength in what was the last age when grandees still had the confidence to commission large houses.

A characteristic that Lutyens borrowed from Shaw was to change with the times. His Deanery Gardens in Sonning (1901) was Arts and Crafts Tudor. In the same year he adopted English medieval for *Country Life*'s owner, Hudson, at Lindisfarne Castle (1901). Yet for the same magazine's Covent Garden offices he designed a town house in the style of Wren. Working there in my twenties I sensed its high ceilings and rich furniture drawing me back to the seventeenth century. We had a rebellious receptionist who adorned her alcove with an enormous poster of the actor Steve McQueen, to the dismay of more conventional contributors.

It was Wren to whom Lutyens became most firmly wedded. In the 1900s he was the inspiration for Lutyens' masterpiece, the Queen Anne mansion of Salutation in Sandwich (1911). This contrasted with his baronial Castle Drogo in Devon (1910), built for the Home and Colonial store chain tycoon Julius Drewe. Drogo was never fully finished and the building was so costly it spawned the saying that no man is so rich that an architect cannot break him. Lutyens went on to produce City banks, war memorials and cenotaphs, some in a 'stripped' classicism, others pure Wren revivals.

As if of necessity, the Anglican Church felt obliged to answer to an old tune. No sooner had the Catholics opted for Byzantine at Westminster Cathedral than a competition was launched for a new Anglican cathedral in Liverpool, with the veterans Bodley and Shaw among its assessors. But again the question arose, should it be Gothic or classical? The committee recorded such comments as 'Gothic produces a more devotional effect upon the mind than any other which human skill had invented.' A firm classicist, Reginald Blomfield, disagreed. Gothic was 'a worn-out flirtation with antiquarianism, now relegated to the limbo of art delusions'. Editorials appeared in national newspapers but the issue was left open.

Submissions poured in from most of the leading architects of the day, but under pressure from Bodley the decision went to a twenty-two-year-old grandson of George Gilbert Scott named Giles, on the strength of a handful of drawings. Scott was a mere apprentice, a Catholic and a relative of Bodley's by marriage, who had 'never designed more than a pipe rack'. The nepotism sparked outrage. Yet Bodley was adamant and Scott got the job. To the surprise of no one, it was Bodley who designed the first part of the building to open, the Lady Chapel, but he died shortly after. The cathedral then proceeded in fits and starts, with Scott remaining in post and with the project persistently short of money. He eventually died in 1960 and the cathedral was not finished until 1978.

Liverpool Cathedral was in the style of a great European Gothic church. It lacked the innovative vitality of Gaudi's Sagrada Família, then rising as slowly over Barcelona. I visited them in succession in the 1970s. While Barcelona was already an exhilarating example of Spanish Gothic reborn, the unfinished Liverpool in its damp quarry seemed helpless and grim. Since then Liverpool has been finished and Barcelona almost so. While the latter I regard as a sensation, Scott's work has grown on me. His mastery of proportion and his sense of space are astonishing. To stand in the crossing, pierced by the sun's rays on a clear day, is to feel the true potency of the Gothic style that classicism has never quite equalled.

Despite being outsmarted in the Liverpool controversy, the classical revival went from strength to strength. Its champion Blomfield (1856–1942) was a creature of his age. His attachment to English tradition was rooted in what would be less welcome today: ethnic authenticity. He saw style as about racial origin, and in the case of the English that meant the Celts and their descendants. Style should emerge naturally in the course of a building's design, and to discuss it was to deny it. This 'deniability' of style was a common theme among architectural purists.

Blomfield was an admirer of the Oxford architect Thomas Jackson. Designer of the university's neo-Elizabethan Examination Schools (1876), Jackson was favoured by colleges eager for a continuity with their past. His Renaissance 'Bridge of Sighs' at Hertford College, ostensibly sixteenth-century, was actually built in 1913. Appropriate to Oxford as 'the home of lost causes', Jackson was a last revivalist of Tudor Gothic. Blomfield became a practising architect, with a clientele among conservative homeowners usually eager to restore classical dwellings. He declared himself available to any house that offered him a weekend's shooting. His daughter denounced his reactionary views by shouting 'Votes for Women!' at the king during the annual debutante ball.

Meanwhile, in architecture's backwaters, surviving members of the Art Workers' Guild were buoyed by one of Shaw's former assistants, William Lethaby (1857–1931). He became an inspiring teacher as well as an architect. Lethaby brought the light of scholarship to bear on a subject rarely studied: the origins of architectural style. His *Architecture, Mysticism and Myth* (1891) delved deep into the symbolism, even the magic, of building. He carried Arts and Crafts concepts to their limit, finding significance in such banalities as 'simple well-off house-keeping in the country, tea in the garden, boy-scouting and tennis in flannels'. At a time when public architects were dressing their buildings in classical orders, he simply asked why.

The nearest Lethaby came to an answer was in his church at All Saints Brockhampton (1901), with its floor-to-roof concrete arches. A strange structure, it might be late twentieth century were it not for its thatched roof. It was Gothic in mood but not in vocabulary. One scholar whom Lethaby took under his wing was an official at Germany's London embassy named Hermann Muthesius. In a widely read book, *Das Englische Haus* (1905), Muthesius analysed the Arts and Crafts movement more thoroughly than any English scholar. Applauding 'the absolute practicality' of traditional English building, he celebrated its 'restraint and honesty, its domestic utility in both town and country'. An admirer of Shaw, Muthesius declared his houses 'in every way a higher form of life' with their emphasis on historicism and simplicity. His was the final seal of approval on the age of sweetness and light.

★

Other architects struggled to keep alive enthusiasm for the 'free style' of the 1870s. Harrison Townsend's Horniman Museum and Whitechapel Art Gallery in London (both 1896) are hard to place other than in a sort of muscular neo-Romanesque. Two veterans of the Art Workers' Guild, Edward Prior and Charles Voysey, travelled from Queen Anne to art nouveau. Their houses had steep roofs, asymmetrical windows and white walls. In Voysey's case such features were later to be hailed as foretastes of modernism. His most remarkable work was the old Sanderson wallpaper factory in Chiswick, where he once worked.

The socialist ambitions of Morris and his friends were carried into the new century by another architectural eccentric, Charles Ashbee (1863–1942). He was fond of pointing out that Arts and Crafts architects had built almost exclusively for a moneyed minority. 'We have made our movement,' he said with more than a little truth, 'a narrow and tiresome little aristocracy working with great skill for the very rich.' He seemed to exonerate his own Guild of Handicraft and in 1902 set up a colony of like-minded craftsmen in Chipping Campden in the Cotswolds. Ashbee went on to serve as a conservation administrator in Jerusalem, join a secret order of homosexuals and build Arts and Crafts houses in the Chelsea artists' colony. They were hardly for the poor.

Of these Arts and Crafts survivors the most celebrated was not a Londoner but a Scotsman, Charles Rennie Mackintosh (1868–1928). Scotland at the turn of the century, and particularly Glasgow, was prospering. The Clyde shoreline was lined with wealthy clients open to new ideas. Mackintosh pleaded that 'we must clothe modern ideas with modern dress, adorn our designs with living fancy'. In this he was the opposite of the prolific and energetic John James Burnet, his Glasgow contemporary who was lining Scotland's city streets with every style from Wren to Scots baronial before moving down to London. His most

Fit for Empire (1900–1920)

prominent work was to be the impressive King Edward VII Galleries at the rear of the British Museum, opened in 1914.

Mackintosh's short career saw few completed buildings. Some displayed a gable or other decorative device and most echoed Shaw's fascination with the disposition of windows. Central to Mackintosh's work was a belief in the fusion of exterior and interior design: the furnishing of a building was to him integral to its character. He borrowed from Japanese styles, best seen in his Willow Tearooms in Glasgow, designed in collaboration with his wife, Margaret Macdonald Mackintosh, and since restored to their translucent, stained-glass glory.

Mackintosh's most celebrated work was the Glasgow School of Art. Its high walls and generous windows appeared protomodernist, yet its furnishings, chairs and cupboards were clearly in the tradition of art nouveau. The high point of the building was the two-storey library. Its wavy lines and subtle lighting created a sense of space redefined, with books as mere decoration. The school carried Mackintosh's signature motif, an elegant rose. It was twice gutted by fire and is now being again restored. It remains the cardinal monument of the promise offered by the Arts and Crafts movement to British architecture at the start of the twentieth century, but never fulfilled.

These architects were establishing links with developments on the continent. Mackintosh was invited to the Viennese Secession exhibitions, to find himself alongside Antoni Gaudí, Victor Horta, Otto Wagner and Frank Lloyd Wright. He was admired by his contemporaries, though how influential he was over them is debatable. The buildings of Ashbee, Voysey and Mackintosh constituted the makings of a new direction, but as Ashbee pointed out, they appealed only to a small number of rich patrons. They were used neither for public buildings nor by the growing market for suburban homes.

This market was now by far the most distinctive realm for new

British architecture. An urban social reformer, Ebenezer Howard, shared the ambition of many late-Victorian progressives to bring human habitation closer to nature. His *To-Morrow: A Peaceful Path to Real Reform* (1898) followed the work of housing philanthropists such as Peabody and Hill, but he, unlike them, saw existing cities as beyond redemption. Ideally, they should be replaced by new 'garden cities' built afresh in the countryside.

In 1903, Howard set up a trust to found a new town at Letchworth in Hertfordshire, designed by two young architects, Raymond Unwin and Barry Parker. It was to be planned for an 'ideal population', declared by Howard to be 30,000. Such settlements would replace old ones by 'scientific methods'. A novel union of town and country, said Howard, from which 'would spring a new hope, a new life, a new civilization', governed and run on socialist principles. It was the first shoots of what was to become a modernist fixation with architecture as the agency of utopia.

Though it had much in common with Bedford Park, Letchworth was more radical. It was to have trees and grass galore, modest houses for the rich and (fairly) poor, hedges not fences and a full complement of communal services. Its road users enjoyed what was said to be Britain's first roundabout. As for architecture, a ruthlessly plain cottage style applied to most of the houses, though Letchworth's town hall was firmly Queen Anne. The town soon inspired the more celebrated Hampstead Garden Suburb (1906), founded by philanthropist Henrietta Barnett and designed by Raymond Unwin for a wealthier clientele.

The formal public sector was not far behind. Battersea council in 1901 produced at Latchmere a high-density estate of terrace houses barely distinguishable from the surrounding Georgian streets. Hendon council's Watling Estate was of a quality comparable with nearby Hampstead Garden Suburb. LCC estates appeared in 1912 at White Hart Lane in Tottenham and Old Oak

Common in Hammersmith. The garden city concept attracted attention from local authorities across Europe and proved a rare British contribution to early-twentieth-century architecture.

Meanwhile, away from this idealism a different type of new town was emerging. It was suburban, private, rented or owner-occupied, and marketed to an aspiring lower-middle class of 'white-collar', mostly clerical workers. Its stimulus came from the outward spread of London's underground railway network that was now attracting migrants in their hundreds of thousands from the rest of Britain. The unplanned and unrestrained expansion into Middlesex of the Metropolitan Railway Company's line lent its name to a new designation: Metroland.

Town planning was all but non-existent. Some closer-in neighbourhoods took Bedford Park as their lodestar. Others saw a lower-density diversity. Miles of woods and fields disappeared under pitched roofs and mansard windows. Gables everywhere carried Tudor black-and-white decoration. Walls were pierced by oriel bays and hung with tiles. Doors were flanked with pilasters and corbels.

Developers went to great lengths to attune their architecture to each level of class. Streets were tree-lined and called drives, parks, groves, walks, crescents and dales. House prices varied from £300 (about £14,500 today) to £1,000, with care taken not to mix cheap and expensive in one neighbourhood. Wanstead's Aldersbrook was priced at £500. The Wimbledon House Estate was of detached mansions in Tudor, Queen Anne and Dutch styles and nearer to £1,000. Few suburbs had much in the way of shops or public services. All that mattered was closeness to a station to London.

Most remarkable of these early suburbs was Gidea Park, outside Romford. Here an enlightened developer, Herbert Raphael, was eager for east London to have its own Hampstead Garden Suburb. He duly held a competition in 1900 for houses priced at

£375 or £500. A hundred architects submitted proposals, including most of the prominent names of the period. These included Ashbee, William Curtis Green, Mackay Baillie Scott, Charles Holden, H. Percy Adams, Clough Williams-Ellis and Hampstead Garden Suburb's Raymond Unwin.

Almost all were chosen to contribute designs and 159 were eventually built, almost all detached. This first phase of Gidea Park was completed in 1911 and the style was overwhelmingly one that would have been recognized by Norman Shaw, in the spectrum from Tudor to Queen Anne. It was the British suburb at what became its most typical, secure, green, characterful and individual. Gidea Park today forms a remarkable and little-known gallery of English domestic architecture, as it emerged uncertainly into the twentieth century.

16.
Homes for Heroes (1920–1930)

Britain emerged from the First World War a nation traumatized and eager to turn a new page. On that page was written one word: houses. The legacy of the Victorian slum was a blight from which victory in war was thought to have earned a release. Architects and builders were to be marched out of the trenches and onto a new battlefield, to confront Lloyd George's demand of 'homes fit for heroes'. The king, George V (r.1910–36), declared that the 'solution to the housing question is the foundation of social progress'.

Edwardian suburbs were already encircling every English city and particularly London. Building had ceased during the war and a housing shortage was declared after it. This led in 1919 to the Addison Act, launching a national programme of building in both public and private sectors. Local councils were told to create new rental estates, unlimited in size and with their budgets guaranteed by the Treasury against loss. Private house-builders too were subsidized, to the tune of between £160 and £260 a house (£7,000–11,000 today – roughly 20 per cent of cost). The result was construction on a scale unprecedented even during the pre-war suburban boom. An average of 200,000 new units a year were created, sustained for twenty years. Of these, a million were to be built by local councils and three million by the private sector. There was no stipulation of where they should be, or that there be any related infrastructure.

The result was phenomenal and not a little chaotic. By the late

1930s when the suburban boom came to an end, London's built-up area had expanded sixfold since the 1880s, to be halted only by another war and the introduction of green belts. Nowhere else in Europe was comparable in the lavishness of its housing. Most suburban properties, public as well as private, had some sort of garden. This was barely conceivable on the continent, where the norm was blocks of flats. The use of valuable land bordered on reckless.

The Addison Act initiated a new responsibility on local authorities to house not just the homeless and slum-dwellers but ordinary in-work citizens. Estates that had previously been the isolated endeavours of private philanthropists and committed councils sprouted everywhere. The LCC's largest estate, at Becontree in Barking, had by 1935 100,000 residents. This was a settlement whose population was greater than that of Darlington or Bath. It was followed in 1928 by the next largest, the St Helier estate at Morden in south London. These were described as 'cottage estates', in terraces and semi-detached villas, almost all with some form of private garden. Tenants were imported chiefly from the overcrowded East End, the sole qualification being that they be in employment. They were described as 'prosperous working class'.

For the best part of a decade, Becontree had no infrastructure of schools, hospitals or shops. Houses were unheated and water tanks would freeze in winter, rendering flush toilets unusable. Residents had to trudge down muddy builders' tracks to get to work or services. In many places unschooled children ran wild over construction sites. It was British town planning at its most barren, and target-led housing at its most mindless. Yet Becontree famously produced celebrities such as Dudley Moore, Sandie Shaw, the Dagenham Girl Pipers and George Carey, Archbishop of Canterbury.

Histories of the suburbs rarely touch on the question of style.

Homes for Heroes (1920–1930)

A collection of essays by Paul Oliver, Ian Davis and Ian Bentley entitled *Dunroamin: The Suburban Semi and Its Enemies* (1981) was an exception. It emphasized the stark distinction that arose between the public and private estates. Council housing departments turned for advice to professional architects, who viewed their designs in quasi-political terms. To them the houses were expressions of communal collectivity. Rules of egalitarianism required that no house be different from any other and forbade it being 'improved' to make it so. Houses belonged to the council, not the tenant.

As a result, estates were not fragmented into separate enclaves, let alone individual properties. As Ian Bentley pointed out in *Dunroamin*, equality had to be rigid. 'At all scales, from the layout of the estate, through the form of the public spaces to the design of the houses themselves, the council estate spoke the language of community.' That community was defined by the council, which put style firmly in the hands of one group of people: council architects.

These architects were drawn, as if by professional instinct, to what came to be called 'stripped Georgian'. As Bentley put it, 'its horizontal roof-lines, string-courses and plinths could join terraces of houses into a single unified composition expressing community. Its simple regular forms suggested economy, rationality and order.' As such, 'Georgian' became the standard style for public housing throughout Britain. It firmly replaced the previous dominance of the Arts and Crafts tradition inherited from philanthropic and early council housing before the war.

What was meant by Georgian became moot. Becontree's plain facades reached the point where a house, terrace or semi-detached, needed only a pitched roof, a front door and three windows to be dubbed Georgian. When asked why virtually no houses in the then booming private sector looked anything like this – why neo-Georgian went completely out of suburban fashion – one private owner was quoted as replying that no one would want their home to look like a council house.

This clash of styles reached an extreme at Cutteslowe in north Oxford in 1934. Here a council estate was built at one end of a road that had 'Queen Anne' private houses at the other end. The private owners promptly erected a seven-foot wall across the road with iron spikes to separate them from the council tenants. It took twenty years – and mass demonstrations including by my then undergraduate mother – to negotiate the barrier's removal.

Elsewhere the private sector was picking up speed. Farms vanished. The countryside swarmed with labourers' camps. The fields of Middlesex, Essex, Surrey and Kent sprouted the names of Costain, Laing, Wimpey, Wates and Taylor Woodrow. The annual Ideal Home Exhibition at Earls Court, begun by the *Daily Mail* in 1908, attracted thousands of eager visitors. New settlements were advertised as (initially) rural villages, surrounded by sloping hills and trees. The estates themselves were carefully grouped into neighbourhoods of equal social value. The joke was that a woman saying 'my husband' should not find herself living next to one saying 'my Bill'.

As for style, families who had spent their lives crammed into city terraces or flats wanted above all to have somewhere distinctively theirs. It had to signify escape from the metropolis. They might not have found a real country cottage or village manor, but they sought an approximation. The aspiration was one that Shaw had honoured in Bedford Park. The desire for redbrick neo-Tudor with seventeenth-century dressings that had characterized the Edwardian period showed no sign of abating. Just as the resident of centralized Georgian London aspired to a classical square, so the new suburbanites aspired to a rural retreat. It was a democratization of taste.

Alan Jackson's *Semi-Detached London* (1973) charted the efforts of private builders to meet this demand. He recorded advertisements promising 'no pair of houses alike in the road'. Asked to explain the popularity of 'Queen Anne', a housing magazine reported in confusion that 'one person loved it for its homeliness, another for its dignity and picturesque grace; one admired it for being domestic and unpretending, another for being rich and queenly. For everyone, it was pure English, pure Flemish, pure Italian.' In other words, no one spoke the language of architecture. They just knew what they liked. It was a land, in the words of its greatest fan, John Betjeman, of 'gnomes and ordinary people'.

The response of architectural critics was almost entirely hostile to the private suburb, often with an extraordinary overlay of snobbery. To the newly arrived German émigré Nikolaus Pevsner, bourgeois taste in England was a matter of half-heartedness: he declared it semi-detached, half-timbered, 'sub-urban' and middle-class. It was, he said, as if the English could never make up their minds. Private developers made desperate attempts to find a terminology for their various styles. They rang changes on 'Tudor, Elizabethan or Old World' (sometimes Olde Worlde). Some fell back on codes, 'Type A5' or 'Plan B', but this proved unpopular. The self-conscious Laings invented 'Olympia', 'Malvern', 'Filey', 'Jubilee' and 'Coronation', the references meaningless.

The new suburbs were lampooned from right and left – though not by those who lived there. The cartoonist Osbert Lancaster described the two classes of private estate as 'By-pass Variegated' and 'Stockbroker Tudor', later adding a third: 'Pseudish'. The first was down-market and meant a scatter of gabled frontages: 'Houses disposed to ensure the largest possible area of countryside is ruined with the minimum of expense.' The up-market Stockbroker Tudor was firmly retro, 'a glorified version of Anne Hathaway's cottage', stopping short only of thatch. Pseudish was neo-Egyptian or neo-anything. Owners were fierce in wanting all mod cons and indeed were adventurously modernist in their interiors. But their face as shown to the world was unequivocal. Nothing should interfere with old oak beams, bottle-glass windows and wrought iron light fittings. They were sacred emblems of the suburban liturgy.

If any period revival was most hated by the purists it was Victorian. Each generation famously rejects the taste of its predecessor, and so it was between the wars. Wodehouse's narrator, hardly a modernist, remarked of the Victorians, 'It's pretty generally admitted that few of them were to be trusted within reach of a trowel and a pile of bricks.' To critics, the Ideal Home Exhibition, drenched in neo-Tudor, was a national humiliation, a festival of vulgarity. It was packed with people who considered themselves neither true townspeople nor true country people. They were zombies.

Worse, they were zombies who seemed to know what they liked. A poll taken c.1930 on what should be the British 'national style' of architecture would almost certainly have yielded 'Tudorbethan'. The authors of *Dunroamin* suggested that what architects and critics could not tolerate in the new suburbanites was that they appeared rather happy in their surroundings. Indeed, they had felt no pressing need for the service of architects. A developer's pattern book would do fine.

Meanwhile, the architecture of the public realm was a different world. After the war, the practitioners of the Edwardian Grand Manner remained in the lead. Lutyens and his contemporaries still regarded classicism as the national style. Lutyens himself veered towards megalomania. Again, cathedrals were in the frame. Lutyens' commission to build a new Catholic cathedral in Liverpool was intended to rival Scott's Gothic version down the road. It was projected to be the biggest church in the world, bigger than St Paul's and St Peter's Rome, but this never rose above its crypt. After the Second World War it was replaced by a modernist cathedral by Frederick Gibberd (1962) dubbed 'Paddy's Wigwam'.

35. Regent's Park Ionic: Cumberland Terrace, completed 1826

36. Soane's 'Battle of the Styles'

37. Classical-on-Sea: Brighton's Brunswick Square, 1820s

38. City of grace: Newcastle's Grey Street

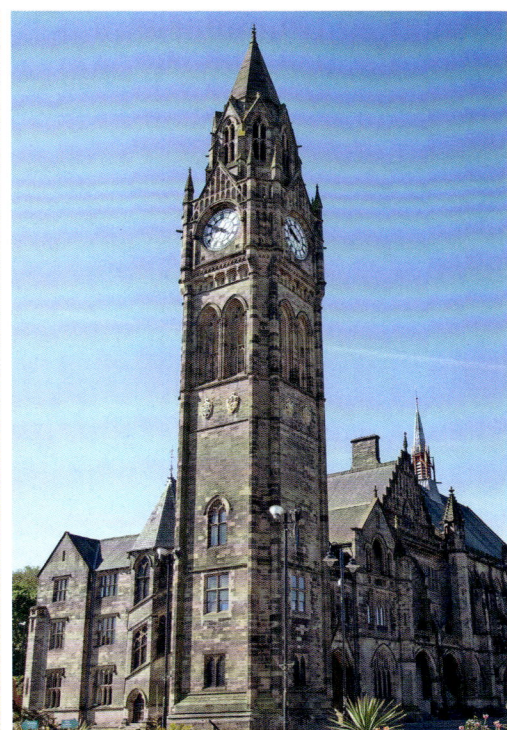

39. Yorkshire Renaissance: Leeds Town Hall, 1853

40. Rochdale Town Hall's Gothic splendour, 1866–83

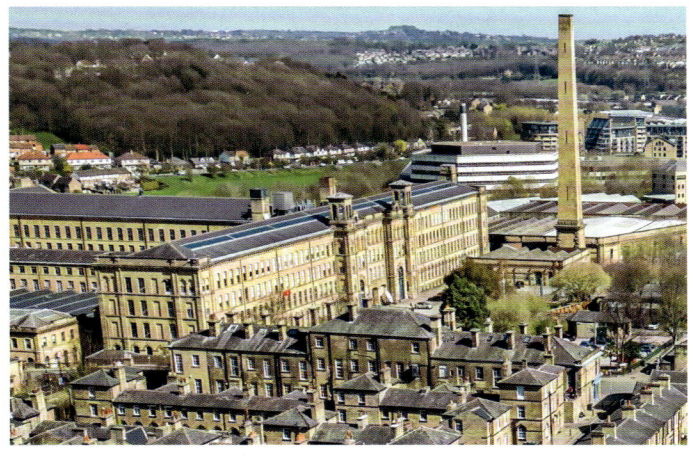

41. Saltaire, city of the future

42. Patriotic Gothic: Palace of Westminster, 1835 onwards

43. Patriotic Italianate: Foreign Office, completed 1873

44. Railways too can fight: St Pancras v. King's Cross

45. Technicolour Gothic: All Saints, Margaret Street, 1849–59

46. Rebirth of the Tudor: Cragside, 1869

47. Anglo-Dutch Fantastical: Harrington Gardens, 1880s

48. Welsh pride: Cardiff Town Hall, 1901–04

49. Breath of the new: Glasgow School of Art, 1907–09

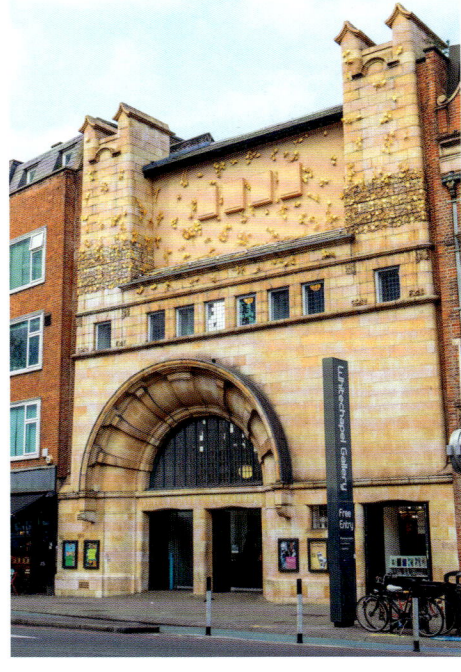

50. Whitechapel's Art Nouveau Romanesque, late 1890s

51. Liverpool's Three Graces, early twentieth century

52. Last cry of the Goths: Liverpool Cathedral, 1904–78

Lutyens was the last of the classical fundamentalists. He wrote of the Vitruvian orders of capitals as if they were holy – despite their being pagan. To him the orders were messages from the past, to be 'so well digested that there is nothing but essence left . . . nearer to nature than anything produced on impulse or accident-wise'. The architect might vary them only in such a way that 'every stroke must be endowed with such poetry and artistry as God has given you'.

The Grand Manner was certainly on display as Nash's Regent Street was steadily demolished. Its rebuilding was in the hands of baroque revivalists, mainly Reginald Blomfield and Albert Richardson. When Vincent Harris was commissioned for government buildings throughout the 1920s and 30s, his style was restrained classical. His elegant Sheffield City Hall (1920) had a giant loggia fronting a Georgian entrance, that might have been dated any time since the 1840s. Within Curtis Green's Wolseley Motors offices building (1921) next to the Ritz in Piccadilly, with an arched ground floor and paired columns above, has all the confidence of Liverpool's Oriel Chambers from sixty years earlier. These were not buildings suggesting a style on its way out. Indeed, the vigour of Georgian 'survival' was such that Richardson and others in the Society for the Protection of Ancient Buildings went on to found the Georgian Group in 1937.

Greater individualism emerged from Edward Maufe, whose Guildford Cathedral (1932–61) was a sort of stripped Perpendicular revival rising on its Surrey hill with the personality of a power station. At my Surrey primary school, children were asked to contribute a brick each to help finish it. When we went to see it, some cried because they couldn't tell which brick was theirs. Giles Gilbert Scott moved on from Liverpool Cathedral to create the brick-encased Battersea Power Station, begun in 1929, and later Bankside after the Second World War. The art deco interiors of Battersea have been magnificently restored, while Scott's familiar red telephone kiosk, the K2, won a Post Office competition in 1925. Followed by the smaller K6 in 1936, the kiosks were erected across the land in their thousands. They supplied a bright splash of red to soot-grimed streets and greenest countryside alike. Their mildly Greek design served as Britain's dying tribute to classicism into the twenty-first century.

One event that seemed briefly to set a new architectural course was the 1925 Paris Exposition of Decorative Arts. Its radicalism took its name from that of the exhibition itself: art deco. It posited a shift from the sinuousness of art nouveau to the angularity of cubism. Art deco celebrated the hard lines of industry, the excitement of the motor car and washing machine and the glamour of jazz and the cinema. The style lent itself to new forms of interior design, startling yet spare and light, galvanized by its use of coloured lighting. This had a decorative freshness, the antithesis of Edwardian conservatism. It was matched by a revolution in women's fashion from full-skirted dress to the 1920s Flapper style and Coco Chanel.

Elements of art deco can be seen in inter-war buildings by Voysey and Mackintosh and in the geometry of Roger Fry's short-lived Omega Workshops design studio (1913–19). Overseas, the style was prominently displayed in New York's Chrysler building. Critics hesitantly dubbed it international, Jazz Age, moderne, even streamline modern, as if to give it a formal place in the stylistic lexicon. Its historian, Bevis Hillier, admitted it could too easily be dismissed as a concept of 'frivolous commercial novelty, in stark opposition to modernism's pious reforming zeal'. Yet it did offer, briefly, the hint of a stylistic way forward. When the V&A staged an art deco exhibition in 2003, it described the style as 'the most glamorous and popular . . . of the 20th century'.

Where art deco found a welcome was in the new consumer economy. Factories designed by Wallis, Gilbert and Partners included that for Firestone tyres (1928) in west London, scandalously demolished by its owner in 1980 a week before it was to be listed for protection. The same firm's Hoover factory (1931) survives, showing how a basically classical facade can be brought to life when an architect feels he can play with every feature and a pot of paint.

Another prominent art deco work was the neo-Egyptian factory for Carreras cigarettes in Camden Town. This was crammed into every spare foot of Mornington Crescent Gardens. It sparked such anger as to precipitate legal protection for all London's squares. The most spectacular art deco interior still standing is Owen Williams's former Daily Express foyer in Fleet Street. With its gleaming surfaces, jangling images and jagged corona you can almost hear the jazz band playing.

Outside London, only in cinemas did art deco make much impact, promoting the exoticism of the new medium of film. By 1929 cinemas had become 'super-cinemas', designed as oriental, Egyptian, Moorish, anything that might draw the eye down a high street. In 1930 the first Odeon, in a Moorish style, opened in Perry Barr in Birmingham, with a hundred more of the chain following over the next seven years. The most sensational of the super-cinemas was the Granada Tooting. Its fantasy Venetian Gothic auditorium was designed in 1929 by a Russian émigré, Theodore Komisarjevsky, briefly husband of Peggy Ashcroft. It was the first cinema to be Grade I listed.

Perhaps the oddest of the 1920s free spirits was Harry Goodhart-Rendel, a scholar and historian but also an architect happy to turn his hand to bricks and mortar when the opportunity came his way. His contribution to Hay's Wharf (1930) on the south bank by London Bridge is hard to pigeonhole but has the feel of art deco. It is a rare example of a modern building that is both unlike any other, yet also sits contented with the older dock buildings on either side.

Of traditional country houses between the wars there was a sense of a dying fall. Alan Powers, in his history of twentieth-century houses, titled his chapter on the 1920s, 'Forgetting the Future'. Almost daily there was news of sales and demolitions, of insufficient staff and impossible repair bills. Where new works were undertaken, the style was eclectic. The D'Oyly Carte family's Coleton Fishacre by Oswald Milne was art deco. The Sassoon family's Port Lympne in Kent by Herbert Baker and Philip Tilden was South African Dutch revival. The decline was relieved by the National Trust moving from protecting landscape to guarding historic houses. Its country house scheme was set up in 1936, enabling families to give their houses to the Trust to look after and open to the public; in return, the families were allowed to continue living there.

There remained, as always, the outliers. In Wales an Arts and Crafts enthusiast, Clough Williams-Ellis (1883–1978), was a champion and restorer of vernacular buildings. In 1925 he acquired a small ravine at Cardigan Bay in Wales and began to build a village in the style of Italy's Portofino. For half a century he added terraces, cottages and a hotel, as well as rescuing galleries and halls from various English and Welsh houses facing demolition. Portmeirion was treated by Williams-Ellis's contemporaries as a folly, if not a joke, satirized as a care home for elderly buildings. To him it was a serious attempt to match a style of architecture to a particular site, that of a hillside by the sea. If anything, it was in the spirit of Nash and Repton. Portmeirion swiftly became a tourist attraction and, in the 1960s, a location for a surrealistic television series, *The Prisoner*. Its most telling boast is of being the only twentieth-century settlement that visitors in their thousands will pay to see.

One architect of originality who was able to take advantage of London's suburban boom was the designer of its Underground stations, Charles Holden (1875–1960). A rare northern product of

Homes for Heroes (1920–1930)

the Arts and Crafts movement, he had a retiring personality, entering competitions under a pseudonym and working most of his life for the Percy Adams practice. Holden and his wife were socialist ascetics, described by Ashbee as existing 'with bananas and brown bread, no hot water, plain living, high thinking and strenuous activity for the betterment of the world'.

Between the wars, such modesty was hardly reflected in what turned out to be Holden's two biggest buildings yet erected in London, probably in Britain. No. 55 Broadway (1926) in Westminster was headquarters for the new Underground Electric Railways Company, later London Transport, with statues on the facade by Jacob Epstein, Eric Gill and others. It was followed by the even larger Senate House (1931) in Bloomsbury for London University, upheld by two massive buttresses. Both displayed the gigantism of so-called 'stripped classicism', a noble style apparently in its death throes. The Senate House was thought appropriate for Orwell's Ministry of Truth in the film version of *1984*. It was supposedly the first stage of a Soviet-style redevelopment for the university for almost all of Bloomsbury.

Holden's most significant work arose from his closeness to Frank Pick, boss of the Underground. They were much influenced by a visit to Stockholm in 1930 and, by Holden, to Russia in 1936 to see the new Moscow Metro. Scandinavia had in the 1930s acquired the status of a mini-grand tour to young architects, thanks to Stockholm's new town hall. The result was a series of stations by Holden remarkably free of stylistic inhibition. Mostly built in the 1930s, they included Piccadilly Circus, Gants Hill, Arnos Grove, Sudbury Town and Southgate. Some were mildly art deco. Others, such as the Gants Hill concourse, mimicked the Moscow model: virtually a ballroom. Southgate's escalator could be a set for a Tchaikovsky ballet.

The 1920s thus ended on a question mark. Architecture could offer public buildings in an ongoing if rather exhausted classicism.

Art deco could supply the new commercial economy with designs suitable for its expanding market, as could Tudorbethan the equally booming suburbia. These were not styles that were speaking to each other. None the less they reflected an extraordinary stylistic range that continued through the 1930s. In his bullish history of these years, Gavin Stamp compared the period to the diversity of the nineteenth century. Its vitality should not be downplayed because of the new stylistic thundercloud that was gathering over the horizon.

17.
Modernism Emergent (1930–1940)

A feature of European architecture in the twentieth century was a growing sense of internationalism. Muthesius had carried news of the British Arts and Crafts movement to Germany. Rennie Mackintosh was invited to the Austria Secession exhibitions and British architects studied developments in France, Sweden, Austria and Germany. Nowhere was more innovative than the German Bauhaus school of design, founded in 1919 but suppressed by the Nazis in the 1930s, its work considered 'degenerate' and left-wing. In Moscow, the Russian Vkhutemas academy experienced similar suppression by the communists. The result was a remarkable diaspora of architectural refugees, those who arrived in Britain including Walter Gropius, Peter Behrens, Erich Mendelsohn, László Moholy-Nagy and Berthold Lubetkin. It released a gush of talent into Britain's then shallow architectural pool.

The movement's presiding genius was a man of intellectual charisma, the Swiss-French architect Charles-Édouard Jeanneret, later Le Corbusier (1887–1965). He was a Swiss art nouveau house designer who moved to Paris, but his eccentric temperament won him few commissions. He was a talented artist, but contact with Adolf Loos in Vienna led him to regard ornament of any sort as 'a crime'. He admired Nietzsche, disliked parties, approved of monastic living, believed in 'the revolutionary possibilities of reinforced concrete', and wanted to rebuild half of Paris. For obscure reasons he came to loathe streets, calling them 'disgusting'. The café he called 'a fungus that eats the pavements of Paris'. Le Corbusier's motto was that the street had to die: *'Il faut tuer la rue-corridor'* (We must kill the street). Street aversion became a badge of Corbusianism – and still is.

To a profession seemingly lost between a desiccated revivalism and council housing, Le Corbusier offered what was so rarely permitted to architects, a vision. In 1923 he wrote *Toward an Architecture*, an all-encompassing plan for modern habitation. Its message was that there could be only one plan, his, and no role for disagreement. For no particular reason, he declared the ideal city to be of three million people, its population living in sixty-storey towers interspersed with slabs. The perfect house, defined as 'a machine for living in', would have 2,000 occupants and just one front door. As for style, he said, it was 'a lie . . . but our eyes unfortunately don't yet know how to see it'. Architecture was about engineering and technology, 'the magnificent play of volumes brought together in light'.

Twelve years later came Le Corbusier's follow-up, the Ville Radieuse (Radiant City – 1935), which he planned as his utopia. This city would be a giant structure sitting in the country, with him living fifty kilometres outside it under a palm tree. He criticized 1930s New York for its skyscrapers being too small and gathered on streets. In future, human contact would be essentially by car or plane. His city planning, all of which featured residences in vast anonymous blocks, rarely made mention of people. He wondered at the smooth-running efficiency of the new Ford factory, its workers as automatons. To his biographer Charles Jencks, 'it was this confusion of the factory with the good state that made him rather easy on fascism'.

Architectural taste is often regarded as a function of psychology. The pre-war utopias of Ebenezer Howard had reflected his experience in the American Midwest, convincing him that cities would succeed best as a genuine fusion of town and country. He

Modernism Emergent (1930–1940)

had studied how people lived and favoured an ideal of individual houses set in gardens. Settlements should be small enough for people to stay in contact with nature and to form village-like communes. Modernism was deaf to Howard's message.

Le Corbusier leaves the reader wondering if he ever saw his creations as about human beings at all. He viewed communities as lumpen groups. In 1928 he founded the Congrès Internationaux d'Architecture Moderne (CIAM), whose aim was to reject all styles and rebuild the world afresh. He conveyed this with a cult-like passion that to modern observers would render him little short of mad, certainly possessed of a misanthropic egotism. Yet this eccentric individual held an extraordinary appeal to a generation of young British architects, though he was never to design a single building in Britain.

It is hard to dissociate CIAM's appeal from the atmosphere of interwar Europe. Its politics were depressed and messianic ideas were at a premium, from whatever source they came. Le Corbusier seemed to mesh with the authoritarianism of both left and right. His Ville Radieuse openly welcomed 'the strong ideas . . . emerging in Moscow, in Berlin, in Rome', where 'little by little the world approaches its destiny'.

In 1933 members of CIAM, including a full quota of Britons, went on a Mediterranean cruise that took on the character of a pilgrimage. It went from Marseilles to Athens and 'away from the urban reality of industrial settings', in the recollections of one architect at the time, Lionel Esher. What he called the 'Jesuits of the new faith' returned with a proclamation that was dismissive of all styles or ambitions other than their own. It was expressed in language oddly elitist even by the standards of architectural feuds. The now rampant English suburb was declared a particular horror, 'a symbol of waste, a place of bleak ugliness . . . a squalid antechamber, a scum churning against the walls of the city, one of the greatest evils of the century'. CIAM's Roger Fry declared that Britons were 'a populace whose emotional life has been drugged by the sugared poison of a pseudo-art'.

A British branch of CIAM called the Modern Architectural Research Group (MARS), formed that same year of 1933, was to be greeted by Le Corbusier as a call 'to see architecture as a social art . . . an economic and political tool that could improve the world'. Architects should go out and 're-equip whole countries . . . to enable us to carry out our vast undertaking'. It should be noted that early members of MARS included such traditionalists as John Summerson and John Betjeman.

The challenge was taken up by London's Architectural Association, a private college formed in 1890 as an alternative to traditional apprenticeship. It was also championed by the *Architectural Review*. Both school and magazine treated what came to be termed modernism as a new orthodoxy. It was perhaps the promised 'national style' sought by theorists for so long. As such it might have been no more than the rebirth of the stylistic orthodoxy of the Burlingtonians or the Arts and Crafts movement. But British modernism mutated into far more than this, into a political programme.

The outspoken Canadian leader of MARS, Wells Coates, saw Le Corbusier's modernism as the route to extreme socialism. 'Architecture has to serve the purposes of the people as well as the purposes of beauty,' he avowed, both purposes being as defined by MARS. Coates declared that space in the proposed housing blocks should not be wasted on furniture. If really needed, seats should be built into walls. As for cooking and washing, they would be more efficiently performed in a central facility. Above all, there should be no scope for dissent. One architect, Maxwell Fry, instructed his colleagues 'to address ourselves only to those capable of understanding us, and let the rest go hang'.

At the time, CIAM and MARS attracted little attention. Their impact on the 1930s was largely rhetorical, a stimulus reminiscent of Pugin and Ruskin and to many young architects not unwelcome. An early star of the movement, Oliver Hill, wrote admiringly of the new materials that modernism might unlock: 'concrete, steel, glass, rubber, cork, asbestos, plastic and metal alloys'. He felt their 'cleanable and durable surfaces' gave them an intrinsic beauty of colour and texture that needed no adornment. New machines for moving, cooking and cleaning were sufficient 'to compound a new aesthetic'.

These ideas, essentially of urban planning, were of a different order from previous innovations but they still had an impact on architectural style. This was reflected in the limited number of buildings the movement created between the wars. The first truly modernist house was New Ways in Northampton, designed by Behrens in 1927 for a local business friend. Its bare, almost windowless facade had the character of an abstract sculpture, with echoes of Mackintosh and Voysey. Another was Joldwynds (1932) near Dorking in Surrey, built by Oliver Hill for a Lord Greene, whose wife later recalled it as 'the coldest and draughtiest house we have ever lived in . . . not a house but a film set'. It still stands and is treasured. As for flats, Wells Coates's Isokon block in London's Belsize Park (1934) adopted the Bauhaus concept of external deck access to its upper floors, antecedent of the 'street in the sky'.

A few adventurous local councils dipped their toes into the same water. Impington College in Cambridgeshire (1935) was designed by Gropius and Maxwell Fry in a glass-walled, flat-roofed modest style that became widespread after the war. Lubetkin's more ostentatious High Point flats rose over Highgate in 1933, precursor of the luxury tower block. These were followed by London Zoo's gorilla house and, for nature's most art deco of creatures, the penguin pool.

Closer to commerce were a handful of modernist stores, including Peter Jones in Sloane Square by William Crabtree (1932) and Simpson (now Waterstones) in Piccadilly. A different sort of modernism was displayed by the first prominent building designed by a woman. The Shakespeare Memorial Theatre in Stratford (1931) was by a member of the Scott dynasty, Elisabeth. It had the spare, unadorned outline of modernism, but its brick-built massing was closer to her cousin Giles Gilbert's power stations.

Modernism was a style so alien that some architects tried it almost in secret. J. R. Scott, retained by the Southern Railway, had designed the baroque entrance to Waterloo as well as Georgian stations at Margate and Ramsgate. In 1937 he turned to Surbiton and clearly felt he could let go. He created an undeniably dramatic modernist structure in dazzling white, admirably restored today. But such buildings were a minuscule proportion of those erected in the 1930s. In his history of this period Alan Powers managed to find only a handful of pre-1940 constructions that he could classify as modernist.

Despite Fry's remark, the rest did not go hang. Britain's suburban expansion was continuing apace. While CIAM was sailing the Mediterranean, developers were not immune to new ideas. In 1933 a number of private builders did wonder if they were missing a trick, and decided that the Ideal Home Exhibition should make a bold move. For one year it would abandon 'Tudorbethan' and present houses in a modernist style, under the headline 'The Village of Tomorrow'. Houses would boast flat roofs, grey facing bricks, cavity walls and rubber-floored bathrooms. The roof was the centre of attention. It was to be a new floor, a place of openness and fresh air. Homeowners would do physical jerks in 'suntraps' during the day, and at night 'enjoy the peace of the moonlight and sleep al fresco'. The term Suntrap was even applied to the style as a whole. One futuristic example was declared 'the house of 1950'.

Some builders went even further. A scatter of modernist show houses was erected on new London estates for buyers to inspect. Jackson assiduously traced surviving examples by Wates, Laing, Haymills and Howard Homes to Edgware, Hendon, Bromley and Bexley. Keen not to miss out, the developers of Gidea Park 'exhibited' a further thirty-five houses by Tecton and others. These included 64 Heath Drive, which, now restored, is the epitome of the new British modernism. No. 62 next door was given a dissenting hipped roof, presumably to help it sell. Builders realized that Suntrap minimalism, shorn of all adornment, was cheap. The smallest semis were priced as low as £395 (around £30,000 today).

Few of these houses sold. The 1934 exhibition was a blind alley. Modernism had been given a fair run, but by 1935 Howard's West Molesey Estate was hurriedly rebuilt with pitched roofs. Upper storeys were being tiled in green. Travellers to Heathrow through Chiswick can see opposite Hogarth's House a Suntrap property all alone, naked with a flat roof and rounded corner windows. Modernism had made its offer but when the buying public was presented with a choice it said no thanks.

This was curious. The interwar modernist style was not unattractive and had none of the harshness of what came in the 1960s to be called brutalism. Le Corbusier's rare creation, Villa Savoye (1928), had an exquisite minimalism that was widely imitated. The clear white walls and spacious windows of Amyas Connell's High and Over in Amersham in Buckinghamshire were nothing if not handsome. The sparseness of line and lack of decorative clutter can be seen as descending from the work of Voysey, Ashbee and Mackintosh. Architects such as Serge Chermayeff, Ernő Goldfinger and Leonard Manasseh were designing and living in such houses themselves. It might have seemed that modernism would catch on.

In reality, Europe in the 1930s was anything but normal. The old world in all its manifestations was thought to have failed. The First World War, the Great War 'to end all wars', had not delivered stability and security. As conflicts resumed in 1939, individualism and innovation went into decline and governments everywhere instinctively moved towards ever greater control over public policy. War required it, and so would the need to recover from war.

That need embraced an absolute authority over the built environment. The destruction wreaked by the Second World War presented a landscape of ruins across Europe from which all appreciation of the past lost validity. Governments, autocratic or democratic, felt they had a licence to do as they wished. Nothing could have offered a more fertile soil to the apostles of architectural utopia. The day for a new modernism had arrived, one fused as never before with politics.

18.

Modernism Triumphant (1940–1965)

In the aftermath of the 1940–41 Blitz, young men could be seen wandering the wreckage of London's battered streets, notebooks in hand. They were seeking the names of desperate owners open to an offer on their wrecked premises. The immediate postwar property boom related in Oliver Marriott's 1967 book of that title told the story of these young men. He estimated that over a hundred British developers became millionaires by fast-track deals in the unregulated chaos of wartime London.

Elsewhere in Britain, bombed cities were less open to opportunity. Those most severely damaged, such as Liverpool, Glasgow, Plymouth, Hull and Coventry, struggled to rehouse their populations and get businesses back to work. Building materials were tightly rationed and black markets were active everywhere. Aircraft factories were urgently converted to produce prefabricated houses, the celebrated 'prefabs'. They were not a success, costing more per unit than houses built in the private sector. A treasured few survive in south London's Catford, still fiercely defended by their proud occupants.

Whitehall's priorities were differently articulated. In the 1920s Le Corbusier had advocated the demolition of much of Paris and its replacement with avenues of blocks. Even as the bombs were falling on London in 1941, the MARS group published a not dissimilar plan. It was for a new city based on a sort of millipede, with the river as its back and gargantuan buildings as legs stretching north and south. It was the work of a Marxist émigré, Arthur

Korn. The biographer of modernism, David Dean, later described it as 'beyond the Luftwaffe's wildest dreams'.

An article in the *Architectural Review* that year by William and Aileen Tatton Brown – modernists with the architects Tecton – proposed a different city of the future with 'a completely new ground level for pedestrians'. The existing ground would be for the 'man-in-the-motor-car' while the 'man-on-the-pavement' would be elevated to live and work on an upper-level podium, 'a vast area of display free from the perils of the motor car'. Without any streets – residential towers would rise from expanses of deck – pavement man 'could sit and rest and watch the world go by'. Indeed, he could 'come into contact with architecture on a more human and intimate scale than has ever been possible in the centre of any great city'.

The postwar city was thus seen as dominated by adjustment to traffic. Two other radicals, Alison and Peter Smithson, likewise declared that 'we live in moron-made cities', created before the age of the car. For them, 'the diseased quarters' of cities should be overtaken by streets in the air, while below extended 'a grid of expressways for cars . . . that represent escape and freedom'. A forest of towers would rise skyward to become the city's 'acupuncture that would reanimate the nervous system'.

Ordinarily such thoughts would have been confined to academic journals. But the 1940s were what Le Corbusier meant when he wrote of the days of Louis XIV and Napoleon, of 'the golden moments when the power of the mind dominated the rabble', when the unthinkable could be thought. Gropius too had proclaimed old cities to be so absurd that 'nothing less than the complete overhaul of their sclerotic bodies can turn them into healthy organisms'. The language of architecture was as colourful as it had been in the eighteenth century. It was as if the fantasy lurking beneath every architect's imagination was suddenly unlocked.

Modernism Triumphant (1940–1965)

This talk took hold of Whitehall. In 1940, with Britain's cities facing apparent obliteration by the Luftwaffe, Winston Churchill, the new prime minister, appointed the former director of the BBC Sir John Reith as Minister for Reconstruction. He was not an easy colleague and his authoritarian style – he had admired Hitler's 'magnificent efficiency' – saw him sacked from the Cabinet after just two years in office. Yet in that time Reith brought dynamism to his brief. He planned the rebuilding not just of buildings and streets but of whole cities, fit for the age of the motor car.

Reith summoned a Liverpool planning academic, Patrick Abercrombie, chairman of the Council for the Preservation of Rural England, whose experience lay chiefly with garden cities. His first plan in 1943 was for the badly damaged Plymouth and comprised old-fashioned Beaux Arts boulevards. The plan for Greater London emerged in 1944, the first vision of a new metropolis since the days of Wren, and on a near Corbusian scale. The capital's population was to be curbed to reduce overcrowding. So-called surplus families, possibly a million people, would be deported to 'new towns' in the Home Counties beyond a 'green belt'. In London, half a million 'dwelling units' would be created, or ten times the number destroyed in the Blitz.

The major premise of Abercrombie's plan was that urban Britain was, to use his favourite word, 'obsolete'. In particular it was wholly unsuited to what was seen as an unavoidably rising volume of vehicles. This concept of obsolescence, driven in large part by the assumption that existing thoroughfares were more suited to horses and carts than to motorized traffic, was to dominate British architecture for some three decades. Its solution lay in a world designed afresh by architects and by architects alone.

At this point such utopianism would normally run up against considerations of cost, practicality and even unpopularity. But times were not normal. Britain's bruised cities had in the 1940s a task of reconstruction facing them and an ideology suited to that task. It was an ideology allied to the hand of power able to bring it to pass. The fastidious, monocled Abercrombie emerges from Nick Barratt's history of London planning, *Greater London: The Story of the Suburbs*, as an other-worldly figure. He had 'the love of neatness and beautiful shapes on maps that is endemic in planners, but sadly takes little account of what is already there . . . He itched to demolish and rebuild.'

Abercrombie asserted, on no evidence, that what he was proposing was 'what the working man needs'. He sent his plan to schools and army units throughout the country. A copy even found its way into the notorious German prisoner-of-war camp Stalag Luft III, where a lecture was given in its honour. In a publicity film, *The Proud City*, Abercrombie and his colleagues described the metropolis as 'obsolete, inchoate and unsuitable . . . haphazard, jumbled together in a hopeless confusion . . . scattered and piecemeal, without any order or plan'. Its street system was 'dreadfully narrow and winding – and most of its houses should have been pulled down long ago'. He seemed blind to economics, to the need of all cities to have informal areas, back-street districts of small-scale manufacturing and services.

Of Abercrombie's wartime plans only that for Plymouth was put into place with immediate effect. It (sadly) survives to this day. His plan for Hull was rejected by its council. A plan for central Coventry proposed not to restore its historic core but to rebuild it with large concrete blocks. In Germany and Poland flattened Lübeck and Warsaw immediately reconstructed their ancient centres. They are today celebrated by UNESCO. Coventry is not.

Abercrombie's plan for London proposed that the metropolis be divided into development zones, divided by six orbital ringways and ten radials. The inner two rings would run north and south of Regent's Park. In one version, a grand avenue drove straight into the West End, terminating at Marble Arch. The inner area would still contain precincts of existing activity, but the numbers living in them would be restricted. It would no longer be a market-driven city but a state-conceived one. To the *Architectural Review* it was a triumph, 'the liberation of the imagination' – the imagination of architects. To the sceptical novelist Evelyn Waugh, 'the kingdom seemed to be under enemy occupation'.

The postwar Attlee government welcomed the London plan enthusiastically. It seemed to complement the optimism of the new welfare state. The plan went to the LCC for implementation. Crucial was the issue of traffic. Here the radicalism of the Tatton Browns and the Smithsons for radical separation was taken forward in what amounted to a part two to Abercrombie, Colin Buchanan's *Traffic in Towns* report (1963). This regarded the prospect of traffic as so cataclysmic that London would be 'strangulated' unless something like half the physical fabric of the inner city was demolished to make way for cars. Buchanan said that, 'if we are to have any chance of living at peace with the motor car, we shall need a very different sort of city' – in effect two cities, one for traffic and an elevated one for people. Modernists and planners were singing from the same hymn sheet.

As so often with plans, the devil in Abercrombie's lay in its first contact with reality. The Greater London Plan had the support of both central and London governments. Absolute power was conferred on local governments in a 1947 planning Act, giving them control over every aspect of renewal. It also proposed a 'betterment levy' or tax on the profits of private development, supposedly to pay for public reconstruction. All seemed possible.

The London plan ran into the same headwind as had Wren's in 1666. This was the overriding need of any big city to return to work as fast as possible. The government was subject to intense lobbying from businesses, developers and local councils and found it hard to resist. Like Wren, Abercrombie had seemed unconcerned by the human beings inconvenienced by his utopia.

They would need to be evicted and sent to new towns elsewhere. London would somehow start again.

On the ground reigned near anarchy. One developer, Joe Levy, had served as an air-raid warden at night during the war and returned to buy the blitzed shops from their owners the next morning. Another would tell his staff, 'Bombs last night: bargains this morning.' Sites might be purchased on the spot from owners who could not imagine any future for them. As for rules, they were shambolic. Damaged buildings designated as dangerous could be licensed for demolition, which gave value to that condemnation. Residential premises could become more profitable offices if those offices were 'for exporters'. This was easily arranged.

The 1947 Act, intended to control rebuilding and promote depopulation, proved so badly drafted that it did the opposite. One loophole stipulated that owners could add 10 per cent to their cubic volume if they rebuilt rather than repaired a damaged property. This so-called 'third schedule loophole' was dubbed a 'spiv's charter'. It allowed a developer not to restore an existing facade but replace it with a featureless new building that had two or three extra floors. The result can be seen to this day, jarring the view down central London's most historic streets. Portland Place became a bruised and battered mess – though not entirely through bombing.

The property boom of the 1940s and 50s saw a metropolis frantic for office space that led to corruption, exploitation and competition for building materials. There was no planning discipline. Cities elsewhere in Europe, often hit far worse than London, took immediate steps to safeguard their heritage and appearance. In Britain there were none. Every demolition became a precedent for the next.

One consequence of the chaos was to torpedo Abercrombie, at least in London. A central feature of the 1947 Act, the betterment levy to aid councils in their renewal, was never

Modernism Triumphant (1940–1965)

implemented. A crucial factor was the obligation on councils to find more space for traffic. Councils owned little land and had no money with which to build. Their only marketable resource was the value of their planning permissions. This gave both parties a mutual incentive to break rules, leading to negotiated deals between developers and planners, usually for a wider road or crossroads in return for a bigger building than the old zoning or height rules allowed.

In 1951 an event took place intended by the Labour government to boost morale. The Festival of Britain – on the centenary of the 1851 Great Exhibition – was erected on a plot of publicly owned land on the South Bank. Designed by Hugh Casson, it was characterized by critics as 'herbivore', or 'picturesque modernism'. One commentator, Michael Frayn, called it 'all Victorian balloons, penny-farthings, Emmett trains, the sweet ration, Ealing comedies'. There was a delightful tree-railway through Battersea Park. The exhibition happily combined English tradition and 'contemporary' design. One characteristic was the copious use of colour in a city immersed for decades in soot and blackness.

The exhibition's most prominent modernist features were the Dome of Discovery and a delicate spike called the Skylon. Both were treated by Churchill as symbols of the outgoing Labour government, so hated that he had them demolished on taking office that year. The festival did leave one building of character, the Royal Festival Hall, designed by three prominent LCC modernists, Leslie Martin, Peter Moro and Robert Matthew. Today it looks almost picturesque alongside the concrete brutalism of its neighbours. It was an early example of a building designed on a podium, which tended to mean an uncertain entrance.

As a contribution to the festival, the LCC architects decided to build an estate of council houses in Stepney. Martin and Matthew were in command and Esher recalled the excitement as young modernists 'flocked to the colours'. Service in 'a great organization dedicated to the rehousing of the people of London met their political as well as architectural aspirations'. The only hurdle was the familiar one, a battle over style. Should the new London be low-rise, perhaps with a few small towers, or should it have high-rise deck-access slabs? The two approaches were swiftly labelled soft and hard, a rift that was to cast a long shadow into the 1960s. To Esher, the soft party 'were content to humour and persuade' the citizens of the new London, whereas 'the hard men were ready to confront and amaze . . . that English eyes be opened'.

Stepney's Lansbury Estate, initially of 2,000 acres, was soft. Terrace streets damaged in the war were not repaired but wiped out. Its core was a community shopping centre surrounded by low-rise council blocks and green spaces. The development was erected in a hurry and was characterless and bland, with none of the vitality of east London's existing Mile End Road or Brick Lane. Yet it became the model for hundreds of such council estates in the 1950s across the country.

An alternative already under way was from the LCC's 'hard' faction, a Corbusian estate in Pimlico designed by two Architectural Association graduates, Philip Powell and Hidalgo Moya. Churchill Gardens was of deck-access slabs said to have required the demolition of more houses than Westminster lost in the Blitz. Begun in 1946, it was regarded as the first and only development along strict Abercrombian lines actually to see construction. A walk down Lupus Street today offers a contrast of what was then seen as the future and the past, LCC to the south, Cubitt to the north. As for the soft and hard dichotomy, it was bizarrely repeated in the sylvan suburbs of Richmond Park. 'Soft' Alton East was a mix of low-rise houses and 'point' blocks, while 'hard' Alton West was an estate of five slabs explicitly based on Le Corbusier's Unité d'Habitation then rising in Marseilles. The Unité became a rallying cry for the more assertive modernists across Europe.

Modernism Triumphant (1940–1965)

One regulation that quickly went by the board was a long-standing limit of 100ft on a building's height, purportedly the length of the tallest fire brigade ladder. Officials simply dropped the rule in return for a developer offering a new bridge, tunnel, roundabout or road widening. When in 1951 an incoming Tory government said it would 'let the people free . . . to help those who do things, the developers who create wealth', the help was hardly needed. The names of Marriott's millionaires had already become synonymous with riches: Harold Samuel, Joe Levy, Jack Cotton, Charles Clore, Harry Hyams and Max Rayne.

Across London there duly rose the first generation of towers that later came to coat the metropolis. These were not, as was customary in cities, clustered in groups. They were located at any road junction where a borough felt the need for road widening. These included Centre Point in Holborn, Euston Tower on Euston Road, Stag Place in Victoria, Notting Hill Gate and traffic gyratories at Aldgate, Hammersmith and Elephant and Castle. The last was named after a famous pub dominating a hub that was known as the Piccadilly Circus of south London. The hub was replaced with a double-roundabout gyratory traffic scheme across which no one could walk. South London lost its heart.

At the junction of Oxford Street and Charing Cross Road – in need of just a traffic light – the planners decided on a grassy knoll, like that at Marble Arch. The local developer Harry Hyams suggested he create a larger roundabout if in return he were allowed an office tower on the knoll, called Centre Point. He then negotiated an ever wider roundabout for an ever higher tower that eventually became London's tallest building. Hyams left its thirty-four storeys empty, relieved of taxes while it rose in value on his balance sheet. Built in 1966, it has lain mostly empty to this day. The roundabout was never needed and became a bus park. It stands as an emblem of London's postwar planning incompetence.

The regulation of London's architecture was not helped by constant interventions from central as well as local government. The prime minister Harold Macmillan had his arm twisted by Shell Oil (1961) and Conrad Hilton (1963), both threatening to 'leave London' if they were refused zone-busting towers, one on the South Bank, the other overlooking Hyde Park. The tower for New Zealand House at the foot of Haymarket was allowed in 1963 to break every rule and soar incongruously over St James's on the grounds that the occupant was a Commonwealth country.

The developers' favourite architect, Richard Seifert, became a master negotiator. He insisted on meeting planning officials and chairmen in secret until permission was a done deal. All publicity was to be avoided lest protests occur. That is exactly what occurred when my colleagues and I leaked that Seifert intended to demolish the historic City Club in Threadneedle Street for his NatWest Tower. He invited me into his Rolls-Royce and drove to the site, saying he was going to save it after all.

The appearance of London was at the mercy of what seemed random individual decisions. When in 1964 someone suggested to economics minister George Brown that there were too few hotels in London, he blandly offered a subsidy of £1,000 a room to get more built. Characterless towers with tiny rooms promptly scarred the West End and the surroundings of Hyde Park at public expense. There was no need for such a subsidy and the scars remain to this day.

At least London's anarchy saved it from Abercrombie. Other cities less infested by private developers were not so fortunate. Following Buchanan in the 1960s, urban motorways became the principal galvanizing force for planning departments. These were often staffed by traffic engineers rather than professional planners, and were in receipt of plentiful funds from central government. Almost overnight Britain lost some of Europe's finest Victorian town centres and the vitality that went with them.

Modernism Triumphant (1940–1965)

Birmingham found its future in the hands of a chief engineer, Herbert Manzoni, who publicly stated he could see 'no tangible value of links with the past'. They were 'more sentimental than valuable' and there was 'little of real worth in Birmingham's architecture'. To make way for his inner ring road he duly demolished his city's Market Hall, Central Library, Mason's College, Liberal Club and countless works of Victorian distinction. Pugin's Bishop's Palace (1840), a pioneering work of early Victorian Gothic, was destroyed after Manzoni demanded the diocese pay a prohibitive sum to divert one of his roads.

Le Corbusier's influence was ever-present. Glasgow's city engineer, Robert Bruce, proposed the virtual flattening of the city centre for new dual carriageways. Drastic demolitions began in 1945 and were to continue through the 1960s. The Bruce plan was curtailed four years later by a replacement plan from Abercrombie himself, based on decanting residents to two new towns at East Kilbride and Cumbernauld. But the new M8 still ploughed its way north and west of the city centre until some twenty-five kilometres of urban motorway had been completed. There have since been suggestions to turn its ten-lane Kingston Bridge into a pedestrian boulevard. Manchester's chief planner, Rowland Nicholas, complained that 'in the last century buildings were designed to last too long . . . long after they have been rendered obsolete by changes of function and progress in building technique'. At least in central Manchester he did not progress with too drastic a correction, though he was less kind to districts such as Moss Side and Hulme.

Newcastle's egotistical leader, T. Dan Smith, announced that the city would become 'the Brasilia of the North'. When Dobson's Royal Arcade, perhaps the loveliest Regency arcade in England, stood in the way of his Central Motorway East, the Royal Fine Art Commission pleaded for it to be dismantled and erected elsewhere. Smith agreed, demolished it, numbered the stones and threw them away. He then pulled down a quarter of Dobson's historic Grainger Town as well as his handsome Eldon Square (1825) for a shopping centre. The mall's architects, Chapman Taylor, rebuilt one side of the square with a continuous wall of black brick that survives today. Smith's grander plans were cut short when he went to prison for corruption.

The most drastic prospect after Glasgow was that offered to Liverpool. Two LCC veterans, Walter Bor and Graeme Shankland, arrived in the early 1960s to declare it 'glaringly obsolete'. They declared the whole of 'the inner crescent of twilight areas and two-thirds of the central area are due to be rebuilt'. The head of Abercrombie's old architecture school, Charles Reilly, likewise dismissed any proposal for 'just a new block here and a curly suburb there'. Instead, 'whole sections of towns, now decaying and never anything to be proud of, must be destroyed, replanned and rebuilt, or new towns must be started and the old left to rot'. It was Corbusianism writ large.

Bor subsequently resigned and repented such extremism. He was among the first architects to appreciate the importance of the street to communal cohesion. He went on to champion the 'preservation and rehabilitation of whole areas with their street networks, pedestrian alleyways, scale, colour and texture'. But his was initially a voice in the wilderness. Shankland showed the radicalism of a committed communist. On Merseyside, he planned to replace acres of low-rise housing in Everton and Toxteth with an inner ring of 'system-built' towers, six of which were of twenty-two storeys. At one point there was even talk of a hundred Liverpool towers. On the outskirts would be new towns at Kirkby, Runcorn and Skelmersdale.

When I visited the city at the time, Shankland showed me a model of his new Liverpool with pride. It was simply a new city with bits of the old lingering in the cracks. The energy and money required to clear so many buildings, not to mention the consequent human and communal disruption, were mind-blowing. Shankland was oblivious. I later unkindly compared him to Bomber Harris, the RAF's wartime commander responsible for the razing of Dresden. The plan collapsed when Liverpool found it did not receive its required 'share of rising national prosperity' to pay for it. By then a swathe of land round St George's Hall had been demolished and replaced by one of the most depressing vistas in an English city, a desert of tarmac, a six-lane urban highway and the bland exterior of a tired shopping centre. Shankland allegedly later regretted his plan.

Most ironically, the one body that came nearest to implementing the modernist doctrine was the most conservative: the City of London Corporation. Its ancient privileges had kept it outside the LCC's strategic authority, but with local government reform in the air its aldermen thought it wise to keep up with the times. They duly prepared a mini-Abercrombie plan for their square mile. North and south, highways were driven along London Wall and Upper and Lower Thames streets. The latter's four-lane carriageway wiped out the riverfront of Victorian warehouses that gave the City its 'walled' character when seen from the water. The historic Coal Exchange went with them. Come the twenty-first century, this bleak carriageway was reduced back to just two lanes, to curb rather than assist the traffic.

The City then commissioned the modernists Chamberlin, Powell and Bon to rebuild its north-west Barbican quarter in its entirety. This involved the clearance of some forty acres of severely damaged buildings. In accordance with Buchanan, three floors of car parking were built to support a supposed new 'street level' or podium in the air. Here was where 'pavement man could sit and watch the world go by'. On this podium were erected 2,000 flats in three forty-three-storey towers and seven-storey slabs. The ground level was to be strictly for cars. The encircling thoroughfares were stripped of shops and houses and rendered impassable to pedestrians by covering their edges with high cobbles. The aversion to humanity was fanatical.

Apart from its novelty, the Barbican has little to do with Abercrombie. Visitors must traverse a maze of concrete passages, bridges, signs and stairs to get anywhere. The podium failed completely as a 'street in the sky'. Forty acres in the centre of Europe's busiest city are almost permanently deserted. The shopping area never took off, with almost no shops opened in fifty years. The area's popularity was salvaged only by the late addition of an arts centre with a view over the gardens. When the Barbican opened in 1982, even the *Architectural Review* commented that it was 'stillborn while the rest of the world moved on'.

The Barbican is popular with its residents, for whom it is a gated high-security pied-à-terre in the city centre with parish parking. It contributes nothing to London's urbanism, contrasting with the bustle of the streets, shops and activity of conserved Smithfield to its west and Hoxton to its north. It is a textbook case of modern architecture's inability to bring to urban renewal the vitality that comes with old buildings.

19.
The Dawn of Hesitation (1965–1973)

I will not forget the day in 1968 when we heard news that a twenty-two-storey block of council flats called Ronan Point in east London had collapsed, just two months after it had opened. Four residents died. Newspaper offices were besieged by engineers saying they had known this would happen. A wider body of opinion suggested that high-rise living was neither civilized nor safe, especially for families with children. Even the *Architectural Review* complained that modernism had met its Waterloo. It had created too many 'badly fitting buildings, grotty concrete steps, cheap twisting aluminium trim, rough precast panels and broken plastic infills'. Having championed such architecture for half a century, the *Review* was now offering a half-apology.

The days of towers appeared to be numbered. A category error had been recognized. It was reported that towers disappeared overnight from LCC drawing boards and low rise became the theme of public housing. In his analysis of this period, the urban historian Otto Saumarez Smith wrote that the 'presumption that cities would be totally transformed through urban renewal and radical architectural forms was increasingly untenable'. Both the architects and the politicians on whom they relied were caught in what amounted to a political bind. Politicians had been shown the route to a new Jerusalem and had acted accordingly. If the architects had let them down, it was unclear who was obeying whose orders – and which orders either should follow. There was conveniently no one to blame.

The reality was unfolding on the ground. Among the most celebrated projects was the Park Hill Estate in Sheffield by J. L. Womersley, completed in 1966. Like many others it was explicitly inspired by Le Corbusier's Unité d'Habitation, though the two seemed to have little in common. A sinuous seven-storey wall of flats curved round a hilltop outside the old steel town. It was visible for miles around and probably the most prominent council estate in Britain. Yet its much-vaunted 'streets in the sky' did not work as streets, any more than did the Barbican's podium. There seemed no active concourse or venue for casual meeting, and almost no garages. Parents could not see their children playing outdoors. Public spaces were disrespected. Lifts were used as toilets and the flats became run down and vulnerable to crime, the tenancies hard to let.

Anyone visiting Park Hill at the time could see it was in trouble. The flats were starting to empty. Walking round its eventually gutted interior in the 1990s, I felt I was in a Levantine citadel from which the crusaders had just fled. In the early 2000s the council admitted defeat and the estate was handed to developers for sale. Park Hill was converted chiefly for private ownership and partly for student flats. The state had paid millions to build what became a private development.

A similar fate confronted Peter and Alison Smithson's Robin Hood Gardens in Poplar in 1972. Again, a wall of flats defined an isolated community. Again, there was much talk of 'streets in the sky'. The flats became hard to maintain and to let. As the Pevsner of modernism, Owen Hatherley, commented, it showed why 'composing a public building primarily as a means of carrying on theoretical debates in architecture schools is not a good idea'. Although some residents were ready to grin and bear it and supported its rehabilitation, in 2012 75 per cent of those still occupying the estate voted for its demolition. Veteran modernists lined up to protest, arguing that architectural celebrity should trump the residents' wishes. The pleas fell on deaf ears and the estate was half demolished in 2018 for a planned replacement. Peter Smithson had claimed that the failure of Robin Hood Gardens was due to 'social issues rather than architectural ones', an odd view from an architect so long motivated by social ambitions.

One example of 'wall architecture' that was considered a success was in Newcastle. Here the one-and-a-half mile Byker Wall begun in 1969 by Ralph Erskine offered a colourful contrast to Park Hill and Robin Hood Gardens. What passed for its streets were on the ground, not in the sky. A striking jumble of facades encircled an estate of maisonettes. Every flat was given some degree of personality, a change of material, balcony or angle of view. Local people were consulted throughout the construction process, and were rehoused on the estate as their old houses were demolished. Ground floors had front doors and thus recaptured some of the spirit of the terraces they replaced. Whether or not such spatial sensitivity held the key to Byker's success, it is at least plausible.

What was called, including by its champions, the brutalist style was developed in the 1960s, supposedly based on the French word for raw, *brut*. It adopted heavyweight proportions and gloried in empty expanses of wall, relentless decking and Le Corbusier's 'loyal, truthful' concrete. In appearance it had little of the charm of pre-war modernism, though it borrowed from it an attachment to abstract geometry and shape. Significantly, the promoters of Byker expressly pointed out that it was *not* brutalist.

Supporters of brutalism had difficulty finding terms in which to discuss it – as did its critics. Few on either side made any pretence that it was about beauty. They rather adopted the language of architectural machismo. Thus the Barbican's publicity material championed its 'brutalist qualities: the scale and rhythm of the columns, edge beams and the use of bush-hammered concrete'. Admirers pointed to its amassed strength and dynamism. They felt it lent aesthetic quality to large and otherwise boring residential and commercial buildings.

According to the Smithsons, the essence of brutalism 'was to make a raw, emotional point', though they never said what it was. Almost all its buildings were commissioned by public authorities or institutions, usually as housing blocks, car parks, shopping centres and new universities. The expansion of higher education in the late 1960s coincided with the climax of the brutalist era, hence the concrete layers of Denys Lasdun's University of East Anglia and Robert Matthew and Stirrat Johnson-Marshall (RMJM)'s disjointed pavilions on the campus at York. Basil Spence's spartan University of Sussex made few concessions to the idyllic folds of the South Downs in which it was set.

Two prominent London examples were by the pre-war modernist Ernő Goldfinger. His Balfron Tower in Poplar (1967) and Trellick Tower in North Kensington (1972) were both described as 'vertical streets'. He declared they would create far stronger urban communities than horizontal ones, the sort of vacuous statement that should have been tested empirically before being implemented. Trellick was described by its developer, the GLC, as 'replacing outdated social accommodation', by which it meant houses. At a time when towers were already unpopular, Trellick was dubbed 'the tower of terror' and near impossible to police. After watching a mother trying to wrestle a pram into Balfron, I wanted to grab Goldfinger by the scruff of the neck as I saw him luxuriating in Mayfair's Savile Club.

When Goldfinger was challenged actually to live in Balfron Tower, he did so with his wife for two months. He even gave a cocktail party for his neighbours, whom he described as a 'focus group'. He swiftly retreated to the Hampstead house that he had built for himself in 1939 in a strictly non-brutalist modernist style. Its rectangular outline and refined fenestration were later rated sufficiently historic to be acquired by the National Trust. Both

The Dawn of Hesitation (1965–1973)

towers reached a familiar crisis of decay and joined Park Hill in facing privatization. They remained impossible to humanize. That said, I did meet a private owner in Trellick who had bought his flat and loved its scruffy environs. One of the flats sold in 2020 for £277,000. There is a London for every taste.

The most public work of brutalism was the LCC's 'farewell' to London before its disbandment in 1965. This was the Hayward Gallery (1968) on London's South Bank, together with its neighbour, Lasdun's marginally more civilized National Theatre (1976). Lasdun regretted the theatre's bare concrete, he said the result of parsimony. He had wanted it covered in the same flint chippings as his IBM offices next door. As for the adjacent Hayward, it was described as a 'nuclear facility' by Prince Charles. Surrounded by a warren of decks, blind alleys and empty corners, it defied all attempts by the South Bank board to make them less hostile. A street market was attempted but soon retreated to the pavement below.

Brutalism came at a time when the arts were seeking a new virility and seemed to embody its fascination with violence. Young writers were angry. Art was abstract, music was atonal and films were raucous. I and others who founded the Thirties (later Twentieth Century) Society in 1979 did so primarily to save art deco and modernist buildings. We frequently found ourselves asked to champion postwar architecture but found brutalism a challenge. Its apologists rarely claimed its works were lovely, only 'important'. They described them as heroic, strong, noble and emphatic, safe in the knowledge that they were unlikely to be living in them.

For some in the 2010s, brutalism became a conservation fashion, with sympathetic surveys by Elain Harwood, Alan Powers and Owen Hatherley, admiring of its vigour and forcefulness when photographed under a blue sky. But the percentage of people who welcomed being confronted by a 'raw emotional point' every time they went shopping was limited. Few styles in history can have been met with so many pleas from its users to see it destroyed.

Eight of the twelve 'candidates for demolition' in a 2005 television series on most-hated British buildings were brutalist. They included Park Hill, Gateshead's Trinity Car Park and Cumbernauld new town. Almost all are no more. Pressure to demolish the Hayward Gallery failed and Preston Bus Station was saved, but Portsmouth's Tricorn Centre, Edinburgh's St James Centre, half of London's Robin Hood Gardens and John Madin's Birmingham Central Library all went. The cost of erecting buildings unable to survive one generation of use was ridiculous.

It should be said that similar brutalist developments in the suburbs of Paris were so raw as to make Britain's seem positively quaint. Catalogued by Nigel Green and Robin Wilson, blocks such as Beaugrenelle and Chêne Pointu now lie derelict, their lifts unpowered and squatters in their basements. Back in the 1970s, France's culture minister André Malraux enthused that 'nothing like them has been done since France's great Gothic cathedrals'. Most silently await demolition.

Brutalism was not the only style for public commissions in the 1960s and 70s. The partnership of Darbourne & Darke showed that traditional London red brick could make a less aggressive impression. Their Lillington Gardens in Pimlico, completed in the early 1960s, proved both popular and lasting. A similar search for variety was shown in the Uxbridge (now Hillingdon) Civic Centre of 1973, designed by RMJM. Of brick and with pitched roofs, it was accused of every pre-modernist sin, of employing decorative detail and strange windows. So ingrained was modernism at the time that the building's eccentric charm was dismissed at the time as 'weird'.

A few traditional buildings poked their heads above the parapet. In 1960 the Georgian revivalist Vincent Harris repeated his

The Dawn of Hesitation (1965–1973)

Sheffield City Hall with a grandiloquent public library for Kensington. Within five years the local council appeared to get cold feet and approached Basil Spence for a new town hall next door. He delivered them a brutalist block of brick and concrete. A battle of the styles was thus refought in just one decade on either side of a west London courtyard.

The last phase of the postwar era came as thirteen years of Conservative rule ended with the election of a Labour government in 1964. The final decision from the outgoing Tories early that year was a truly grandiose modernist gesture. They commissioned Leslie Martin to replan the entire government enclave in Whitehall as a new 'government quarter'. Even for its day, the proposal was drastic. Martin proposed a highway driven in a tunnel from Victoria Street under Parliament Square along the Thames and up to the British Museum. He decided to flatten the entire south end of Whitehall from Downing Street to the river, including the Foreign Office, the Home Office, the Treasury, New Scotland Yard and Richmond Terrace. Nash's Carlton House Terrace overlooking St James's Park had already been scheduled for demolition.

A government minister, Lord Hailsham, eager to be thought approving of the new age, declared that 'keeping the past means destroying the future'. A new Whitehall would arise as a 'horizontal megastructure', a series of office ziggurats round courtyards. Only one side of Downing Street and the Banqueting House would be left untouched. A measure of the times was that there was virtually no public reaction. Government had spoken and the future was decided.

In 1968 a long-awaited plan to redevelop seventy acres of the Covent Garden district was finally tabled. This involved an area twice the size of the Barbican and was a pet project of the new Tory-controlled Greater London Council, which had replaced the old LCC in 1965. The plan proposed the demolition of 60 per cent of the buildings lying between the Strand and Holborn, with new through roads sweeping round its edges. A traffic engineer at a public inquiry accused objectors to his dual-carriageway Strand of 'wanting to bring London to a complete halt'.

A final talisman of what was portrayed as the Swinging Sixties was the determination of a brash developer, Jack Cotton, to demolish Piccadilly Circus. In 1962, Cotton's architect Lord Holford proposed to deck over the circus and surround it with slabs and towers coated in advertisements. Various versions were successively proposed and dropped throughout the sixties until in 1972 Holford put forward a dramatic triple-tower podium in the Buchanan fashion. This too was rejected by the now reinstalled Tory government, not for wiping out a much-loved neighbourhood but because it provided space for only 20 per cent more vehicles. Ministers wanted 50 per cent more. Motor traffic was still the ruling obsession in the government's handling of London.

These three planned comprehensive redevelopments of London's West End – Whitehall, Covent Garden and Piccadilly – came on top of proposals already described for cities throughout England and Scotland. Sites of the most intense local history, not to mention architectural diversity and character, were to be obliterated. Swathes of inner cities would be demolished, possibly to lie waste for decades, as did indeed happen to areas of inner Liverpool and Manchester. Thousands of businesses would be driven out of town centres, emasculating their economies. This was 'the new Britain' pursued by a consensus of architects, planners, councillors and politicians. Even the incoming Labour government of 1964 had accepted this future without demur, driven by a near hysterical optimism as to the resources that would be needed.

Saumarez Smith portrayed those participating in planning at the time as almost numb to what they were doing. Liverpool's Shankland claimed to 'see the city as art'. He professed himself particularly sensitive to the 'crumbling and chaotic' northern

The Dawn of Hesitation (1965–1973)

cities 'whose unity and character enabled them to be comprehended'. He even went on to conserve much of central Bolton. Yet he presided over the destruction of an estimated 33,000 Liverpool homes, not far short of the 50,000 lost in London during the Blitz. Blackburn was even sadder. A macho Corbusian councillor boasted he had 'the sense and the courage to knock down the whole town centre in accordance with modern needs and ideas', which indeed he did. The centre was replaced by today's huge shopping mall and car park.

As the 1960s drew to a close, politicians still adhered to the faith. Figures on the left and right, such as Hugh Gaitskell, Anthony Crosland, Richard Crossman, Keith Joseph and Geoffrey Rippon, were all implicitly Corbusian. Obsessed with 'obsolescence', they regarded implementing the modernist agenda as an inherited duty, however Herculean. Even as towers were privatized and brutalism was demolished, they flicked maps, shuffled charts, totted up statistics and dismissed critics. As for coping with the human fallout from their plans, that was the job of local government.

The most extraordinary feature of this period was the docility of the victims, almost as if they had been persuaded of historic necessity. One of my most depressing experiences was to witness the implementing of Rowland Nicholas's Manchester clearances from the city's Hulme district at the end of the 1960s. We observers were invited to watch fleets of coaches lined up in the rain outside a community centre to transport the residents with their cases to new towns miles away. Hulme was undeniably a slum – the council had neglected it for decades – but these people had spent their lives attached to its streets, families and community of friends. They needed only heating and plumbing. No one asked them if they wanted to move.

The community centre was full of bemused and miserable faces. We compared them to wartime refugees awaiting transportation. I do not recall a single smile. We later saw aerial photographs of their abandoned neighbourhood, a flattened landscape identical to that of wartime Warsaw after its bulldozing by the Wehrmacht. Apologists now say the architects meant well and thought they were offering Mancunians a better future. I find that hard to believe. Officials on the ground behaved as if they were 'only obeying orders'.

At Hulme, Hugh Wilson and Lewis Womersley, architect of Park Hill, designed a new estate of deck access crescents, boasted as the biggest public housing project in Europe. It opened in 1972 to house 13,000 people. The crescents came immediately under attack, described by the *Architects' Journal* as 'hideous, system-built deck-access blocks ... Europe's worst housing stock'. Within two years tenancies were declared 'for adults only'. The estate was crime-ridden and the police refused to visit it, claiming it was 'private'. Rents were not collected and by the late 1980s the new Hulme was abandoned as its tenants just walked away.

In 1991, just twenty years after their construction, the Hulme crescents were demolished as uninhabitable. After £400 million (nearly £900 million today) had been spent trying to rescue it, the estate was turned over to the private sector. I know of no inquiry in the Hulme fiasco. Any of Hulme's few once-slum terrace houses that managed to escape demolition now fetch £250,000 on the open market.

This raised a question rarely discussed in planning circles. In all the debates about housing after the war, the question of class was seldom mentioned. For thirty years in Britain, architects were designing buildings unlike any in which they or their friends and associates were likely to live. They were forcing working-class people into properties that were soon proving uninhabitable, so that many had to be demolished at enormous public expense. Yet there was no inquiry, no evidence of second thoughts, let alone of apology. Nothing illustrated the gulf in British society in the decades after the war so much as did its

The Dawn of Hesitation (1965–1973)

experience of architecture. The resulting damage to the social and economic life, particularly of northern towns, served to hasten their migration south.

There was one category of development that fell mostly outside these traumas, one that as the 1960s came to a close was reaching maturity, the new-towns movement. It was an attempt to bring to the chaotic house-building boom of the interwar years some of the ideological discipline of the early garden cities movement. It seized on hostility to the overcrowding and 'obsolescence' of the city and replaced it with the new utopianism. The only question was, should it be the utopia of Howard's sylvan suburbia or Le Corbusier's virile brutalism?

Initially some two dozen settlements were planned, to be set in open countryside round existing cities. Those founded in the 1940s were mostly in London's Home Counties, such as Crawley, Basildon, Stevenage, Bracknell, Harlow and Hemel Hempstead. The Midlands was given Corby and the north Peterlee. To the 1945 Labour government these had been in the image of the council estate en masse. The minister in charge, Lewis Silkin, said of Basildon, 'It will become a city which people from all over the world will want to visit.' The angry residents of the once-rural village of Stevenage called it Silkingrad. Foreign visitors were few.

Much like interwar council architecture, the style of these estates was broadly Georgian 'cottage vernacular'. Most had small gardens and were spaciously laid out. Harlow was designed as 'town in country'. Its principal architect, Frederick Gibberd, insisted on 'green wedges' penetrating to its centre. He persuaded his friends to design individual buildings, much in the manner of Gidea Park. As a result, Harlow was host to works by Powell and Moya, Maxwell Fry and Jane Drew among others. It gained a reputation of being effete, but then that had been true of Bedford Park.

By the 1960s most of the 1940s new towns were settling down, albeit unevenly. Those that relied heavily on daily commuting to work elsewhere proved vulnerable to 'new town blues', a loneliness and lack of the sense of community afforded by the urban streets they had left behind. New towns were poor at supplying social infrastructure. A second wave of towns followed in the 1960s, mostly attempting to be more urban in character. These were in a more aggressively modernist style, in particular Skelmersdale, Telford and Cumbernauld.

Of these, Glasgow's Cumbernauld was the most radical. It resulted from the reversal by Abercrombie of the Bruce plan for the rebuilding of inner Glasgow with towers. The thirty-storey cluster of eight towers and slabs in Gorbals' Red Roads was the biggest estate in Europe and utterly soulless. Residents bewailed the end of the tradition of tossing food to children from Glasgow tenement windows: 'Ye cannae fling a jeely [sandwich] oot a twenty-storey flat,' went a local song. The estate's spectacular destruction in the 2010s was even staged as an explosive launch of the 2014 Commonwealth Games.

The new town of Cumbernauld was a spread of low-rise terraces and maisonettes, but its centre was to be a brutalist rebuttal of the now despised 'prairie planning' favoured by the first generation of new towns. Designed by Geoffrey Copcutt and Hugh Wilson, the core took the form of a single multi-storey block on a hill with a throughway below it. This was surrounded by a maze of pedestrian access tunnels and bridges, opened in 1967. Ubiquitous concrete walls were intended, said the publicity, 'to elicit new codes of community behaviour'. The means by which brutalism intended to achieve this patronizing outcome were never made clear.

Saumarez Smith recounted a visit to Cumbernauld in 1965 by the then housing minister Richard Crossman and his permanent secretary, Evelyn Sharp. Both were modernists and Cumbernauld

The Dawn of Hesitation (1965–1973)

delighted them. Sharp recorded her pleasure at 'the good, solid, hard town'. She admitted that most people preferred houses and gardens, but 'even if they don't want to like Cumbernauld, they would come to like it once they live in it'. Crossman agreed. The place was 'done in a tremendously austere, exhilarating, uncomfortable style'. These were extraordinary epithets for a place they expected others to call home.

The following week Crossman paid a visit to one of the earliest garden cities, Welwyn. Here he admitted his doubts. His diary recorded that Welwyn in comparison with Cumbernauld was 'charming and I am sure delightful to live in'. He still preferred Cumbernauld's architecture but he could understand 'that the vast majority of British people probably prefer to live in Welwyn'. To him such a preference should clearly have no impact on the architecture. It was a nadir of class arrogance.

Cumbernauld was the purest of Corbusian developments and duly won a number of architectural awards. Outside the profession the response was different. It was voted Scotland's 'most hated town' and was twice declared 'Carbuncle of the Year'. The original central block was eventually to join the toll of brutalist demolitions and the town never achieved more than two-thirds of its planned 70,000 population. Twice in a generation areas of the great city of Glasgow had been rebuilt and had had to be destroyed, in deference to a failed architectural cult. Back in London, Crossman suppressed any guilt and Sharp appointed Cumbernauld's architect Wilson as her housing adviser.

Another new town of this period had been struggling to surface since the early 1960s. On the outskirts of east London, downstream from Woolwich, the LCC's modernists had long been determined to show they could do their own Barbican. The area was blighted with power stations, pylons and sewage outfalls and needed an uplift. The riverside settlement of Thamesmead would be a resort of sailing and water sports, of brutalist blocks and terraces overlooking the water. Parallels were drawn with Port Grimaud in the south of France.

Begun in 1967, the town was ill-conceived from the start. The site was prone to flooding and millions of tons of sand had to be shipped in to stabilize it. Ground floors had to be made watertight or confined to garages. No yachts appeared in the harbour, shops were few and council tenancies were hard to let, even to new immigrants. The terraces were used as a set for the violent 1971 film *A Clockwork Orange*.

By the 1990s the population target of 60,000 was nowhere near being reached and was abandoned. In 2010, Thamesmead went the way of so many failed housing developments: a third of the houses, mostly on the outer roads, went for private sale and the rest were handed over to a housing association, the Peabody Trust. The trust estimated it would need £1 billion to make Thamesmead 'lettable', a mind-blowing sum. Parts of outer Thamesmead, where it tries to be an ordinary suburb, are attractive but the enterprise was clearly a failure. There has never been an inquiry into why. Thamesmead is rarely mentioned among new towns, largely because it was lost within the maw of LCC council housing.

To read accounts of the new-town movement is to realize that they worked best where they came closest to what their creators had most detested. This was the traditional out-of-town suburb, the 'houses with gardens' deplored by Evelyn Sharp. The best illustration was the brightest light on the new-town horizon, Milton Keynes in Buckinghamshire. This was doubly fortunate. Its location was midway between London, Birmingham and other centres of Midlands prosperity, and it was laid out by its architect Derek Walker as the antithesis of Cumbernauld, in effect a garden city.

The model for Milton Keynes published in 1967 was for a new Los Angeles. There would be a grid of one-kilometre-squares, each block said to form an explicit 'village'. The sovereignty of the car was accepted as dominant, but cars as extensions of human activity. Houses had garages and there was road space aplenty. Milton Keynes was declared 'a new model for urban life in Britain for a quarter of a century ahead', a strangely modest ambition.

The settlement was criticized as a 'community without propinquity'. Personal bonding was supposed to occur in the villages and there was no formal town centre or hub. There was merely a business and shopping avenue fronted with faceless glass-fronted blocks. A shopping mall was named The Centre and, as if in kindness, was later listed as historic. In an effort to avoid new-town blues, the authorities persuaded the Open University to relocate there. They installed an artist in residence and persuaded the jazz musician Johnny Dankworth to visit and perform. There was later a theatre.

For all this, Milton Keynes ranks among the successes of the new-town movement. The designers understood that a development intended predominantly for young families meant that mobility outside the home would be on wheels. Such community as existed was to be supplied by neighbourhood contact on foot. Planners were replicating the private suburb. With some irony, Milton Keynes was to be the only new town later granted the accolade of city status.

In 1974 an American academic, Stephen Elkin, published a comparison of British and American planning practice over this period. It included a detailed study of major London projects, such as Centre Point and Euston Centre. Elkin expressed astonishment at the lack of public participation in Britain. At Euston, local residents on the site of one of the biggest towers in London were kept in the dark until virtually the moment of their eviction. The first they knew of their fate was when builders sought keys to the central garden to park their bulldozers.

In other words, British planning was entirely top-down. 'Consultation' meant the sponsors of a project discussing it among themselves. Officials on the ground were almost always in favour of redevelopment and had an interest in keeping quiet. Local democracy was a broken reed. Elkin saw this as the reason why so many projects came unstuck. Their 'shortcomings went largely unnoticed and unpunished . . . their claims largely untested'. In America similar pressures would invariably involve local people, often in fierce opposition. America's 'more populist and participative kind of political system' kept planning and architecture on their toes. In America, the saying goes, 'all politics is local', in Britain it is central.

20.

The Conservation Counter-Revolution (1973–1986)

By the early 1970s urban Britain was in a state of neurosis. The utopian fantasies that the 1960s had inherited from the 1940s were fast dissolving. Plans that were never going to see the light of day lay in local government offices. Councils ploughed on with projects in which few had much faith. They continued to erect deck-access flats, push through bypasses, build car parks and develop shopping centres. Everywhere they were spending huge sums of public money backed by an increasingly powerful construction lobby. But the character of the settlements they were still hoping to create was unclear.

The arrival of a new Tory government in 1970 had seen headwinds begin to blow. A shock rise in the price of oil in 1973 led to a recession and a widespread taking of stock. Redevelopment for a while went into abeyance as local councils realized they simply lacked the resources. At the same time there was increasing public unease at the destruction of the familiar. Back in 1957 a Tory MP, Duncan Sandys, had founded a national body called the Civic Trust to promote more sensitive town planning. It was followed a year later by the founding of the Victorian Society, drawing attention to the types of buildings most under threat from renewal. The Civic Trust led to the setting up of trusts in towns across Britain, complemented by often militant local amenity societies.

A new architectural language came to the fore, that of conservation. Lionel Esher, a modernist in his time, warned the RIBA's

1964 annual conference to 'beware of contempt for old buildings', which he called 'a sort of architectural fascism'. Not all slums needed to be treated as such, 'but as potentially decent places to live'. Many architects had declared Victorian slum housing 'obsolete' for the working classes, yet were themselves now restoring and living in just such properties.

In 1967, Sandys made a second move. He won a private member's bill, the Civic Amenities Act, establishing in statute the concept of the conservation area. It sought to curb development in neighbourhoods that had been built before the twentieth century, banning the demolition of old buildings and forcing new ones to respect their context. The new areas were to be designated and enforced by local planning authorities. This meant that councils at last had both the responsibility and the power to save their past. In this they were assisted by market forces. Older properties proved attractive, so conservation could be paid for through private ownership. Over time, prices of pre-twentieth-century houses in conservation areas tended to run at one-third higher than for modern buildings.

Coupled with the rapid advance of listing of historic buildings, Sandys's 1967 Act was the most radical innovation in British planning history. It signalled what Alan Powers was to dub the 'Heroic Period of Conservation'. The movement went from being the preserve of historians to a much wider upsurge of public opinion. Amenity societies were now armed with a legal weapon with which to defend the character of cities. Under the 1967 Act councils had to consult them. Architecture moved from the realm of professional consensus to a cockpit of divisive politics.

A growing group of architectural writers championed the conservationist cause, including Ian Nairn, Nicholas Taylor, Roger Scruton, Christopher Booker, Theo Crosby, Marcus Binney, John Harris and the veterans Osbert Lancaster and John Betjeman. Newspapers carried headlines such as the Sack of Bath and the

The Conservation Counter-Revolution (1973–1986)

Rape of Westminster. Bloomsbury was described as being 'vandalized' by London University, Bayswater by the Church of England and the entirety of the Victorian railway by British Rail.

The direction to be taken by urban planning was more intractable. Abercrombie's utopian vision for London might be disintegrating, but it remained the official plan for the capital under the GLC. In 1970, however, the incoming Tory government of Ted Heath made a seismic decision. It abandoned the 1965 Martin plan to rebuild Whitehall. A devastated Martin wrote a farewell letter to his minister, ending, 'Please do not bother to reply.' A year later, the GLC plan for Covent Garden faced something new in British planning: a concerted public revolt of the local people it had long been evicting from their homes. A Covent Garden community association took to the streets, championed by the vicar of St Martin-in-the-Fields.

Unlike much of working-class east London, Covent Garden was not a bombed ghost town. It had a resident population that was mixed middle and working class, replete with creative businesses and articulate activists. Despite the district's ageing fabric, it was not 'obsolete' but a still-vibrant city-centre district, subsequently revealed as home to no fewer than 17,000 small businesses. Apart from the usual urban utilities of transport, repair, catering and entertainment, these included thirty-four publishers and twenty-six stamp dealers. All were at risk from the proposed redevelopment. Modernist town planning was revealed as what it was: a systematic assault on an inner-city economy.

The campaigners went on marches, recruited media allies and hogged headlines. In a sensational move, they persuaded the chairman of the GLC's pro-plan Covent Garden Committee, Lady Dartmouth, publicly to resign her post and join them. After months of relentless pressure, even the Tory planning minister, Geoffrey Rippon, switched sides. In January 1973 he personally listed for protection some 250 mostly Victorian buildings in the Covent Garden area, meaning none could be demolished without specific permission. This sabotaged the GLC's plan, effectively crashing the entire project. The various plans for Piccadilly also died the death at much the same time. The circus had made a narrow escape and was allowed to survive into the age of conservation.

The worm now turned. In 1974 a similar local rebellion against clearances in Cheshire's Macclesfield was led by the architect Rod Hackney. It initiated a wider movement to resist mass housing redevelopment, crucially winning grant-aid from central government for conserving and updating old terraces. Shortly afterwards, another revolt occurred among Liverpool residents, this time against their eviction from the city's battered Vauxhall docks area. The residents demanded the right to stay put and be consulted about, indeed to decide, what style of new housing they would enjoy. The resulting Eldonian Village estate bore little relationship to inner-city public housing. It was uncannily similar to the Tudorbethan cottages and terraces of the Liverpool suburbs. The new Eldonian did not face demolition but became the most popular public housing in Liverpool.

Such developments galvanized public debate at a time when the national mood was uncertain. In 1973 the Heath government was dealing with an enforced three-day working week, mass industrial strife and every corner of the public sector under pressure. Architecture too was suffering. Its image was changing in the public mind from the creation of the new to the destruction of the old. In 1975 the Royal College of Art was refused permission to demolish part of Italianate Queen's Gate in Kensington. The college had recently erected a large modern block next to the Royal Albert Hall and wanted to put up another. Nine distinguished architects duly wrote a letter of protest at the refusal to *The Times*. Ten years previously the letter would have overruled all objection. Now it had zero effect.

The Conservation Counter-Revolution (1973–1986)

Esher wrote that people were now taking notice of how the buildings around them looked, 'and for the most part they do not like what they see'. He declared architecture to be 'in the dock, charged with being banal, inhuman and impossible to love'. Even the elderly Pevsner took to the airwaves to declare he had 'emphatically lost faith in what is happening now'. A public seminar organized by the critic Nathan Silver, an adviser to the Prince of Wales, asked 'Why is British Architecture so Lousy?' That it was lousy seemed unexceptionable at the time. I recall a heckler shouting the answer: 'Corbusier'.

In 1974 the Victoria and Albert Museum staged a strident exhibition on the Destruction of the English Country House, recording that such houses were being lost at the rate of almost one a week. In the previous six months there had been 334 applications to demolish listed historic buildings. The exhibition, largely of photographs of vanished mansions, stimulated a burst of protest and the formation the following year of SAVE Britain's Heritage by a group of architectural writers, led by Marcus Binney. The group devoted itself to alerting public opinion to impending demolitions, and to stimulating opposition. It concentrated on press releases and photographs, making the point that many beautiful buildings lurked behind a surface of neglect and decay. Capturing the spirit of the times, the Council of Europe declared 1975 European Architectural Heritage Year.

A Labour resurgence in the mid-1970s saw the Conservatives lose power both at Westminster and on the GLC. An incoming Labour regime seized the public mood. It formally abandoned the London Motorway Box, most of Abercrombie's road proposals and the Covent Garden plan. The London ringways subsided into the background, leaving fragments at Shepherd's Bush and the East Cross Route at Blackwall Tunnel. A ghost of the Motorway Box can still be seen at the White City flyover, where a stub points over the roofs of North Kensington like a defunct cannon.

Outside London, the question was how many horses had fled before the conservation door was even half bolted. The M8 was already being driven across central Glasgow and throughways snaked through Liverpool. A portion of Newcastle's Grainger Town had gone. An urban highway named Maid Marian Way cut a destructive path through old Nottingham in the shadow of its castle.

A close shave came to Halifax. Its famous Piece Hall was an enclosed and colonnaded square built in 1779 and a majestic work of eighteenth-century architecture. It was also a monument to the Yorkshire cloth trade, whose market it once hosted. None of this was enough to save it from the local council, which in 1970 declared it obsolete and proposed its demolition. Only a national campaign secured its reprieve, with councillors complaining that their planners had never told them conservation was an option.

A similar battle occurred in London over St Pancras Station, which British Rail hoped would follow the nearby Euston Arch into extinction. A campaign led by the Victorian Society and the then poet laureate John Betjeman eventually secured its listing. But its survival was then threatened with dereliction by a BR that used it for storage. Not until the late 1970s was £1 million spent on roof repairs. As so often in these cases, the philistines eventually turned proud owners. At the reopening of St Pancras in 2007, assembled railway executives celebrated with royalty at a magnificent concert in the station's great train shed. They were the same executives who had tried to destroy it.

I recalled that in my art class at school our teacher, a keen modernist, had suggested we spend a term designing a new city. He handed out rulers and compasses and asked us to plan roads, houses, factories and offices, all to be in different colours. I had no clue what he meant and felt a rising panic as I saw fellow pupils

The Conservation Counter-Revolution (1973–1986)

drawing lines, circles, sectors and squares. To me a city was the only one I knew, London. I duly drew a river and tried to recall the functions of the various neighbourhoods adjoining it, filling the sheet of paper with tiny squiggles. It ended up looking like a Jackson Pollock painting. The teacher gave me an angry nought out of ten and I was mortified. I later realized that I had not 'designed' a city but merely described one that seemed to work.

Over the years my London had, like other British cities, prospered not through planning diktat or draughtsman's ruler but by organically adapting to the demands of its inhabitants. These mutated from large-scale activities such as manufacturing, dockworking, offices and bureaucracy into retail, entertainment and hospitality. Once dismissed as obsolete, a residential terrace or shopping street could see its rooms extended, walls adjusted, floors added and plumbing renewed. Even in old industrial districts, workshops, storehouses, lofts and basements were easily converted to meet a desire for unusual or informal city living, as in Covent Garden. Such flexibility was near impossible in large buildings made of reinforced concrete.

The centres of most of Britain's cities were, by the last quarter of the twentieth century, facing the need drastically to adapt their buildings from formerly Victorian activities. The assumption had been that this required their demolition. Yet it was noticeable that in London two of the world's most technically advanced industries – diagnostic medicine and film post-production – were concentrated not in new suburbs but in the most heavily conserved districts, Marylebone and Soho. Their buildings dated from the eighteenth century and were mostly terraces of town houses that could hardly be less suited to high-tech purposes. The fact was, their interiors were easily adaptable to the changing needs of advanced technology while their surrounding streets were popular with their staff.

Everywhere in Britain, post-war planning had simply disregarded the utility to a modern urban economy of what was second nature to an ancient one, a hinterland of informal and adaptable properties and courtyards, catering to a hierarchy of activities. These embraced building, distributing and servicing, ranging from small-scale enterprises such as lawyers, accountants and consultants to bars, galleries and restaurants, hairdressers and tailors. Their premises were no more 'obsolete' than their occupants. Such was the demand of the movie industry for once-scruffy Soho properties in the 2020s that they were priced second only to the City of London per square foot.

Given the frequency of conference references to the American urbanologist Jane Jacobs and her *Death and Life of Great American Cities* (1961), this neglect of the complexity of a modern city was puzzling. To Jacobs, streets were the arteries and veins of urban life. Buildings fronting onto pavements were 'eyes on the street', with passers-by enabling it to become 'self-policing'. A street was a fusion of indoor and outdoor activity that was the essence of neighbourliness. Jacobs' attention to the psychology of street behaviour was completely alien to most British urban architecture at the time; it was still attuned to Le Corbusier's cry: 'We must kill the street.'

Throughout the postwar period almost no traditional streets were created anywhere in Britain, while thousands were demolished. Architecture was concerned solely with building. Beyond walls was just space, like the Barbican's relentless podium. This drained cities not just of the diversity of old buildings and variegated facades, but of the diversity that fuelled their microeconomies. This was particularly crippling to the often marginal commercial activities of northern cities as their primary industries, extractive and manufacturing, began to close. It widened the gulf between them and London. If there was a name for the dominant planning style of the 1960s and 70s it might be that of 'streetlessness'.

*

The Conservation Counter-Revolution (1973–1986)

The balance of power in urban architecture was now shifting. The agency of urban renewal was no longer an all-powerful planning committee and its officers, restrained by little more than their available resources. Listed-building control – saviour of Covent Garden – and the wider impact of conservation areas were becoming major obstacles to comprehensive redevelopment. Renewal now depended on historical facts, the age and character of existing buildings and the power of local amenity lobbies. Traffic engineers who had dominated planning in cities such as Birmingham and Glasgow no longer had carte blanche. Planning became a matter of compromise.

What this meant in practice was that urban renewal would increasingly mean architectural renewal. Councils that had for twenty-five years regarded their principal role to be builders of public housing saw that role become redundant. Victorian properties once seen as fit only for demolition were now moving into the private sector for sale. This in turn led to new pressures. In London many of the Victorian neighbourhoods built for the middle classes had drifted downmarket and become home to working-class occupants. Leaseholdings had become mile upon mile of slums. The expense of restoring these slums drove existing residents out. Renewal often began with squats and hippy housing, gradually attracting young improvers or 'gentrifiers'. The 1960s estate agency named after its founder, Roy Brooks, glamorized this process. Pimlico, Islington and North Kensington were advertised for sale each Sunday, to 'excite a destitute artist . . . pose a challenge full of promise . . . respond to a loving owner'.

In the London boroughs of Islington and Camden, though some towers had been built, much social housing was obtained at lower cost by the council itself buying and improving Victorian streets. I lived next to one myself, and watched it mature into a model of stable, communally integrated housing, what balanced urban renewal should be. More generally, social housing meant direct aid for renting privately owned properties or those owned by housing charities. During the 1980s, council-house building was slashed, but housing subsidy did not diminish. It switched to housing benefit.

A new generation of architects was emerging, whose approach to urban design was less hidebound by Corbusian tradition. A survey conducted by the RIBA in 1979 asked architecture students to outline where they expected to work. The answers indicated a transformation since the 1960s. It was reported that 'disturbingly few wanted to influence the environment through their work'. A public sector that had sustained the profession for generations now appealed to a mere 4 per cent of students. It was as if they had gazed at modern British architecture and agreed with the public. They wanted nothing to do with it.

This scepticism reached a peak with the intervention of one public figure whose views were unlikely to be ignored. Prince Charles, usually the master of platitude, hurled himself into architectural controversy. A speech to the RIBA in 1984 and another in 1987 were followed by a seventy-five-minute television diatribe in which he expressed his hatred of modernist buildings. Architects, he said, had created 'god-forsaken cities . . . of huge, blank, impersonal buildings'. They had 'consistently ignored the feelings and wishes of the mass of ordinary people in this country'. They did so because they were trained to do just one thing: 'tear down and rebuild . . . for the approval of fellow architects, not for tenants'.

The prince was happy to name names, or at least cases. A proposed steel-and-glass extension to the National Gallery in Trafalgar Square looked like a 'village fire station . . . a monstrous carbuncle on the face of a much-loved friend'. A proposed Mies van der Rohe tower in the city was 'yet another glass stump better suited to downtown Chicago'. The Hayward Gallery was 'a nuclear facility' and Colin St John Wilson's British Library 'an academy for secret police'. As for Madin's Birmingham Central Library, it looked more like 'a place where books are burned'. It was the nineteenth century's battle of the styles returned with a vengeance.

Many of the architects responsible were sitting in the audience and fumed. Some accused Charles of being 'undemocratic' – as if they themselves had ever put their buildings to a referendum. He replied that he had no more legal status in planning decisions than they had. The difference was in the response. After the prince's National Gallery reference, the Palace reportedly received thousands of letters in support. It was as if the public had, for the first time, been invited to debate architecture and eagerly accepted. In the ensuing publicity, the RIBA's president and prominent brutalist, Owen Luder, inelegantly proposed that architects stick to their guns and tell the public, 'Sod you.' The press described his buildings as 'sod-you architecture'.

The prince courted further controversy by practising what he preached. He commissioned a new town called Poundbury on his Duchy of Cornwall land outside Dorchester. This would be high-density, traffic limited and designed by Léon Krier, an apostle of the American New Urbanism. This stressed respect for traditional townscape and its social and environmental character. Krier's motto was, 'I'm an architect, because I don't build.' Poundbury was original. Its central core was a Palladian composition that turned to vernacular in its side streets and courtyards. Though initially ersatz and frigid, it matured over time to accommodate a population of over 6,000, a third of it in social housing.

To walk round Poundbury is to sense what the new-town movement never grasped: that a town is not a village or a suburb. It needs a dense and active core and spaces of congregation and diversity. It also needs areas of privacy and intimacy. As it grew, Poundbury acquired all these. It responded to the new concept not of space-filling but place-making. This was an ethos awash in abstraction but, in essence, it meant treating public spaces with the care shown to private ones, places described as for 'Sunday afternoons, walking your dog, running into friends, people watching and losing track of time'. Many architects felt Poundbury was a comment on their failings – as it was – and deploring it became a badge of honour. I once drove two of them through it and they pleaded with me to leave, as if they were in a horror movie. Undaunted, the Cornwall estate repeated Poundbury in a new settlement at Nansledan, outside Newquay in Cornwall.

The royal intervention had been preceded by a similar eruption in America, where the novelist Tom Wolfe savaged the Corbusian modernists in his *From Bauhaus to Our House* (1981). He complained that they hated decoration and forced tedium and ugliness on their users. Architecture to Wolfe was 'a gallery we can't walk out of, a book we can't close, an art we can't even turn our backs on because it is there facing us on the other side of the street as well'.

One of the few observers to penetrate the professional culture that lay behind the modernist eye was Owen Hatherley. In *A Guide to the New Ruins of Great Britain* (2010) and *A New Kind of Bleak* (2012) he traipsed round British towns and cities with a sympathy few writers were able to tolerate. Happy with modernism, Hatherley talked with its practitioners. He visited Preston, original home of Building Design Partnership (BDP), one of Britain's leading public sector architects. The firm was responsible for some of the dreariest schools, universities, hospitals and public buildings back to the early 1960s. A former BDP chairman, Keith Scott, was remarkably frank. He admitted that the postwar period 'was a disastrous period . . . we had to produce a building stock quite quickly, with cheap methods . . . we produced a lot of shoddy architecture.' When Hatherley asked him whether his approach to style changed in the 1970s and 80s, he said, 'I don't think anything to do with style entered my head.' He confessed to being a fan of Prince Charles.

The Conservation Counter-Revolution (1973–1986)

Conservation in the 1970s had told architecture that its consumers wanted to be surrounded by clear links to the past. Designing within the context of history was hardly new. Inigo Jones had demanded that Lord Bedford's new Covent Garden take a lead from ancient Rome and Renaissance Paris. Pugin had done the same with medieval Gothic. William Morris had preached a revival of Arts and Crafts, of the tools and materials of a pre-industrial age. Form should indeed follow function, but there could be nothing wrong in decorating it with the reassurance of history.

Some architects continued to meet this challenge. Raymond Erith and his business partner Quinlan Terry were neoclassicists throughout the postwar period. Terry's Richmond Riverside (1984), a parade of different Georgian facades, was too much for many architects to tolerate but has remained popular locally. It was another battle of the styles revived. With Terry were John Simpson and Julian Bicknell, the latter perfectly recreating Palladio's Villa Rotonda at Henbury Hall in Cheshire as if he were Burlington reincarnated. John Outram's New House in Sussex (1982) for the Rausing family was so rich in classical and Egyptian references as to rank as postmodernist (see next chapter).

The modernist tradition was becoming almost historic. Anthony Hudson's Baggy House in Devon (1994) was a flamboyantly 1930s arrangement of oblongs and cubes, with the flat roofs and expansive windows recalling the interwar Bauhaus. Michael and Patty Hopkins' house in Hampstead was indeed nothing but a flat roof and windows in the manner of Mies van der Rohe. In commenting on the private houses of the last years of the century Powers felt obliged to point out that, in matters of style, 'in order for one of them to be right, the other does not have to be wrong'. He thought architecture in these years was 'as much involved in historical references as was classicism'.

As conservation advanced, some architects were able to attune their style in its direction. In the rescued Covent Garden, Terry

Farrell adapted its vernacular in his extraordinary Comyn Ching Triangle, an unobtrusive blend of modernism and conservation in a neighbourhood idiom. William Whitfield, a master of contextual modernism, designed a dignified new office block opposite Downing Street in Whitehall. Peter Barber showed that modern design could exploit the intimacies of the back streets with his extraordinary Edgewood Mews in Barnet and others like it. Piers Gough's warehouse-style flats enlivened Victorian docks without abusing them. The salvaging of Liverpool's Albert Dock was a masterpiece of renewal, yielding a buzzing waterfront in contrast to Manchester's bleak modern equivalent at Salford Quays.

The 'big four' house-builders, Wimpey, Laing, Persimmon and Berkeley, continued to give little time to modernism – any more than they had since the 1930s. They offered the market what they thought it wanted, the standard twentieth-century style, a mix of stripped neo-Georgian and neo-Tudor. In the decontrolled 2010s this was replicated in identikit housing estates located at random in fields across southern England. It was the architecture of a comfort-seeking, unobtrusive Britain, rarely with reference to locality or setting, and seldom with an architect in sight.

In the 1970s the magazine *New Society* took antagonism to modern planning to an extreme. Reyner Banham, Paul Barker, Peter Hall and Cedric Price founded the 'non-plan' movement, rejecting outright not just the modernists' style of urban renewal but the very idea of planning itself. They argued for 'the removal of regulations in favour of the spontaneous urban development that would follow'. They positively derided the notion 'that the planner has the right to say what is "right" . . . an extraordinary hangover from the day of collectivism in left-wing thought'. As if in desperation, the authors cried for communities to be left to rule themselves and the market to decide. They did not explain whether it was communities or the market that should have the final decision. Anarchy would be the probable victor.

If my litany of the sins of modernism in the 1960s and 70s has been relentless, it is because I believe its impact on Britain's built environment to have been one of the greatest errors of modern British government. The public officials involved, like the architects, seemed to have no sense of accountability, either to the past they were destroying or to their fellow citizens whose lives they were upheaving. When I took an Italian friend from Rome to show him the present London skyline from Waterloo Bridge, he was aghast. 'I come from the most corrupt city in Europe,' he said. 'Even we would not let this happen.'

Most societal calamities – fatal accidents, building collapses, terrorist incidents or epidemics – are subject to public inquiry, to audit and testing for lessons to be learned. When the medical, legal or engineering professions are found to be responsible there are demands for accountability. Yet the misjudgements of the three decades of postwar urban renewal were never investigated. Billions of pounds were wasted, notably in demolishing recently constructed buildings. The misery caused almost exclusively to poor communities was beyond calculation. Yet it was as if no one cared, no one should be blamed and nothing was to be learnt. Modern architecture seemed to be saying to a sizeable portion of the British people what was said by the president of the RIBA: 'Sod you'.

21.

The Age of Spectacle (1986–2020)

By the 1980s the old guard of postwar British architecture had mostly passed on. Richard Seifert, Frederick Gibberd, Richard Llewelyn-Davies, Basil Spence, Denys Lasdun and Leslie Martin had brought to the nation's townscape the styles and concepts most had learned in architecture schools before the war. They had produced quantities of hospitals, government offices, universities, new towns and housing estates almost all at public expense. The built environment we see round us was, at least in most urban centres, dominated by their work, though I rarely find people who can cite favourite buildings from this era. Few go beyond Coventry Cathedral, the Post Office Tower, the National Theatre and perhaps Milton Keynes. Many hold that modern buildings are just buildings rather than architecture.

As we saw in the last chapter, the 1980s were a period of architectural depression, but a new cast was now coming on stage, self-promoting, ambitious and innovative. In 1986, London's Royal Academy offered its first show of British architecture since the war. It presented works by three personalities, the jet-setting master of the commercial glass wall, Norman Foster, glamorous Richard Rogers of the 'inside-out' building and the cerebral James Stirling, specializing in academic buildings as abstract sculptures. The show's theme was to be controversial, the fact that these British architects were best known for buildings abroad, not at home. Each was invited to display a built and an unbuilt project.

The intention was summed up by the academy's president, the

artist Roger de Grey, who began with an acknowledgement that all was not well in the architecture camp. His introduction pointed to 'the antagonism with which many new buildings are greeted at home'. Britons were negative towards their architecture, de Grey's implication being that the fault lay with the public and not the architects. A different note was struck by the exhibition's organizer, the critic Deyan Sudjic. Architects, he said, had recently passed through 'a period of uncertainty and doubt'. He pointed out that modernism's 'long-cherished convictions and dogmas since the 1920s are being subjected to an unparalleled degree of questioning . . . indeed to a public outcry'. The promised utopias had been 'manifest failures'. The 'feeble attempts to copy the work of their movement's pioneers had produced monotonous and dispiriting environments from which city life has been driven out'.

This was a gloomy preface, but the exhibition was an attempt to clear the air and establish a new departure. On the one hand, Sudjic admitted that the works on show had not resolved what was to him the principal failure of modernism, 'an inability to insert new buildings into an existing urban fabric'. On the other, the exhibits were exciting and it was undeniably refreshing to see architecture presented as art. Foster's glass HSBC tower in Hong Kong (1985) was radical in shifting the solid service core to make way for space and light. It had a gracefulness that foretold of his later Gherkin for the City of London (2004). His (unbuilt) headquarters for the BBC in Langham Place was serene, but nakedly glassy for a traditional London street.

Rogers's Lloyd's building had already captured public attention and was at least in Britain. Like his Pompidou Centre in Paris (1976), built with Renzo Piano, its entire internal structure, floors, lifts, ducts and drains, was open to view behind great sheets of glass. It was a building impossible not to admire. Rogers's unbuilt structure was a new bridge over the Thames at Waterloo. Stirling's Staatsgalerie in

Stuttgart (1984) was the star of the show, a swirl of variegated stone and angled glass, bursting with slopes and planes. The exhibition was a success. It put architecture on the map and a point was made. It was the birth of the 'starchitect'.

The modernist style, insofar as it was definable, was already diversifying. In 1977 the historian Charles Jencks had attempted to supply a new nomenclature in his *Language of Post-Modern Architecture*. He accepted that it was hard to describe a movement merely as 'post' its predecessor. He suspected that 'the only way to kill the monster [of modernism] is to find a substitute beast'. Postmodernism (or Po-Mo) had already been recognized in America, in Robert Venturi's *Complexity and Contradiction in Architecture* (1966). Venturi discussed departures from modernism in the same terms as Mannerism and baroque had departed from classicism.

American postmodernism embraced Venturi's neoclassical variants of the 1960s and the comic commercialism of Los Angeles and Las Vegas. It ran to Philip Johnson's pedimented Sony Tower (1984) in Manhattan and went on to endorse a ragbag of buildings shaped as binoculars, a basket of fruit, a Venetian gondola and other eccentricities, from both Johnson and others such as Charles Moore and Michael Graves. Leading the age of the postmodern starchitect was Frank Gehry and his Bilbao Guggenheim (1997), which appeared to stimulate the economic revival of an entire city. Like the Pompidou Centre and Sydney's Opera House, it showed that truly distinctive buildings can survive any criticism and pack a punch.

Venturi complained that modernism had lost the ability to communicate in a new language. The result had been an impoverished urban landscape in the 1950s and 1960s. He rebutted Mies van der Rohe's maxim of 'less is more' with the crisp reply, 'less is a bore'. He also practised what he preached. Venturi's winning entry for the National Gallery extension (1991) took Wilkins's original as its theme and stretched it. His building replicated its classical pilasters and then, as it turned the corner onto Pall Mall, syncopated them and adorned them with Egyptian motifs. Venturi said he wanted to respect the context of Trafalgar Square and hoped to make people smile. That was rare in an architect.

As Jencks had pointed out, to be postmodern meant little more than applying some eclectic variety to what had been modernist. All three Royal Academy architects merited that title. Rogers's Lloyd's building was a veritable cathedral of Po-Mo. Others rallied to the call. Terry Farrell's London Breakfast TV studio (1981) was decorated with boiled eggs and became Eggcup House. His Charing Cross station building (1990) was a giant double arch, as if welcoming trains to a cavern under London. John Outram's Cambridge Judge Business School (1995) looked like an Egyptian mausoleum awaiting Tutankhamun. At Bryanston School the columns on Piers Gough's portico were giant-sized corkscrews. The parliament building next to the Palace of Westminster was crowned by Michael and Patty Hopkins with Quaker stovepipe hats as chimneys. British architects were at the very least becoming interesting.

They were also learning to sell themselves, obsessively. The Dutch critic Reinier de Graaf in 2021 totted up the number of architectural awards and found they far outstripped those given to actors, let alone artists or writers. Of British architects, Rogers had amassed 217, Zaha Hadid 234 and Foster a staggering 400. Eighty per cent of the awarding bodies charged a hefty entry fee for the potential publicity. If all else failed they would hand out prizes for 'lifetime achievement'. From 2006 there was even a 'carbuncle cup' for the year's worst building, in which it seemed architects took a grim pride. It was won variously by Rafael Viñoly's top-heavy Walkie-Talkie in the City (2004) and Chapman Taylor's bleak Drake Circus shopping centre (2006) in Plymouth.

Buildings too were taking on personalities. They became 'experiences'. In contrast to the run of faceless structures erected in the 1960s and 70s, they were intended to make people stop and notice. In trying to define the new mood, the critic Tom Dyckhoff called it the Age of Spectacle. In the early 2000s he interviewed John Prescott, Tony Blair's planning minister, whose job it was to approve or reject high-profile projects. It was a task that, with no qualification, he performed with abandon. When Dyckhoff asked what he looked for in a building, Prescott replied, anything that made him say, 'Bloody 'ell!' or perhaps, 'Wow!' Dyckhoff christened the result 'Wowhaus architecture'.

An early exercise in wow had already been seen in Manchester's deserted Salford dockland. Acres of disused land and water had left planners with a craving for something 'iconic'. There first appeared a scatter of office blocks and a media centre, but the site was eventually dominated by two waterside buildings, an auditorium and a museum, both in the postmodern style termed 'deconstructivism'. Michael Wilford's Lowry Centre (1995) was a crafted pile of curved shapes that he called 'a collage, a mass . . . an abstract sculpture'. It seemed an attempted imitation of Gehry's Bilbao. While bearing no relation to its purpose, it was undeniably striking. To the west the rival attraction was by the American Daniel Libeskind, his northern Imperial War Museum (2002). Here much the same description could apply: sculptural.

Both buildings were visually diverting and remained, as Wilford implied, works of architectural abstraction. Yet they seemed curiously isolated from their context, devoid of any surrounding activity. They had not exorcized modernism's curse of repelling rather than congregating people. Salford Quays is no Albert Dock, Camden Lock or Gas Street Basin.

The new Labour government's favoured buildings of the early 2000s were mostly wows. They included Foster's Sage Gateshead auditorium (now The Glasshouse), a great metal bulge of a

53. New dawn: the art deco Daily Express building, 1932

54. Public Sector Hygenic: Stripped-Georgian Becontree, completed 1935

55. Pop-up Tudor in 1930s Ealing

56. Purist Moderne: New Ways, Northampton, 1925–27

57. Cinematic Revivalism: Granada Tooting, 1929–31

58. Playing with people for a new Glasgow

59. Sorry for the mistake: the new Glasgow falls

60. Tomorrow's London: people in the sky from *Traffic in Towns* (1963)

61. It can work, just: Newcastle's Byker Community Trust

62. Brutalist Desert: Barbican Podium, 1962–82

63. Inside-out: Lloyd's of London, 1978–86

64. Post-modern at Cambridge Business School, 1991–95

65. London in the twenty-first century

66. Art peopling space at The Lowry, Salford Quays, 1995–2000

67. Today and yesterday: Borough Market and the Shard

building. There was Future Systems' Selfridges in Birmingham, like a whale stranded in the Bullring shopping centre, and there was Prescott's personal offspring, the St George Wharf Tower at Vauxhall. The last was a foreign investment vehicle some 80 per cent of which lay unoccupied, as if nothing had been learned since Centre Point. Prescott reportedly overruled the local planners and approved it because it stuck out.

Labour's prize exhibit was the 2000 Millennium Dome in North Greenwich by Mike Davies of Richard Rogers and Partners, not strictly a dome but a tent of lightweight PVC. The exhibition inside of British design – widely criticized as uninspiring – included pavilions by architects such as Hadid and Eva Jiřičná. The Dome afterwards mutated into a successful sports and entertainment venue, at least defeating the 1951 Dome of Discovery by surviving.

Areas where wow architects might still display their wares were in post-industrial 'brownfield' sites where, as in Salford, redevelopment had been delayed. Most spectacular was arguably London's best-known monument, Battersea Power Station. Its restoration and the demand that its developers fund a new Tube station proved so expensive that one after another withdrew over some twenty years. Eventually a Malaysian consortium agreed to proceed, but only if it could squeeze the maximum return from the surrounding land. In effect it was allowed to build at will.

The result abandoned all customary curbs on density or demands for more than token affordable housing. The site was crammed with slabs and walls of luxury flats, at times obliterating views of the power station itself. The overdevelopment was supposedly mitigated by using starchitects for the residences, with facades by Frank Gehry and Norman Foster. Thoroughfares were named after Malaysian cities in the hope of attracting overseas money. London's mayor Boris Johnson even travelled to Kuala Lumpur to help sell the flats. The use of London buildings so blatantly as depositories for foreign cash bordered on the obscene. Together with the adjacent Nine Elms tower cluster, the district was the closest a European city came to modern Hong Kong.

A second mega-development lacked even a derelict power station to lend it character. The industrial wasteland of Stratford in east London was cleared in 2012 for the Olympic Games. Olympic sites are usually blighted by the near impossibility of feasible reuse. In Stratford a 'legacy authority' was appointed to handle regeneration. A proposal to integrate the site with the streets of neighbouring Hackney was rejected, though it would have housed thousands and recouped some of the Games' £13 billion cost. Instead the authority became obsessed with finding a purpose for architecture rather than architecture for a purpose.

Stratford's Olympic stadium was eventually donated to West Ham football club, whose fans complained that they must watch their team from a distance across what had been a running track. There was also a 'helter-skelter' and a swimming pool by Hadid. Only the 'athletes' village' was swiftly converted and sold as a housing estate. An attempt was then made to render the development creative with some top-down sponsorship. Sites were donated to the V&A, the BBC, Sadler's Wells and University College London. It was noticeable that the most prominent new architecture of the twenty-first century tended to be for museums, galleries and theatres rather than houses, hospitals and schools. In eighteenth-century terms culture was the new aristocracy.

One new project that was a success was for the renewal of the railway goods yards at London's King's Cross. Here an early proposal for a 'new town' was rejected and conservationist pressure led to the retention of the old canal basin, warehouses, gasholders and a so-called German gymnasium. This fusion of old and new by the architects Allies and Morrison was then developed piecemeal. The warehouses were first a 'pop-up' university of the arts, which swiftly brought people and activity to the canal area. The gasworks became flats and the old 'coal-drops' sheds a shopping street, deftly converted by the designer Thomas Heatherwick. Even a nature reserve was created.

The south of the site behind King's Cross was the price that had to be paid, an overdeveloped cluster of office blocks. They were supposedly mitigated as at Battersea by the use of star architects, such as David Chipperfield, Demetri Porphyrios and John McAslan. This created what became a high-rise 'cold zone' between the station and the canalside. Yet the prominence of the canal area rescued the project and gave the neighbourhood a personality that was undeniably popular. Modern architecture and planning had got the point.

Elsewhere opportunities were missed. Cardiff in the 2000s could have located Wales's new Senedd building by Richard Rogers and its opera house next to its century-old civic centre. It would have composed a fitting architectural grouping for a national capital. Instead assembly and opera house were exiled to the docks, two miles away. More successful was Scotland's new parliament (1999), designed by a Spaniard, Enric Miralles. By fracturing its various components across the site, it slotted relatively unobtrusively between the old town and Holyrood palace.

Most noticeable about British architecture from the 2010s onwards was a change in its tone of voice. An uneasy marriage of modernism and conservation had bedded down and could be seen in the ubiquitous architectural prize lists. In the 1990s and early 2000s the shortlists for the RIBA's annual Stirling Prize were dominated by spectacle buildings, often for well-funded arts and university institutions. With the 2010s they became more contextual. In what was dubbed the 'new eclecticism', judges praised the restoration of medieval Astley Castle, Damien Hirst's gallery in a converted Vauxhall street and a Lake District jetty museum.

These were discreet rather than ostentatious works, the successful adaptation of a building or setting to a new use.

In 2019 the prize caused a stir when it went to a new council estate in Norwich, Goldsmith Street, composed of a streetscape of terraces, modern in style but traditional in plan. The streets were not wide and were overlooked by front doors and windows, Jane Jacobs's 'eyes in the street'. By Mikhail Riches and Cathy Hawley, Goldsmith Street was a true attempt to recapture the virtues of neighbourhood architecture. This revival was promoted in 2013 by the Create Streets consultancy of Nicholas Boys Smith, unsuccessful bidder for a network of residential streets at Mount Pleasant in Clerkenwell. Laid out round a resurfaced River Fleet, it would have been at a higher density than the conventional slabs that were eventually built, yet traditional in plan. The very concept of a new street was still toxic to British town planners.

Equally significant was the number of times the Stirling Prize went to a Maggie's Centre for terminal cancer patients. Commissioned by Charles Jencks from leading architects in memory of his late wife, the one requirement was that each centre should be small, of just a few rooms. Jencks wanted to forestall modernism's occupational disease of bigness. The result was a collection of some twenty-five minor masterpieces from Foster, Rogers, Gehry, Hadid, Gough, Ted Cullinan, Richard MacCormac and others. Each was a gem mostly of postmodern design, of architecture in tune with its users. The centres formed a modest gallery of British twenty-first-century design.

The 1960s utopians did not go down without a final fight. In the early 2000s a coalition of northern councillors, planners and building contractors convinced housing minister John Prescott to donate £2.2 billion of taxpayers' money for the clearance of remaining run-down areas to use as 'land-banks' for future rebuilding. The project was tastelessly named Pathfinder, after Bomber

The Age of Spectacle (1986–2020)

Command's wartime targeting German cities. An extraordinary tally of 100,000 houses were slated for demolition, but with no money allocated for rebuilding.

After a burst of public opposition, the programme was abandoned in 2011, a Whitehall statement explicitly condemning 'bulldozing of buildings, knocking down neighbourhoods and pitting neighbour against neighbour, with people trapped in abandoned streets'. It was a bizarre comment on half a century of Whitehall's own policy. Yet £70 million of 'transitional' money survived to complete existing schemes, a third of it going to Liverpool's Welsh Streets in Toxteth. This area, originally of some 10,000 houses, had been designed in the late nineteenth century for Welsh immigrants, many in tidy grids, some even tree-lined. Houses that in London would be snapped up for restoration were dismissed by the council as 'obsolete . . . relentless rows for Welsh navvies'. Years of council evictions had rendered the area a ghost town, though one house left standing was the early home of the Beatle Ringo Starr. One street was used as a film set for the television series *Peaky Blinders*.

Battle ensued and eventually the council, which had spent £21 million amassing properties in the neighbourhood, sold the lot to a local developer for £1. A number of councillors were later arrested on suspicion of corruption. Survivors such as Madryn and Powis Streets were restored and a characteristic part of Liverpool's heritage was rescued. Welsh Streets won architectural prizes and tourist buses visited Starr's birthplace, but they still compose a sad memorial. It was the last gasp of a policy that had for half a century wreaked havoc across Britain's Victorian cities.

This concept of architectural fusion, of the built environment as a marriage of past and future, was reflected in new visions of the city. Two urbanists, America's Edward Glaeser and Canada's Richard Florida, offered contrasting perspectives. To Glaeser the issue was sustainability. Big modern inner-city spaces such as

Manhattan should be the new capitals of green living. Their residential densities were high, infrastructure was intensively used and journeys to work were short and energy efficient. To Glaeser, people should be encouraged to live, if not in Manhattan, then efficiently in close proximity to as many other people as possible.

Clearly, more density meant taller buildings. In practice the quantity of floor-space in a metropolis had little to do with height, more with street width and need for open spaces, at least outside the crammed megalopolises of east Asia. British cities are famously low density. Inner Paris, its streets relatively low-rise, has a population density four times that of inner London, for all the latter's towers. The average British household has 4.7 rooms, far above the European average. This is largely the result of low-density suburbs and regressive property taxes with no incentive to downsize. In Britain, 80 per cent of homes also have gardens, against 58 per cent in France and 27 per cent in Spain. One survey had London so tree-filled it was classified ecologically as 'forest'.

By the 2020s urban think tanks such as the Centre for London and the Centre for Cities were advocating 'gentle densification'. London's densest populations were concentrated not in tower estates but in the crowded terraces and mansion flats of west and north London. The developer Ben Derbyshire pointed out that if all London had been built at the density of Victorian Islington it could have doubled its population. Gentle densification undoubtedly meant confronting strong defenders of the sylvan suburbs. But frequent studies, such as one in 2013 by the London estate agents Stirling Ackroyd, concluded that merely by building on vacant, mostly former industrial sites, a million more Londoners could be housed in the capital. Similar studies of Manhattan have reached the same conclusion.

Florida's message was different, directed at the nature of these inhabitants. To him, the future economy of prosperous cities lay in activities broadly defined as creative, stretching from tourism, entertainment and leisure to design, marketing and digital technology. These new uses were those most likely to interest bright young people, 'the human capital which in turn attracts innovative, technology-based industries'. The cliché holds that it was the hippies who brought high-tech to California. Such people respond in turn to what Florida called 'street-level culture'. They were particularly drawn to the 'bohemian enclaves' that live on in most though not all of the world's big cities. For all its cost of living, London has the youngest working population of any city in Britain.

Creating such 'bohemian' enclaves has proved phenomenally difficult, the reason being that they must be left to create themselves. They tend to develop in areas that have outlived their original purpose, but where older buildings survive and are flexible to new uses. They were New York's Soho and Tribeca, San Francisco's Castro and Haight-Ashbury. In Britain they have proved to be London's Shoreditch and Bermondsey, Manchester's Northern Quarter and Birmingham's Jewellery Quarter. These areas are not smart but 'cool'. When I walked with Bradford's chief executive round the sadly boarded-up Victorian buildings of her city centre, I asked what was her dream. She said it was to make Bradford 'the Shoreditch of Leeds'. It was the right dream, even if its realization seems sadly distant.

These activities require the recognition and preservation of the urban street in all its variety. The biggest disaster for much of urban Britain has been to see it in thrall to the shopping malls fashionable in late-twentieth-century America. In the 1980s these malls dragged shoppers away from town centres to their outskirts, to bypasses and the surrounding country, leaving high streets emptying behind them. Thatcherism favoured out-of-town, car-borne shopping, producing Sheffield's Meadowhall (1990) and Dartford's Bluewater (1998). The Blair government in the 2000s switched back to 're-urbanization', with Bristol's Cabot

Circus and Shepherd's Bush's Westfield (2008). But these too were inflexible sites, while each policy shift disrupted businesses and traumatized shoppers and retailers alike.

In America, shopping malls were soon experiencing serial collapse. A 2022 survey showed that of 2,500 trading in 1980 just 700 were still doing serious business, the rest lying blighted and empty. In Britain the same year it was estimated that 250 malls had closed or were at risk, possibly amounting to half of those built since the 1960s. The fault lay not, at least initially, in online shopping but in failing to understand that shoppers preferred a familiar and granular street environment in the open air. In other words, the architecture mattered.

The most successful food market in London is not in a mall or even a supermarket. It is Southwark's Borough Market. Created as a charity in the ruins of an old greengrocery depot, it draws a phenomenal twenty million visitors a year, more than the Tower of London opposite. Composed of railway arches, wooden stalls, alleys and side streets, it is informal architecture of a high order – the very essence of a street economy. Likewise in the 2010s, Altrincham in Cheshire faced the decline of its town-centre mall. It reconditioned and reopened its old Victorian market hall and spilled it out into the main street. The market boomed.

It is astonishing that British planning in the 2000s – given the history of its experience since the war – could have given so little thought to the psychological interaction of buildings and their users. Copious research has been undertaken into the relationship between architecture and mental health, at least in the case of hospital design. It should extend far beyond that. The Urban Realities laboratory at Canada's Waterloo University has delved into different streetscapes. It has studied their complexity (and greenery) in arousing interest and pleasure in those experiencing them. Architecture must become human-centred if we are to enjoy what the lab calls 'psychologically sustainable cities'.

The Age of Spectacle (1986–2020)

A similar conclusion was reached by the designer Thomas Heatherwick in his refreshing diatribe against modernism, *Humanise* (2023). He investigated how a person's appreciation of a building can be measured biometrically by the time they spend walking past it, by what they notice and by the pleasure indicators registered in the brain. Heatherwick complained that so many buildings could only be described as boring. A rewarding building or street should have variety, decorative interest and pavement activity. Heatherwick called for radical attention to be paid to how people 'use' a building, which can mean no more than walking past it.

For a building simply to hit the ground in a wall of concrete, as so many modern edifices do, should be a planning offence. I used to watch the pavement round New Zealand House at the foot of Haymarket, surely the bleakest patch of architecture in London. I noticed that people do not walk past it, let alone tarry, they scurry. It is so toxic that Nash's beautiful Royal Opera Arcade immediately to its rear has fallen deserted. An architect once told me that he knew a building had fallen short if it needed to disguise its ground floor with a bank of evergreen bushes.

That is why, if new architecture fails to excite us, we must value the old. This may be getting easier. A new generation must face the fact that the construction industry has become the villain of climate change. It reputedly contributes 40 per cent of harmful global emissions. Hence building conservation is shifting its reference from architecture to the environment. A battle in 2023 over the proposed demolition of Marks and Spencer's store in London's Oxford Street turned not on its aesthetic qualities but on its 'embodied carbon'. Similar considerations may be the salvation of hundreds of surviving north country mills. The agency Historic England has calculated that 42,000 homes could be created out of former northern mills currently lying empty.

In 2015 another newcomer arrived on the architectural stage:

artificial intelligence. That year the consultants McKinsey identified construction as the least efficient modern American industry. California's Silicon Valley promptly became a hotbed of digital design. From self-built and self-powered houses to 3D-printed facades, bespoke rooms, craft robotics and decoration, AI promised not just a revolution in methodology; it also proved peculiarly suited to retrofitting. In 2019, Google announced that it could produce 15,000 new and 'affordable' homes in the Bay Area of San Francisco by converting existing and disused buildings with the help of AI.

From that it can only be a short step to machines taking over building sites and robots dancing attendance on owners' instruction. If the world is ready for self-drive cars it must be ready for self-build houses. The only question is how far they will need architects. Indeed, will there be anything left that could truly be called architecture?

22.

Conclusion: Full Shard Ahead

In early 2023 I found myself on a train that was crawling slowly over the viaducts of south London as it left Victoria station. The inner fringes of Europe's great cities are seldom pretty, but most have a sort of coherence. They display some conceptual plan, of straight roads and formal zones of housing, shopping and commerce. Until the Second World War, south London was similar. It was formed of a carpet of modest streets, Georgian architecture merging into Victorian, graced with the spires and ornamental towers of public buildings. This was the south London I knew as a boy, when I rode much the same route on a No. 2 bus to visit my grandparents near Crystal Palace. It was similar to most British cities, a pattern usually of inner Victorian and outer twentieth-century suburbs, with their centres defined by a cluster of nineteenth-century commercial, civic and church buildings.

Such British cities are now mostly in the past. The London I saw from my train had no character or style. Each hundred yards might consist of a fractured Georgian terrace, an Italianate villa, a Victorian library, a 1950s council block or a 'spectacular' luxury tower. Roofs rose and fell at random, streets opened and then vanished, building heights obeyed no by-law. As townscape it was a shambles. Yet I could not bring myself to dislike it. It was a mess, but a mess of absorbing interest, a happening city. It was incorrigibly London, the city I have persisted in loving all my life.

There was one all too prominent novelty: the array of towers thrusting their fingers into the sky. These towers did not cluster, as is customary in the planning of cities. They rose wherever a planning committee had been bullied or bribed into approving one. What I was seeing was the collapse of any strategy for the visual appearance of the capital over the past half century. Instead I saw a city in three parts. One was a series of conservation areas of Georgian and Victorian architecture, bruised but curated enclaves that I assume are now fixed for all of time. The second part was the scattered eruptions of postwar blocks and slabs of council housing, relics of the modernist gigantism of the 1960s and 70s. The third part was the spaces in between, oases of planning anarchy, where developers, architects and councils had fought to win some blend of ostentation and profit. The most noticeable ostentation of all was the tower.

Towers in Britain had become detached from normal planning. A tower is an architectural form unlike any other. Low-rise buildings merely impinge on their neighbours. They may determine the visual composition of a terrace or a square but not of the wider townscape. Above some fifteen storeys a tower is different. It looms above its surrounding streets and open spaces. Above twenty storeys it forms a defining feature of a town or city. This means that if to one viewer it can enhance a skyline, to another it can deface it. While its absence can hardly cause offence, its presence most certainly can. The balance of architectural pleasure and pain is asymmetrical. In addition, allowing one large building increases the precedent for another.

As the erection of towers became ever easier towards the end of the twentieth century, almost all European cities reached a consensus. Historic neighbourhoods were to be guarded enclaves as legacies of the past. The centres of Italian cities were rigidly protected. France's culture minister in the 1960s, André Malraux, created *secteurs sauvegardés*, or conserved zones. Such zones had a collective value and were appreciated as such by residents and tourists alike. They were not to have sheets of glass or towers of concrete looming over them, certainly not close to. Such zones became common throughout Europe, as in Rome, Paris, Amsterdam, Vienna or Barcelona can see the result. In historic districts, intrusive towers are kept at a distance unlike in Britain's more modest conservation areas.

In London the concept of the cluster held tenuously through the 1960s. Buildings above a dozen storeys were mostly confined to the City of London's north-east quarter, with another cluster in Croydon. As we have seen, this zoning was eroded not out of any aesthetic judgement or civic significance, but through the corruption, however defined, of planning-committee decisions. Britain's cities lost control of their skylines. There were no public consultations or referenda. Towers were thought somehow intrinsic to the future of urban living.

London's most conspicuous new commercial development in the 1980s was proposed at Canary Wharf on the Isle of Dogs. What had been emerging as a bohemian quarter of east London was swept aside in a burst of Thatcherite laissez-faire. The new Canary Wharf included Britain's tallest office block, One Canada Square, designed in 1988 by the American architect César Pelli. The market did not respond to this magnet and Canary Wharf went bankrupt in 1992.

The project was on the brink of abandonment when John Major's Tory government rushed to the rescue. A splurge of public spending – probably the most ever committed to what was a private-property development – saw tax breaks and extravagant outlays on infrastructure. The Limehouse tunnel was the most costly stretch of road reputedly in Europe, while a start was made on the new Jubilee Line extension, jumping three places up London Transport's priority list. It was a testament to the power of public investment that Canary Wharf did as a result recover and stagger on to prosperity.

Although by the 1980s high rise was no longer considered suitable for family housing, or even for modern offices needing big floor plates, it came into fashion for luxury flats. They were popular for singles or couples as a first step on the housing ladder or for second homes in town. They were also popular investments for foreign savings of dubious origin. At one point a third of all residential towers in London were reportedly overseas-owned. A Chinese-financed tower in Canning Town had not even fitted out its interiors ten years after its construction. By the start of the twenty-first-century luxury towers were booming. London had 150 towers of thirty storeys (a hundred metres) or more on its skyline, with a reported 400 in the pipeline. Not one was for housing the poor.

The towers came to have a powerful appeal to a new breed of civic leader, notably Tony Blair's new cohort of elected mayors arriving in 2000. Each saw skyscrapers as a symbol of civic potency, so much so that Deyan Sudjic's *Edifice Complex* described modern architecture as 'the unsubtle symbolism of being the biggest or the tallest and so the most important'. It had driven Kuala Lumpur, Shanghai, New York, Chicago and Dubai to seek ever higher buildings. To Sudjic, a tower 'glorified and magnified the individual autocrat and suppressed the individual into the mass'.

The first elected mayor of London, Ken Livingstone, empowered to plan or reject tall buildings. Though of the far-left, he was no exception. He had a fixation that his metropolis should be made to 'look more like Manhattan'. He would shout at planning meetings, 'higher, higher', and claimed his towers would be half filled with council tenants. As he must have known, they would be filled, if at all, with the very rich. A block on the City fringe was sold almost entirely to Chinese buyers for their offspring should they come to university in London. It was believed that the increase in the value of a flat equalled the sum of college fees.

The result was a rush of inner London boroughs to chase tall buildings and the local tax revenue they offered. The City of London abandoned all idea of clustering away from the Thames. Most aggressive was the Chinese-funded 'Walkie-Talkie' by Rafael Viñoly, allowed to rise next to the Monument and bulging in its middle to allow extra floor-space. Universally regarded as ugly, it dominated once-protected views of Tower Bridge and St Paul's. The City then broke its own ban on a 'curtain' of high buildings behind St Paul's with its most overpowering skyscraper, 22 Bishopsgate. The planners hid their shame by giving towers joke names – Cheese grater, Scalpel, Can of Ham, Gherkin – but the Bishopsgate tower defied even that disguise.

Livingstone's successor, Boris Johnson, had been against the towers when in opposition – 'I want no Dubai-on-Thames,' he pledged. Yet in office he was bitten by the same bug as Livingstone. Though he claimed to have turned many down, he permitted over a hundred towers to rise above thirty storeys, ostensibly at random. Charting the changing London skyline during this period, the critic Rowan Moore reflected on the Athenian oath that required citizens to leave their city more beautiful than they found it. Johnson had been 'more like Nero, fiddling with vanity projects while it burned with clumsy overdevelopments . . . bloated, bulging and light-blocking'.

London was not alone. Manchester boasted in 2004 that its Beetham Tower was 'the highest residential building outside London'. At forty-seven storeys it dominated the conserved Deansgate. This was followed in 2016 at nearby Deansgate Square by a four-tower cluster, the tallest being a giant of sixty-four storeys. In 2018 a forty-storey tower was proposed on the site of Manchester's synagogue, crushing the city centre's conservation area. Publicity backing was obtained from Manchester footballers Ryan Giggs and Gary Neville. By 2022 the city was under siege from thirty-two towers either built or under construction. There was no plan for where they should or should not go.

Other cities were running behind. Birmingham in 2022 had thirteen towers of 100 metres or thirty storeys, either built or building. Leeds had three. Norwich tried to erect a tower to rival its cathedral, stopped only by a public outcry. Planners in the west London suburb of Ealing allowed a fifty-four-storey skyscraper to overshadow a neighbourhood of semi-detached villas and side streets, boasted as the 'tallest residential tower outside Canary Wharf'.

In 2002 competitive tower building found its apotheosis. A successful East End retailer named Irvine Sellar sought to seal his career with an aggressively public structure. He would build the biggest tower in Europe. In 1998 he had acquired a plot of land in Bermondsey that Railtrack, owner of London Bridge station, and Southwark Council were hoping to redevelop. He summoned an Italian architect, Renzo Piano, who had collaborated with Richard Rogers on the Pompidou Centre in Paris. They announced what they called a 'shard of glass', to soar over the City of London across the Thames at London Bridge.

In most cities such a structure would have been the source of major public debate. In London, Sellar felt he had merely to request approval from planners and it would come. To any inquiry he claimed that the Shard's tapering outline 'reflected London's maritime heritage'. He said it would shimmer and float like a sail. Or perhaps, said Piano, it would soar 'like a sixteenth-century pinnacle or rise like one of Wren's City church towers'. Southwark Council and Mayor Livingstone gave enthusiastic endorsement to this hotchpotch.

By the financial collapse of 2008, the Shard project was bankrupt. It was rescued, like half of London's big projects at the time, by foreign money, this time from Qatar. The opening in 2013 was attended by massed ranks of Qatari royalty. Britain was represented by Prince Andrew and Boris Johnson. The latter compared it to St Paul's Cathedral and Big Ben.

Conclusion: Full Shard Ahead

The Shard was by far the most prominent tower I could see from my railway carriage. It stood on its own in what had been a low-rise quarter of the capital, where it made no pretence of fusion with its surroundings. It did not sit in a park, like Paris's Eiffel Tower. At one point the owners' courage clearly faltered. Pictures advertising the tower showed the Georgian buildings of neighbouring Guy's Hospital far more prominent in the foreground, as if to reassure potential tenants this was not Dubai. As for being the highest tower in Europe, it was soon beaten by Sellar's rival in egotism, Vladimir Putin, and his tower in St Petersburg.

The Shard regularly features in polls of London's 'top buildings'. Few people actively dislike it and I do not dislike it myself. Its shape, rising to a pointed 'bishop's mitre' crown, is unusual and elegant. The Shard has the virtue of a spire. It honours the space it pierces rather than merely occupying it. It is certainly outlandish, an alien import deposited as if by accident in its corner of London, celebrating Qatar as much as Sellar. But we should recognize that this has been the story of this sort of British architecture down the ages, of buildings intended to instil awe, celebrate individuals and display wealth.

The beauty of a building in itself is one thing. One of the most telling views in London is of the Shard from neighbouring Borough Market, its alleys jammed with London's humanity at work and play. The market's crowds can just see the entrance to the Shard, 200 yards down London Bridge Street. Its frigid glass facade rises from a deserted podium of concrete, empty and lifeless. The view is from a London that attracts thousands to one that is occupied by two security guards and a demand for £32 for entry. All I know is that one of these buildings belongs in London, the other does not.

I still find it hard to persuade people that, had it not been for the counter-revolution of the 1970s, Britain's cities would have looked more like the Shard than like Borough Market. At one point,

London was to lose Piccadilly Circus, Whitehall, Covent Garden and much of its West End. Tens, possibly hundreds, of thousands of houses would have fallen to urban ringways. Planning ideology recited Le Corbusier, claiming that European cities were obsolete and should be cleared and rebuilt. That was the plan. It might have been democratic in that it was decided by elected politicians. But it defied democracy in being done in collusion with an elitist and introverted profession and without participation by its consumers, the citizens of Britain. As George Bernard Shaw had declared, all professions are conspiracies against the laity.

As to whether the prospect was really as extreme as I have described, I can only answer yes. Such utopianism was happening across the world, especially under communist regimes. I saw with my own eyes the bulldozers demolishing the beautiful centre of Bucharest in Romania. I stood with Chinese party officials as they flattened the exquisite old quarter of Chengdu. I witnessed the clearances of Lancashire's Hulme and London's Barbican and Stepney. The Bruce plan for Glasgow and the Shankland plan for Liverpool are there for anyone to read. By 1980, over 30,000 houses had been destroyed in Liverpool to no purpose beyond one of ideology.

Alain de Botton in his study of the relationship of architecture to happiness reflected on how 'a few people, neither particularly sinful nor malevolent' and who 'may love golf and animals', could 'substantially ruin a landscape for 300 years or more'. Cultural banality might produce nothing more harmful than a poor novel or a rotten play, but in architecture it was allowed to, according to de Botton, 'leave wounds which will be visible from outer space'. On much of this era, British architectural history has been conspiratorially silent.

British architecture is now less arrogant. It is more humble and it is safer. Across Britain it is showing that new buildings can be beautiful and considerate of their surroundings. Architects are more concerned with the entirety of place-making and the role that old buildings should play in it. They are also more aware of the costs of construction to the environment and the use of energy. This is all good news.

Good also is that arguments over style have not altogether vanished. Many people find modernism exciting and tall buildings also. Let them make their case to those who do not, as both must share the outcome of their disagreement. Variety and eclecticism remain, witness the popularity of self-build housing programmes on TV. Council-built estates have all but ceased, but they have been replaced by less prominent charitable housing associations. In the private sector, 'stripped' Georgian and Tudorbethan still proliferate, as can be seen in the speculative estates that sprang up round Midlands and south-eastern towns in the 2010s. Their style can seem less aggressive than of old, even if it can be no less boring.

Architecture in the 1950s and 60s was able to give Britain an almighty fright largely because too few people knew what was going on. They were told their surroundings had to change in a particular direction and they believed it. They were hoodwinked. That is why architecture should now be ruthlessly debated. It is engineering as an art form of supreme concern to the happiness of everyone. Its decisions should never be left to a coterie of architects and planners.

The subject should be taught in schools and colleges. New buildings should be reviewed, projects publicized and planning decisions discussed in a media forum. My dream is that people's eyes will be opened instinctively to their surroundings. They might then notice the buildings they pass and understand why they look as they do, causing them to ponder a classical order, a Gothic arch, a clash of styles or a change of texture. I want people to point at buildings, laugh, cry or get angry. I want them to hate and to love what they see. I want them to speak architecture.

Glossary

acanthus: thick-veined leaves forming a Corinthian column *capital*
arcade: colonnade of columns and arches, as separating the aisles of a church nave; 'blind' if attached to a wall
basilica: Roman hall, aisled to form a rectangular church
battlemented: castellated parapet to a wall with indentations
buttress: vertical support for a wall; 'flying' if over an arch
capital: crowning feature of a column, see *orders*
chancel: east end of church beyond *crossing*, traditionally set aside for clergy
chantry: private chapel usually for named beneficiary
chapter house: ceremonial chamber for diocesan meetings
chevron: V-shaped motif, usually on Romanesque arch
choir: part of church where services are sung, usually within *chancel*
clerestory: top storey of nave beneath roof, pierced with windows
cloister: roofed colonnade enclosing a square
crossing: part of church at junction of nave, transepts and *chancel*
deck: pedestrian walkway giving access to elevated flats
dormer window: window projecting from the slope of a roof
entablature: horizontal strip on top of a wall or colonnade, composed of architrave, frieze and cornice
gable: usually triangular feature on top of wall or window, commonly breaking into a roof
hipped roof: roof pitched at the ends as well as sides
lancet: slender, pointed-arch, single-light window without *tracery*
lierne: cross rib linking main ribs in a vaulted roof
loggia: usually colonnaded gallery attached to side of building

Glossary

misericord: shelf under seat of *choir* stall, for rest during long periods of standing
ogee: double curved arch, concave then convex
orders: classical *capitals* are fashioned into one of five orders: three Greek – Doric, Ionic, Corinthian – and two Roman – Tuscan and Composite
pediment: triangular *gable*, forming a portico if above columns
pilaster: classical column flattened in relief against a wall
podium: continuous platform supporting a building
portico: row of columns beneath a *pediment*
presbytery: part of church east of *choir*, usually round altar
rendering: covering of walls for protection or decoration, as with stucco, plaster or cement
reredos: screen behind altar
retrochoir: east end of church behind *choir*
rustication: exaggerated joins of wall masonry to suggest strength
slab: horizontal block usually of multi-storey modernist housing
strapwork: decorative feature of Renaissance facade, as of leather
tracery: decorative ribs in Gothic window
trefoil: pattern of *tracery* formed of three leaves, hence quatrefoil, etc.
triforium: windowless middle storey of church roof below *clerestory*
trilithon: two uprights with a lintel on top

Further Reading

The following books are editions cited in the text or used as sources. I have not included every biography consulted.

General

Bayley, Stephen, *Taste: The Secret Meaning of Things*, 1992
Bell, Colin and Rose, *City Fathers: The Early History of Town Planning in Britain*, 1972
Clifton-Taylor, Alec, *The Pattern of English Building*, 1987
Colvin, Howard, *Essays in English Architectural History*, 1999
de Botton, Alain, *The Architecture of Happiness*, 2006
Florida, Richard, *The New Urban Crisis*, 2017
Gloag, John, *The English Tradition in Architecture*, 1963
Jacobs, Jane, *The Death and Life of Great American Cities*, 1961
Scott, Geoffrey, *The Architecture of Humanism*, 1914
Service, Alastair, *The Architects of London*, 1979
Summerson, John, *The Classical Language of Architecture*, 1963
Thurley, Simon, *The Building of England*, 2013
Watkin, David, *Morality and Architecture*, 1977
———, *English Architecture: A Concise History*, 1979

Early, Medieval and Tudor

Braun, Hugh, *An Introduction to English Medieval Architecture*, 1968

Further Reading

Brook, Christopher and Gillian Keir, *London 800–1216: The Shaping of a City*, 1975
Brown, R. J., *English Village Architecture*, 2004
Cook, Olive and Edwin Smith, *English Cathedrals*, 1989
Girouard, Mark, *Elizabethan Architecture*, 2009
———, *A Biographical Dictionary of English Architecture, 1540–1640*, 2021
Goodall, John, *The English Castle*, 2011
Harvey, John, *English Medieval Architects*, 1954
Hill, Rosemary, *Stonehenge*, 2008
Musson, Jeremy, *The English Manor House*, 1999
Pevsner, Nikolaus, *The Leaves of Southwell*, 1945
Rowley, Trevor, *Norman England*, 1997
Thomas, Christopher, *The Archaeology of Medieval London*, 2002

Stuart and Georgian

Barczewski, Stephanie, *How the Country House Became English*, 2023
Crook, J. Mordaunt, *The Greek Revival*, 1972
Cruickshank, Dan, *A Guide to the Georgian Buildings of Britain & Ireland*, 1985
Jenkins, Simon, *Landlords to London: A Capital and Its Growth*, 1975
Macaulay, James, *The Gothic Revival: 1745–1845*, 1975
———, *The Classical Country House in Scotland, 1680–1800*, 1987
Summerson, John, *Architecture in Britain, 1530–1830*, 1953
———, *Georgian London*, 1962
———, *Inigo Jones*, 1966
Thorold, Peter, *The London Rich*, 2000
White, Jerry, *London in the 18th Century*, 2012
Worsley, Giles, *Classical Architecture in Britain*, 1995

Further Reading

Victorian

Barratt, Nick, *Greater London: The Story of the Suburbs*, 2012
Brockman, H. A. N., *The British Architect in Industry, 1841–1940*, 1974
Crook, J. Mordaunt, *The Dilemma of Style*, 1987
Davis, Terence, *The Gothick Taste*, 1974
Edwards, Arthur, *The Design of Suburbia*, 1981
Girouard, Mark, *The Victorian Country House*, 1971
———, *Sweetness and Light*, 1977
Jones, Anthony, *Welsh Chapels*, 1996
Jones, Edgar, *Industrial Architecture in Britain, 1750–1939*, 1985
Kynaston, David, *The City of London*, 2011
Olsen, Donald, *The Growth of Victorian London*, 1976
Picard, Liza, *Victorian London*, 2005
Porter, Bernard, *The Battle of the Styles*, 2011
Stamp, Gavin, *Gothic for the Steam Age*, 2015
White, Jerry, *London in the 19th Century*, 2016

Edwardian and Interwar

Hillier, Bevis, *The Style of the Century*, 1983
———, *Art Deco Style*, 1997
Jackson, Alan, *Semi-Detached London*, 1973
Jencks, Charles, *Le Corbusier and the Tragic View of Architecture*, 1973
Oliver, Paul, Ian Davis and Ian Bentley, *Dunroamin: The Suburban Semi and Its Enemies*, 1981
Pevsner, Nikolaus, *Pioneers of the Modern Movement*, 1936
Service, Alastair, *Edwardian Architecture and Its Origins*, 1975
Stamp, Gavin, *Interwar: British Architecture, 1919–39*, 2024
White, Jerry, *London in the 20th Century*, 2008
Williams-Ellis, Clough, *England and the Octopus*, 1928

Further Reading

Modern

Abercrombie, Patrick, *The Proud City* (documentary film), 1946 – available on YouTube

Anson, Brian, *I'll Fight You for It! Behind the Struggle for Covent Garden*, 1981

Banham, Reyner, *The Age of the Masters*, 1975

Boughton, John, *Municipal Dreams: The Rise and Fall of Council Housing*, 2019

Christensen, Terry, *Neighbourhood Survival: The Struggle for Covent Garden's Future*, 1979

Crosby, Theo, *How to Play the Environment Game*, 1973

Curl, James Stevens, *Making Dystopia*, 2018

de Graaf, Reinier, *architect, verb: The New Language of Building*, 2023

Dean, David, *The Thirties: Recalling the English Architectural Scene*, 1983

Dyckhoff, Tom, *The Age of Spectacle*, 2017

Elkin, Stephen, *Politics and Land Use Planning*, 1974

Esher, Lionel, *A Broken Wave: The Rebuilding of England, 1940–1980*, 1981

Hanley, Lynsey, *Estates: An Intimate History*, 2007

Harwood, Elain, *Space, Hope and Brutalism*, 2015

Hatherley, Owen, *Militant Modernism*, 2009

——, *A Guide to the New Ruins of Great Britain*, 2010

——, *A New Kind of Bleak: Journeys through Urban Britain*, 2012

——, *Modern Buildings in Britain*, 2023

Heatherwick, Thomas, *Humanise: A Maker's Guide to Building Our World*, 2023

Jencks, Charles, *Modern Movements in Architecture*, 1973

——, *The Language of Post-Modern Architecture*, 1977

Jones, Adrian and Chris Matthews, *Towns in Britain*, 2014

Marriott, Oliver, *The Property Boom*, 1967

Minton, Anna, *Ground Control: Fear and Happiness in the Twenty-First-Century City*, 2009

Moore, Rowan, *Why We Build*, 2012

Further Reading

———, *Slow Burn City: London in the Twenty-First Century*, 2016
Nairn, Ian, *Nairn's Towns*, ed. Owen Hatherley, 2013
Powell, Kenneth, *New London Architecture*, 2001
Powers, Alan, *Modern: The Modern Movement in Britain*, 2005
Powers, Alan and Elain Harwood, *The Seventies: Rediscovering a Lost Decade*, 2012
Rykwert, Joseph, *The Seduction of Place: The City in the Twenty-First Century*, 2000
Saumarez Smith, Otto, *Boom Cities*, 2019
Scott, Peter, *The Property Masters: A History of the British Commercial Property Sector*, 2015
Sinclair, Iain, *Lights Out for the Territory*, 2003
Sudjic, Deyan, *The Edifice Complex: How the Rich and Powerful Shape the World*, 2005
Wolfe, Tom, *From Bauhaus to Our House*, 1981
Wright, Patrick, *A Journey through Ruins*, 1991

Acknowledgements

This book arose from a lifetime's fascination with buildings. It began with my early time on *Country Life* and continued with my work with English Heritage, the National Trust, SAVE Britain's heritage and the Twentieth Century Society. I can only thank collectively the fellow enthusiasts whom I have met over the years and on whose work I have drawn. Many are mentioned in the Further Reading section.

At Viking/Penguin, the inspiration for a short history of British architecture came from Daniel Crewe and my editor Connor Brown. I must thank John Goodall, Jeremy Musson and Matthew Walker for their comments on my text, as well as Tony Travers, Tom Jenkins and my wife Hannah Kaye for reading it in whole or in part. I must also thank my copy-editor Trevor Horwood as well as Penguin's Natalie Wall, Roseanna Battle, Fran Monteiro and Sara Granger. Cecilia Mackay was, as ever, the impresario of the pictures.

As will be apparent in the concluding chapters, the book was stimulated in part by a sense that historians have not done justice to the saga of British architecture in the late-twentieth century. In particular, they have been too timid to address its controversies and failures. That said, I would appreciate any corrections or comments drawn to my attention through Penguin.

Index

A303 (road) 11, 13
Aachen (Germany) 20
Abelard, Peter 31
Abercrombie, Sir Patrick 201–4, 208, 209, 210, 211, 212, 224, 231, 233
Adam, James 103, 107
Adam, John 102, 103, 107
Adam, Robert 5, 102–5, 106, 107, 108, 113
Adam, William 102–3
Adams, H. Percy 178, 189
Addison Act (1919) 179, 180
Aethelbert, King of Kent 20
Age of Saints 20
AI (artificial intelligence) 153, 258
Alan of Walsingham 45
Albemarle, Christopher Monck, 2nd Duke of 86
Albert, Prince consort 143, 144
Aldburgh family 57
All Souls College, Oxford 80, 92
Allies and Morrison (architects' practice) 250–51
Alnwick Castle (Northumberland) 49, 105
Alton Towers and Castle (Staffordshire) 139
Altrincham (Cheshire) 256
Amersham (Buckinghamshire): High and Over 197
Amesbury (Wiltshire) 12
Amiens Cathedral (France) 37, 41
Ammonite order 122

Amsterdam 261
Andrew, Prince, Duke of York 264
Anglo-French entente (1904) 166
Anne, Queen 90, 91, 93
Anne of Denmark, Queen consort 74, 75, 76
Antwerp (Belgium) 69, 83
Appleby Castle (Westmorland) 38, 48
Arbury Hall (Warwickshire) 105
archaeology 14, 17, 19, 103, 104, 108
Archer, Thomas 93
Architectural Association 194, 206
Architectural Review (magazine) 157, 194, 200, 203, 212, 213
architecture, definition and importance 2–4, 7–9, 11, 266–7
Argyll, Archibald Campbell, 3rd Duke of 103
Arkwright, Sir Richard 125
Armadale (Isle of Skye) 125
Armstrong, William Armstrong, 1st Baron 158
Arnold, Matthew 6, 156
art deco 6, 185, 186–7, 188, 190, 217
art nouveau 163, 174, 175, 186, 191
Art Workers' Guild 156, 173, 174
artificial intelligence (AI) 153, 258
Arts and Crafts movement 6, 138, 154, 156–65, 167, 170, 173–5, 181, 188–9, 191, 194, 241
Ashbee, Charles 174, 175, 178, 189, 197

279

Index

Ashcroft, Dame Peggy 187
Ashridge House (Hertfordshire) 107
Aske Hall (Yorkshire) 97
Astley Castle (Warwickshire) 251
astylar design 78, 79
Athens 108, 193, 263
  Parthenon 45, 128, 129
Attlee, Clement Attlee, 1st Earl 203
Aubrey, John 12, 121
Audley End (Essex) 71
Augustine, St 20
Aynhoe Park (Northamptonshire) 119

Baddesley Clinton
  (Warwickshire) 165
Baggy House (Devon) 241
Baker, Sir Herbert 188
Bamburgh Castle
  (Northumberland) 30
Bangor, diocese of 27
Banham, Reyner 242
Bannockburn, Battle of (1314) 48
Barber, Peter 242
Barcelona 261
  Sagrada Família 172
Barker, Paul 242
Barnett, Dame Henrietta 176
Barnsley, Sidney 164
baroque style 5, 44, 82, 83, 89–95, 99,
  120, 167, 168, 185
Barratt, Nick:
  Greater London 202
Barry, Sir Charles 136–7, 139–40, 148
Basevi, George 129
Basildon (Essex) 223
Basing House siege (1645) 78
Bath (Somerset) 3, 12, 34, 99, 117, 132,
  167, 180, 230
  Abbey 53

Bath, Alexander Thynn, 7th
  Marquess of 66
Bauhaus school 191, 195, 241
BDP (Building Design
  Partnership) 240
Beauchamp, Richard 57
Beaumaris Castle (Anglesey) 47
Beauvais Cathedral (France) 41
Beaux Arts style 132, 166–7, 201
Becket, Thomas, Archbishop of
  Canterbury:
  murder 28, 32–3, 34
  relics 34, 35
Beckford, William 107
Bede, Venerable 18, 22
Bedford, Francis Russell,
  4th Earl of 77, 85, 86, 241
Bedford, Francis Russell, 5th
  Duke of 117
Bedingfield family 57
Behrens, Peter 191, 195
Bekker, Koos 17
Belcher, John 167
Belfast 167
Belvoir Castle (Leicestershire) 107
Benedict Biscop, Abbot 22
Benedictines 28
Bentley, Ian:
  *Dunroamin: The Suburban Semi and
  Its Enemies* 181, 183
Bentley, John Francis 171
Berkeley (house-builders) 242
Berkeley Castle (Gloucestershire)
  26, 50, 51
Berkeley family 47, 50, 86
Berlin 132
Bernard of Clairvaux 31, 32
Bernasconi, Francis 125
Bernini, Gian Lorenzo 5, 80, 89

Index

Bertha, Queen of Kent 20
Berwick-upon-Tweed
   (Northumberland) 79
Bess of Hardwick (Elizabeth Talbot,
   Countess of Shrewsbury) 67, 72
Betjeman, Sir John 183, 194, 230, 234
Beverley (Yorkshire):
   Minster 55–6
   St Mary's church 58
Bexleyheath (Kent):
   Red House 156
Bicknell, Julian 241
Bilbao (Spain):
   Guggenheim Museum 246, 248
Binham Abbey (Norfolk) 42
Binney, Marcus 230, 233
Birkenhead (Merseyside) 125
Birmingham 7, 209, 237, 264
   Bishop's Palace 209
   Bull Ring shopping centre 249
   Cathedral 93
   Central Library 209, 218, 239
   Gas Street Basin 248
   Jewellery Quarter 255
   Liberal Club 209
   Market Hall 209
   Mason's College 209
   Odeon cinema, Perry Barr 187
   Selfridges (department store) 249
   town hall 145
   see also Bournville
Bishops Lydeard (Somerset) 56
Black Death (1348) 42, 43, 49, 51
Blackburn (Lancashire) 221
Blair, Sir Tony 248, 255, 262
Blake, William:
   'Jerusalem' 13
Blandford Forum (Dorset) 161–2
Blenheim, Battle of (1704) 91

Blenheim Palace (Oxfordshire) 91–2,
   93, 102, 110
Blickling Hall (Norfolk) 71
Bliss, William 146
Blitz (1940–41) 199–200, 201, 204,
   206, 221
Blomfield, Sir Reginald 171,
   172–3, 185
Bodley, George Frederick 151, 152,
   163, 164, 166, 171, 172
Bolsover Castle (Derbyshire) 72
Bolton (Lancashire) 221
Bolton Abbey (Yorkshire) 61
Bond, Sir Thomas 86
Booker, Christopher 230
Bor, Walter 210
Borromini, Francesco 5, 89
Boston (Lincolnshire) 55
Bournville (Worcestershire) 160
Bowood House (Wiltshire) 110
Boys Smith, Nicholas 252
Bracknell (Berkshire) 223
Bradford (Yorkshire) 255
   mills 145–6
   St George's Hall 145
   town hall 145
   Wool Exchange 145
Bradford-on-Avon (Wiltshire):
   St Laurence's church 21
Bradwell-on-Sea (Essex):
   St Peter's church 21
Bramante, Donato 4, 63
Bramshill House (Hampshire) 143
Brancepeth (Co. Durham) 79
Breadalbane, John Campbell,
   1st Marquess of 125
Brideshead Revisited (television
   series) 91
Brigantes (tribe) 15

Index

Brighton (Sussex) 3, 122
  Brunswick Square 122
  Royal Pavilion 115, 122
  St Peter's church 136
Bristol 8
  Cabot Circus shopping centre 255–6
  Cathedral 37, 47
  Kings Weston House 92
  Queen's Square 88
  St Mary Redcliffe church 46–7
  Temple Meads station 141
British Architect (magazine) 165
British Rail 231, 234
Brixworth (Northamptonshire):
  All Saints church 21
Broadway Tower
  (Worcestershire) 107
Brockhampton (Herefordshire):
  All Saints church 173
Brodrick, Cuthbert 144–5
Bronze Age 13
Brooks, Roy 237
Brough Castle (Cumberland) 48
Brougham Castle (Cumberland) 48
Brown, Ford Madox 155
Brown, George, Baron George-
  Brown 208
Brown, Lancelot 'Capability'
  110–11, 112, 113
Bruce, Robert 209, 266
Brunel, Isambard Kingdom 142, 144
Brunelleschi, Filippo 55, 63
brutalism 197, 205, 215–18, 219, 223,
  224, 226, 239
Bryanston School (Dorset) 162, 247
Brydon, John 169
Buchanan, Sir Colin:
  Traffic in Towns report (1963) 203,
  208, 211, 220

Bucharest 266
building acts:
  17th century 109
  18th century 109
  20th century 179, 180, 203, 204–5, 230
Building Design Partnership
  (BDP) 240
Burges, William 152–3, 157, 164, 168
Burghley, William Cecil, 1st
  Baron 66, 71
Burghley House (Lincolnshire) 5, 66,
  71, 78, 110
Burlington, Richard Boyle,
  3rd Earl of 5, 95–8, 99, 101–2,
  104, 106, 110
Burn, William 158
Burne-Jones, Sir Edward 155, 163
Burnet, Sir John James 174
Burton, Decimus 117, 118, 134, 138
Burton, James 117
Bury St Edmunds (Suffolk) 28
Busby, Charles 122
Bute, John Crichton-Stuart,
  3rd Marquess of 153, 168
Butterfield, William 36, 151
Buxton (Derbyshire) 97
Byland Abbey (Yorkshire) 32
Byzantine architecture 20, 164, 171

Cadbury (confectionery
  manufacturer) 160
Caerhays Castle (Cornwall) 114
Caerlaverock Castle (Dumfriesshire) 38
Caerleon (Gwent) 15
Caernarvon Castle (Gwynedd) 47–8
Caerphilly Castle (Glamorgan) 38
Caerwent (Monmouthshire) 15
Caius, John 69
Calais (France) 55, 59

Index

Cambridge:
  All Saints church 152
  Cambridge Camden Society *see*
    Ecclesiological Society
  Cambridge University 50, 59
    Downing College 128
    Fitzwilliam Museum 129
    Girton College 162
    Gonville and Caius College 69
    Judge Business School 247
    King's College chapel 53–4, 55, 60
    Newnham College 162
    Pembroke College chapel 80
    Queens' College 69–70
    Senate House 94
    Trinity College 84, 128–9
    university library 129
Campbell, Colen 5, 95, 97
  Vitruvius Britannicus 95
Canaletto 82, 110
Cannons (Middlesex) 94
Canterbury:
  Cathedral 26–7, 32–4, 53
  St Martin's church 20
'carbuncle cup' (worst building award) 247
Cardiff 126
  Castle 153, 168
  civic centre 6, 168, 251
  opera house 251
  Senedd building 251
Carey, George, Archbishop of Canterbury 180
Carisbrooke Castle (Isle of Wight) 26
Carlisle, Charles Howard, 3rd Earl of 90
Carr, John 97
Carr, Jonathan 160–61
Casale Roman villa (Sicily) 16

Casson, Sir Hugh 205
Castell Coch (Glamorgan) 153
Castle Acre (Norfolk) 28
Castle Coole (Co. Fermanagh) 107
Castle Drogo (Devon) 171
Castle Howard (Yorkshire) 90–91, 92, 102
castles and castellated houses 8
  Norman 24, 25–6, 30, 37, 50, 133
  later medieval 37–8, 47–8, 49, 50, 251
  Tudor and Stuart 60, 72, 78
  Georgian and Regency 103, 105, 107, 114, 122, 125, 126, 133
  Victorian 139, 140, 153
  twentieth century 171
Catherine of Aragon, Queen consort 61
Catherine the Great, Russian Empress 107
Caus, Isaac de 76
Cavendish, Sir Charles 72
Cavendish, William (*later* 1st Duke of Newcastle) 72
Cecil, Robert *see* Salisbury, Robert Cecil, 1st Earl of
Cecil, William *see* Burghley, William Cecil, 1st Baron
Cedd, St 21
Centre for Cities (think tank) 254
Centre for London (think tank) 254
Chamberlin, Powell and Bon (architects' practice) 211–12
Chambers, Sir William 5, 102, 103–4, 106, 107, 110–11, 113, 114, 119
  A Treatise on Civil Architecture 102
Chambord, Château de (France) 62
Champneys, Basil 162–3, 164

Index

Chandos, James Brydges,
    1st Duke of 94
Chanel, Coco 186
chapels, Welsh 126–7, 153–4
Chapman Taylor (architects'
    practice) 210, 247
Charlemagne, Emperor 20
Charles I, King 72, 76, 77, 79, 85,
    99, 238
Charles II, King 79, 80–81, 89
Charles III, King
    as Prince of Wales 217, 233, 238–40
Chartres Cathedral (France) 32
Chatsworth (Derbyshire) 67, 89, 93,
    110, 143
Cheadle (Staffordshire) 139
Chedworth (Gloucestershire) 16
Cheltenham (Gloucestershire) 3, 123
Chengdu (China) 266
Chepstow (Monmouthshire) 26
Chermayeff, Serge 197
Chettle House (Dorset) 93
Chevening (Kent) 77–8
Chicago 238, 262
Chicheley Hall
    (Buckinghamshire) 97
China 102, 262, 263, 266
Chinoiserie 102, 104, 110, 115
Chipperfield, Sir David 251
Chipping Campden
    (Gloucestershire) 55, 174
Chipping Norton (Oxfordshire):
    Bliss Tweed Mill 146
Christ Church, Oxford 84
Christianity:
    in Britain 4, 16, 19–20, 21, 22, 51, 59,
        126–7, 138–9
    in Roman Empire 4, 16
    see also Reformation

church building *see* ecclesiastical
    architecture
Churchill, Sir Winston 201, 205
Chysauster (Cornwall) 14
CIAM (Congrès Internationaux
    d'Architecture Moderne)
    193–5, 196
cinemas 187
Cirencester (Gloucestershire) 55
Cistercians 28–9, 31, 32
Civic Amenities Act (1967) 230
Civic Trust 229
Civil War, English (1642–51) 50, 78–9
Clarendon, Edward Hyde,
    1st Earl of 79
classicism (style and characteristics)
    1–2, 3–4, 63, 65, 89
    columns and capitals 1, 2, 3–4, 122
    orders 3–4, 63, 122, 185, 270
classicism in Britain 1–2
    Tudor and Stuart 5, 62–4, 65–70,
        72–3, 74–8, 79–84, 89–90
    Georgian and Regency 1, 3, 5–6,
        93, 94–105, 106–7, 108, 109, 113–14,
        119, 120, 121–2, 127, 128–9,
        132, 134–6
    Victorian 1, 5–6, 140, 141–2, 143,
        144–6, 153–4
    twentieth century 166–70, 171–3,
        184–6, 189, 239, 241
Claudius, Roman Emperor 14
clearances, Scottish Highlands
    124–5
Cley next the Sea (Norfolk) 47
Clifford family 38, 48, 61
Cliveden House
    (Buckinghamshire) 140
Clockwork Orange, A (film; 1971) 226
Clore, Sir Charles 206

Index

Coates, Wells 194, 195
Cobham, Richard Temple, 1st Viscount 96
Cockerell, Sir Charles 108
Cockerell, Charles Robert 128–9, 140
Cockerell, Samuel Pepys 108–9
Colchester 15, 19
  Castle 26, 50
  town hall 167
Coleshill House (Berkshire) 78
Coleton Fishacre (Devon) 188
Columba, St 20
Colvin, Sir Howard 105, 132
Commissioners' churches *see* Waterloo churches
Commonwealth Games (Glasgow; 2014) 224
Commonwealth of England (1649–60) 77, 78–9, 85
Composite order 4, 63
Compton, Sir William 61
Compton Wynyates (Warwickshire) 61
Congrès Internationaux d'Architecture Moderne (CIAM) 193–5, 196
Connell, Amyas 197
conservation, building 7, 118, 156, 185, 217, 229–37, 241–2, 250, 251, 257, 260–61, 265–6
Constable, John 46
Constable Burton Hall (Yorkshire) 97
Constantinople 48
  Hagia Sophia 136
Conwy (north Wales):
  Castle 47
  Plas Mawr 70
Cook, Olive 43

Copcutt, Geoffrey 224
Corbusier, Le *see* Le Corbusier (Charles-Édouard Jeanneret)
Corby (Northamptonshire) 223
Corfe Castle (Dorset) 30, 78
Corinthian order 4, 63
Cosin, John, Bishop of Durham 79
Costain (house-builders) 182
Cotton, Jack 206, 220
Council for the Preservation of Rural England 201
council housing 160, 176–7, 179–82, 205–6, 213–15, 216–17, 222, 224, 225–6, 229, 232, 237–8, 252, 260, 267
Council of Europe 233
Country Life (magazine) 165
  offices 170–71
Coventry 199, 202
  Cathedral 244
Crace and Co. (decorating company) 156
Cragside (Northumberland) 158
Crawley (Sussex) 223
Crawshay family 126
Create Streets (consultancy) 252
Crécy, Battle of (1346) 52
Cromwell, Oliver 78, 79
Cromwell, Ralph Cromwell, 3rd Baron 50
Cronkhill (Shropshire) 114
Croome Court (Worcestershire) 110
Crosby, Theo 230
Croscombe (Somerset) 58
Crosland, Anthony 221
Crossland, William Henry 145
Crossman, Richard 221, 224–5
Croydon (Surrey) 261
Cruickshank, Dan 150

Index

crusaders 32, 47
Cubitt, Thomas 123–4, 129, 206
Cullinan, Ted 252
Cullompton (Devon) 53
Culzean Castle (Ayrshire) 105
Cumbernauld (Lanarkshire) 209, 218, 224–5, 226
Cundy, Thomas 146–7
Cust, Sir Edward 135
Cyfarthfa Castle (Glamorgan) 126

Dacre, Richard Lennard, 13th Baron 77
Dagenham Girl Pipers (pipe band) 180
Dale, David 125
Dalmeny (West Lothian) 29
Dance, George, the Elder 97
Dance, George, the Younger 108, 109, 118–19, 120
Danes 22, 27
Dankworth, Sir Johnny 227
Darbourne & Darke (architects' practice) 218
Darlington (Co. Durham) 180
Dartford (Kent):
   Bluewater shopping centre 255
Dartmouth, Raine Legge, Countess of 231
David, Jacques-Louis 120
Davies, Mike 249
Davis, Arthur 167
Davis, Ian:
   Dunroamin: The Suburban Semi and Its Enemies 181, 183
de Botton, Alain 266
de Clare family 57
de Graaf, Reinier 247
de Grey, Sir Roger 245
De Morgan, William 156

Decorated Gothic style 42–6, 48, 52, 56, 121
Delos (Greece) 136
Denmark 74
   see also Danes
Derby, Edward Smith-Stanley, 14th Earl of 149
Derbyshire, Ben 254
Despenser family 57
Destruction of the Country House 1875–1975 (exhibition; 1974) 233
Devonshire, William Cavendish, 1st Duke of 89
Dickens, Charles 147
   Bleak House 128
   Our Mutual Friend 124
Dilettantes *see* Society of Dilettanti
Diocletian, Roman Emperor 103
Disraeli, Benjamin, 1st Earl of Beaconsfield 109
Ditchley Park (Oxfordshire) 94
Dobson, John 132, 209–10
Doncaster (Yorkshire) 148
Dorchester (Dorset) 239
Doric order 3–4, 63
Dorking (Surrey) 195
Dover, Henry Jermyn, 1st Baron 86
Dover Castle (Kent) 25, 48
Downing College, Cambridge 128
D'Oyly Carte family 188
Dresden (Germany) 211
Drew, Dame Jane 223
Drewe, Julius 171
Druids 3, 12, 13, 99
du Pisanie, Nicola 17
Dubai 262, 263, 265
Dumfries House (Ayrshire) 102
Duncombe Park (Yorkshire) 140
Dunrobin Castle (Sutherland) 140

Duns Castle (Berwickshire) 125
Durham:
   Castle 24
   Cathedral 24–5, 27, 29, 30, 107
Dutch style architecture 94, 110, 158, 160, 177
   Pont Street Dutch 159
Dyckhoff, Tom 248
Dyrham Park (Gloucestershire) 89, 94

East Anglia, University of 216
East Kilbride (Lanarkshire) 209
Easton Neston House (Northamptonshire) 90
ecclesiastical architecture, history and development 4, 17
   Saxon 20–22, 26, 29
   Norman 23, 24–5, 26–9, 32, 34, 35
   later medieval 31–7, 42–7, 51–8
   Tudor and Stuart 54, 57, 75, 76, 78–9, 82–4, 85, 121
   Georgian and Regency 92–3, 94, 105, 116, 119, 120, 121–2, 125, 126–7, 132–3, 136
   Victorian 6, 36, 139, 146–8, 150–54, 163–4
   twentieth century 171–2, 173, 184–6
Ecclesiological Society 139, 147
Edinburgh 3, 8, 131
   Calton Hill 131
   Dalmeny church 29
   Holyrood palace 251
   New Town 87–8, 98–9, 124, 131
   Royal High School 131
   Royal Scottish Academy 131
   Scottish parliament building 251
   St James Centre 218
   town hall 167

Edward the Confessor, King 23, 41
   tomb 106
Edward I, King 47–8
Edward II, King 48, 51
Edward III, King 37, 48, 51
Edward IV, King 53–4
Edward VI, King 62
Edward VII, King 169, 173
   as Prince of Wales 166
Edwards, John 114
Egypt:
   Philae 136
   pyramids 5, 12
Egyptian style 146, 187, 241, 247
Eleanor of Aquitaine, Queen consort 32
Eleanor of Castille, Queen consort 48
Elgin, Thomas Bruce, 7th Earl of 129
Elizabeth I, Queen 64–7, 70, 131
   tomb 55
Elizabeth of York, Queen consort 55
Elizabethan architecture 64–70, 71, 72–3, 74, 75
   neo-Elizabethan 135, 141, 143, 172
Elkin, Stephen 227–8
Elliot, James and Archibald 125
Ellis, Peter 152
Elmes, Harvey Lonsdale 132
Eltham Lodge (Kent) 79
Ely Cathedral (Cambridgeshire) 25, 27, 45–6, 147
emigration 14, 126
English Decorated style *see* Decorated Gothic style
Epstein, Sir Jacob 189
Erasmus 59
Erith, Raymond 241
Erskine, Ralph 215

Index

Esher, Lionel Brett, 4th Viscount 193, 205–6, 229–30, 233
Eton College (Berkshire) 51
European Architectural Heritage Year (1975) 233
Evelyn, John 80, 81
Exeter 14
   Castle 26
   Cathedral 37, 42–3, 44, 46
Eye (Suffolk) 55

factories 145–6, 160, 174, 186–7, 192
   see also mills
Fairford (Gloucestershire) 57
Falkland Palace (Fife) 60
Farrell, Sir Terry 241–2, 247
Festival of Britain (1951) 205, 249
Field of the Cloth of Gold (1520) 59
First World War (1914–18) 179, 197
Fishbourne (Sussex) 16
fitz Osbern, William, 1st Earl of Hereford 25–6
flamboyant style 48, 51
Flapper style (women's fashion) 186
Flitcroft, Henry 96
Florence 136, 145
   San Lorenzo church 55
Florida, Richard 253, 254–5
Fontainebleau Palace (France) 59, 62
Fonthill Abbey (Wiltshire) 107
Forde Abbey (Dorset) 28
Foster, John 131–2
Foster, Norman, Baron Foster of Thames Bank 244, 245, 247, 248, 249, 252
Fountains Abbey (Yorkshire) 28, 61
Fox, Sir Charles 144
Frampton Court (Gloucestershire) 105
Francis I, King of France 59, 62

Frayn, Michael 205
French Revolutionary Wars (1792–1802) 113
Fry, Maxwell 194, 195, 196, 223
Fry, Roger 186, 193–4
Future Systems (architects' practice) 249

Gaddesden Place (Hertfordshire) 107
Gaitskell, Hugh 221
garden cities 6, 176, 192–3, 201, 223, 225
   see also new towns
garden design see landscape gardening
Gardiner, Stephen, Bishop of Winchester 70
Gascoigne family 57
gatehouses 37, 38, 49–50, 60–61, 66, 84, 162
Gateshead (Tyne and Wear):
   Sage Gateshead (The Glasshouse) 248–9
   Trinity Car Park 218
Gaudí, Antoni 172, 175
Gehry, Frank 246, 248, 249, 252
Geoffrey de Noyes (mason) 34
George I, King 93, 94
George III, King 106, 123, 128
George IV, King 118, 131
   as Prince of Wales and Prince Regent 108, 114, 115, 116, 122
George V, King 179
George, Sir Ernest 162–3, 170
Georgian Group (charity) 185
Gibberd, Sir Frederick 184, 223, 244
Gibbons, Grinling 83
Gibbs, James 94, 95, 96, 97, 105
   A Book of Architecture 97

Index

Giggs, Ryan 263
Gilbert and Sullivan 163
   Patience 158
Gilbert de Clare, 7th Earl of
   Gloucester 38
Gildas (monk) 18
Gill, Eric 189
Gilpin, William 111
Gimson, Ernest 164
Girouard, Mark 67, 73, 157, 161
Girton College, Cambridge 162
Glaeser, Edward 253–4
Glasgow 7, 8, 125, 146, 174,
   199, 209, 210, 225, 234,
   237, 266
   Ca' d'Oro Building 152
   Egyptian Halls 146
   Grosvenor Buildings 146
   Kingston Bridge 209
   Red Road flats 224
   School of Art 175
   St Andrew's Cathedral 125
   Willow Tea Rooms 175
Glastonbury (Somerset) 34, 61
GLC (Greater London
   Council) 216, 219–20,
   231–2, 233
Gloucester Cathedral 51–2, 53
Godwin, Edward William 154,
   157–8, 161
Goldfinger, Ernő 197, 216
Golding, William:
   The Spire 46
Gonville and Caius College,
   Cambridge 69
Goodall, John:
   The English Castle 26, 37
Goodhart-Rendel, Harry 187
Google (technology company) 258

Gothic architecture 5, 27, 31–48, 51–8,
   72, 79, 121
   see also Decorated Gothic style;
   Perpendicular Gothic style
Gothic revival architecture 5–6, 36,
   41–2, 55, 92, 101, 103, 105–7, 114,
   120, 121–2, 125, 128–9, 130–31,
   132–40, 145, 146–54, 171–2, 173
Gough, Piers 242, 247, 252
Grafton, Henry FitzRoy, 1st Duke
   of 86
Graham, James Gillespie 125
Grainger, Richard 132
Grand Manner, Edwardian
   167–70, 184–5
grand tour 5, 63, 64, 70–71, 74, 78, 95,
   96, 98, 128, 132, 136
Graves, Michael 246
Great Exhibition (1851) 143–4, 205
Great Fire of London (1666) 80, 82,
   109, 134
   post-fire rebuilding 80–87
Great Northern Railway 150
Great Reform Act (1832) 133–4
Great Western Railway 141
Greater Cursus (Neolithic
   earthwork; Wiltshire) 12
Greater London Council *see* GLC
Greece:
   ancient 3
   modern 108, 128, 136
   see also Athens
Greek revival architecture 108, 120,
   128–9, 131, 132, 136, 146, 168
Green, Nigel 218
Green, William Curtis 178, 185
green belt 81, 180, 201
Greene, Wilfred Greene,
   1st Baron 195

Index

Greenwich:
    Hospital 84, 93
    Millennium Dome 249
    Palace 50, 75, 79, 80, 84
    Queen's House 75–6, 77
    Vanbrugh Castle 92
Gresham, Sir Richard 61
Gresham, Sir Thomas 69
Grim's Dyke (Middlesex) 159
Gropius, Walter 191, 195, 200
Guild of Handicraft 174
Guildford Cathedral
    (Surrey) 185

Hackney, Rod 232
Haddon Hall (Derbyshire) 50
Hadid, Dame Zaha 247, 249, 250, 252
Hadleigh (Suffolk) 50
Hadrian's Wall 15
Hagley Hall (Worcestershire) 105
Hailsham, Quintin Hogg, Baron 219
Hakewill, Henry 132–3
Halfpenny, William 105
Halifax (Yorkshire):
    All Souls church 148, 151
    Piece Hall 234
    town hall 140
Hall, Sir Peter 242
hall houses 14, 38–9, 49–50, 51, 61
Hamilton, James 60
Hamilton, Thomas 131
Hampton Court Palace (Middlesex) 60, 62, 84, 90, 93
Hanbury Hall (Worcestershire) 93
Handel, George Frideric 6
Hansom, Joseph 145
Hanwell (Middlesex) 148
Hardwick, Philip 141

Hardwick Hall (Derbyshire) 67–8, 69, 78, 97
Harewood (Yorkshire):
    All Saints church 57
Harewood House (Yorkshire) 97, 110
Harlech (Gwynedd) 21
    Castle 47
Harlow (Essex) 223
Harris, Sir Arthur 'Bomber' 211
Harris, John 230
Harris, Vincent 169, 185, 218–19
Harrogate (Yorkshire) 122–3, 167
'harrowing of the north' (1069–70) 24
Harwood, Elain 217
Hastings, Battle of (1066) 23
Hatfield House (Hertfordshire) 71
Hatherley, Owen 214, 217, 240
Hatton, Sir Christopher 66–7
Haussmann, Georges-Eugène, Baron 159
Hawkhurst (Kent) 148
Hawksmoor, Nicholas 5, 83, 89–91, 92–3, 101, 168
Hawley, Cathy 252
Haymills (house-builders) 196
Heath, Sir Edward 231, 232
Heathcoat-Amory, Sir John 153
Heatherwick, Thomas 251
Humanise 257
Heaton Hall (Lancashire) 107
Hedingham Castle (Essex) 25
Héloïse d'Argenteuil 31
Hemel Hempstead
    (Hertfordshire) 223
Henbury Hall (Cheshire) 241
Hengrave Hall (Suffolk) 61
Henrietta Maria, Queen consort 72, 76, 85
Henry II, King 28, 32, 33

Index

Henry III, King 37, 41, 42, 47, 48, 54
Henry VI, King 53–4
Henry VII, King 50, 54–5
   tomb 55
Henry VIII, King 34, 59–62, 65, 66, 76
Henry, Prince of Wales 75, 77
Henry de Reynes (mason) 42
Hepworth, Dame Barbara 13
Herbert de Losinga, Bishop of Norwich 27
Herculaneum (Italy) 104
Hereford Cathedral 148
Hertford College, Oxford 172–3
Heveningham Hall (Suffolk) 101–2
Hexham (Northumberland) 22
Highclere Castle (Hampshire) 110, 140
Hill, Octavia 160, 176
Hill, Oliver 195
Hill, Rosemary:
   God's Architect 137, 139
   Stonehenge 12–13
hill forts 13–14
Hill Hall (Essex) 64
Hillier, Bevis 186
Hilton, Conrad 208
Hirst, Damien 251
Historic England (government agency) 257
Hitler, Adolf 201
Hoar Cross (Staffordshire):
   Holy Angels church 152
Hogarth, William 97–8, 197
Holden, Charles 178, 188–9
Holdenby House (Northamptonshire) 67
Holford, William Holford, Baron 220
Holkham Hall (Norfolk) 96
Holland, Henry 108, 114, 115

Home and Colonial Stores (retail chain) 171
Honeyman, John 152
Hong Kong 250
   HSBC tower 245
Honorius, Roman Emperor 18
Hooke, Robert 80, 83
Hopetoun House (West Lothian) 102
Hopkins, Michael and Patty 241, 247
Horta, Victor 175
hospitals 240, 244, 256
   Greenwich Hospital 84, 93
   Guy's Hospital 265
   Hospital of St Cross, Winchester 28
   Lord Leycester Hospital, Warwick 69
   Royal Hospital, Chelsea 90
hotels 122, 169, 188, 208
   Great Northern Hotel, King's Cross 150
   Hilton Hotel, Hyde Park 208
   Midland Grand Hotel, St Pancras 150
   Piccadilly Hotel 166
   Ritz Hotel 166–7, 185
   Royal Hotel, Paddington 141
   Royal Spa Hotel, Harrogate 123
Howard, Sir Ebenezer 176, 192–3, 223
Howard, Thomas (*later* 1st Earl of Suffolk) 71
Howard Homes (house-builders) 196, 197
Hudson, Anthony 241
Hudson, Edward 165, 170
Hugh of Avalon, Bishop of Lincoln 34–5
Huguenots 86, 87
Hull 199, 202

Index

Hume, David 131
Humphrey, John 153
Hundred Years' War (1337–1453) 48, 52
Hunt, William Holman 155
Hussey, Christopher 170
Hyams, Harry 206

Ideal Home Exhibition 182, 184, 196, 197
immigration 125, 191, 226
Impington College (Cambridgeshire) 195
India 108–9, 115
industrial revolution 8, 101, 125, 126, 144–6
Inveraray Castle (Argyllshire) 102–3
Ionic order 4, 63
Iron Age 13–14, 17
Islamic architecture 5, 47
Isle Abbots (Somerset) 56
Italianate style 114, 122, 123, 129, 136, 140, 143, 145, 146, 149–50, 158

Jackson, Alan:
 Semi-Detached London 182–3
Jackson, Sir Thomas 172–3
Jacobean architecture 38, 70–72, 74
 neo-Jacobean 141, 159
Jacobite rebellion (1745) 131
Jacobs, Jane:
 The Death and Life of Great American Cities 236, 252
James I and VI, King 12, 70–71, 74, 75
James II, King 87–8
James V, King of Scotland 60
James of St George (architect) 47
Jazz Age 186
Jekyll, Gertrude 170
Jencks, Charles 252

Language of Post-Modern Architecture 246, 247
Le Corbusier and the Tragic View of Architecture 192
Jermyn, Henry *see* St Albans, Henry Jermyn, 1st Earl of
Jerusalem 136, 174
Jiřičná, Eva 249
Joass, John 167
John, King 41
Johnson, Boris 249, 263, 264
Johnson, Philip 246
Johnson-Marshall, Sir Stirrat 216
Joldwynds (Surrey) 195
Jones, Anthony 127
Jones, Inigo 5, 12, 68, 71, 74–8, 80, 89, 94, 97, 136
 Banqueting House 76, 77, 82, 169, 219
 Chevening 77–8
 Covent Garden 77, 79, 84, 85, 87, 100, 127, 241
 Queen's House, Greenwich 75–6, 77
 St James's Palace, Chapel Royal 76
 St Paul's Cathedral 75, 76
 Wilton House 76–7
Jones, William 153
Jonson, Ben 75
 Love's Welcome at Bolsover 72
Joseph, Keith Joseph, Baron 221
Joy, William 43
Julius Caesar 14
Jumièges (Normandy) 23

Keble College, Oxford 151
Kedleston Hall (Derbyshire) 104
Kelmscott Manor (Oxfordshire) 157
Kenilworth Castle (Warwickshire) 30, 78

Index

Kent, William 5, 95, 96–8, 110, 169
Kew Gardens (Surrey) 110
   pagoda 102, 110
   Palm House 144
Kilpeck (Herefordshire) 29, 30
King's College, Cambridge:
   chapel 53–4, 55, 60
King's Sutton (Northamptonshire) 46
Kings Weston House (Bristol) 92
Kingsley, Charles:
   The Water-Babies 143
Kirby Hall (Northamptonshire) 66–7
Kirkby (Lancashire) 210
Kirkwall Cathedral (Orkney) 29
Knightshayes Court (Devon) 153
Knole (Kent) 39, 50
Knott, Ralph 168
Komisarjevsky, Theodore 187
Korn, Arthur 199–200
Krier, Léon 239
Kuala Lumpur 249, 262

Laguerre, Louis 93
Laing (house-builders) 182, 183, 196, 242
Lancaster, Sir Osbert 159, 183, 230
Lanchester, Henry Vaughan 168
landscape gardening 96, 110–12, 114
Lanfranc, Archbishop of Canterbury 26–7
Langley, Batty 98, 130
Las Vegas 246
Lasdun, Sir Denys 216, 217, 244
Latrobe, Benjamin 120
Lavenham (Suffolk) 69
Layer Marney Tower (Essex) 61, 78

LCC (London County Council) 203, 217
   County Hall 168
   housing estates 160, 176–7, 180, 205–6, 213, 225–6
   see also GLC
Le Corbusier (Charles-Édouard Jeanneret) 6, 191–4, 199, 200, 209, 210, 215, 221, 223, 225, 233, 236, 240, 266
   Unité d'Habitation 206, 214
   Villa Savoye 197
   Toward an Architecture 192
Le Vau, Louis 89
Leeds 264
   Corn Exchange 144–5
   St John's church 79
   town hall 6, 144, 168
Leicester 21
   guildhall 69
Leicester, Robert Sidney, 2nd Earl of 86
Leicester, Thomas Coke, 1st Earl of 96
Leonardo da Vinci 59
Leoni, Giacomo 95, 97
Letchworth Garden City (Hertfordshire) 6, 176
Lethaby, William 3, 173
Lever Brothers (manufacturing company) 160
Levy, Joe 204, 207
Libeskind, Daniel 248
libraries 157
   Birmingham Central Library 209, 218, 239
   British Library 238–9
   Cambridge University 129
   Glasgow School of Art 187

Index

libraries – *cont'd*.
  Kensington Public Library 219
  Leicester guildhall 69
  Taylorian library, Oxford 129
  Worcester College, Oxford 74
Lichfield, George Lee, 2nd Earl of 94
Lichfield Cathedral (Staffordshire) 147–8
Lincoln:
  Castle 26
  Cathedral 5, 27, 34–5
  Jews House 30
Lindisfarne (Northumberland) 21
  Castle 170
Lister, Samuel, 1st Baron Masham 146
Little Moreton Hall (Cheshire) 69
Liverpool 7, 8, 210–11, 220–21, 234, 266
  Albert Dock 168, 242, 248
  Anglican cathedral 6, 171–2, 184, 185
  Bank of England 142
  Catholic cathedral 6, 184
  Eldonian Village 232
  Everton 210
  Hope Street 131–2
  Museum of Liverpool 168
  Oriel Chambers 151–2, 185
  Rodney Street 131–2
  St George's Hall 132, 211
  Stanley docks 145
  Three Graces 6, 168
  town hall 167
  Toxteth 210, 253
  Vauxhall docks 232
  Welsh Streets 253
Liverpool and Manchester Railway 140–41

Livingstone, Ken 262–3, 264
Llananno (Powys) 56
Llandaff, diocese of 27
Llandanwg (Gwynedd) 21–2
Llanegryn (Gwynedd) 56
Llewelyn-Davies, Richard Llewlyn-Davies, Baron 244
Lloyd George, David, 1st Earl Lloyd-George of Dwyfor 179
Llywelyn ap Gruffudd 47
Lockwood, Henry Francis 145
Loire chateaux (France) 63, 66, 141
London (history & development) 8
  Roman 15, 39
  Saxon 23
  Norman 26
  later medieval 39–40
  Tudor and Stuart 63, 64, 69, 70–71, 76–7, 78, 80–87
  Georgian and Regency 1, 3, 87, 97, 99–100, 109, 115–18, 123–4, 129–30
  Victorian 1, 6, 159–61
  Edwardian and interwar 169–70, 176–8, 180–84
  post-Second World War 118, 199–208, 211–12, 218–20, 225–6
  late-twentieth century 231–2, 233–5, 237–9, 243, 261–2
  twenty-first century 249–51, 254–5, 259–60, 262–3, 264–6
London (landmarks, buildings & places):
  22 Bishopsgate 263
  55 Broadway 189
  Adelphi 103–4
  Albemarle Street 86
  Albert Hall Mansions 159–60
  Albert Memorial 33
  Aldgate 207

Index

Aldwych 63, 169
All Saints church, Margaret Street 151
All Souls church, Langham Place 116, 118, 121
Alliance Assurance offices, St James's 159
Arnos Grove Underground station 189
Athenaeum Club 118, 134, 135
Balfron Tower, Poplar 216–17
Bank of England 119, 120, 140, 142
Bankside Power Station 185
Banqueting House 76, 77, 82, 169, 219
Barbican 211–12, 214, 215, 219, 225, 236, 266
Barking 180–81
Barnet 242
Battersea 167, 176
Battersea Park 205
Battersea Power Station 185, 249–50
Bayswater 124, 231
Becontree 180–81
Bedford Park 160–61, 162, 176, 177, 182, 223
Bedford Square 100
Belgravia 6, 123–4, 132–3, 146–7
Belsize Park 195
Berkeley Square 100
Bermondsey 255, 264
Bethnal Green 119, 160
Bexley 197
Big Ben tower 82, 139, 145, 264
Blackwall Tunnel 233
Bloomsbury 86, 93, 109, 117, 129, 169, 189, 231
Board schools 163
Bond Street 86

Borough Market 256, 265
Boundary Road, Bethnal Green 160
Breakfast TV centre 247
Brick Lane 206
British Library 238–9
British Museum 129, 133, 141, 169, 175, 219
Bromley 196
Brooks's club 108
Buckingham Palace 118, 133, 141–2, 156, 169–70
Burlington House, Piccadilly 95
Camden 187, 237, 248
Canary Wharf 261, 264
Canning Town 213, 262
Carlton House, St James's 108, 114, 115, 118
Carlton House Terrace 118, 219
Carreras cigarette factory, Camden 187
Catford 199
Cavendish Square 116
Centre Point 207, 227, 249
Charing Cross Road 207
Charing Cross station 247
Chelsea 90, 106, 122, 124, 157–8, 159, 174
Cheyne Walk, Chelsea 159
Chiswick 174, 197
Chiswick House 96, 97, 110
Christ Church Spitalfields 93
Churchill Gardens, Pimlico 206
City Club, Threadneedle Street 208
Clarendon House, Piccadilly 79, 86
Coal Exchange 211
Coliseum 168

Index

London – *cont'd*.
  Collingham Gardens, South Kensington 162–3
  Comyn Ching Triangle, Covent Garden 242
  County Hall 168
  Covent Garden 77, 79, 84, 85, 87, 100, 127, 169, 170, 219–20, 231–2, 233, 235, 237, 241–2, 266
  Crystal Palace 143–4, 259
  Daily Express building, Fleet Street 187
  Deptford 93, 168
  Dome of Discovery 205, 249
  Dover Street 86, 114
  Downing Street 109, 128, 150, 219, 242
  Dulwich picture gallery and mausoleum 119
  Ealing 119, 264
  East Ham town hall 167
  Edgewood Mews, Barnet 242
  Edgware 196
  Elephant and Castle 207
  Ellerdale Road, Hampstead 159
  Euston Arch 234
  Euston Centre 207, 227
  Euston station 141
  Firestone tyre factory, Brentford 187
  Fitzroy Square 100
  Fleet Street 129, 187
  Foreign Office 6, 148–9, 169, 219
  Frith Street 86
  Gants Hill Underground station 189
  Gerrard Street 86
  Gherkin 245, 263
  Gidea Park 6, 177–8, 197, 223
  Gower Street 109
  Granada cinema, Tooting 187
  Great Northern Hotel, King's Cross 150
  Grosvenor Square 100
  Guildhall 108
  Guy's Hospital 265
  Hackney 250
  Hammersmith 176, 207
  Hampstead 159, 216, 241
  Hampstead Garden Suburb 176, 177, 178
  Hanover Square 100, 116
  Harrington Gardens, South Kensington 162–3, 170
  Haymarket 208, 257
  Hay's Wharf 187
  Hayward Gallery 217, 218, 238
  Hendon 176, 196
  High Point flats, Highgate 195
  Hillingdon Civic Centre 218
  Hilton Hotel 208
  Hogarth's House, Chiswick 197
  Holborn 69, 81, 129, 220
  Holland Park 159
  Holy Trinity church, Marylebone 119
  Holy Trinity church, Sloane Street 163
  Home House, Portman Square 104
  Home Office 219
  Hoover factory, Perivale 187
  Horniman Museum 174
  Horse Guards Parade 97, 169
  Houses of Parliament *see* Palace of Westminster
  Hoxton 212
  Hyde Park 33, 143–4, 208

Index

Institute of Chartered
   Accountants 167
Isle of Dogs 261
Islington 237, 254
Isokon building, Belsize Park 195
Jermyn Street 85
Kensington 87, 144, 148, 159,
   219, 232
Kensington Palace 84, 87, 90
Kensington Square 87
King's Cross 250–51
King's Cross station 150, 251
Kingsway 169, 170
Lambeth 167
Lansbury Estate, Stepney 206
Law Courts, Strand 154
Leicester Square 86
Liberty (department store) 156, 158
Lillington Gardens, Pimlico 218
Limehouse tunnel 261
Lincoln's Inn Fields 78, 84, 119, 136
Lloyd's building 245, 247
London Bridge 187, 264–5
London Bridge station 264
London Wall 211
Lower Thames Street 211
Lowther Lodge, Kensington 159
The Mall 169–70
Mansion House 97, 140
Marble Arch 118, 202, 207
Marylebone 99, 115, 119, 235
Mayfair 99, 109, 115, 129, 216
Melbury Road, Holland Park 159
Methodist Central Hall 168
Midland Grand Hotel,
   St Pancras 150
Mile End Road 206
Ministry of Defence 169
Monmouth Street 86

Monument 263
Morden 180
Mornington Crescent Gardens 187
Mount Pleasant, Clerkenwell 252
National Gallery 129, 133, 141, 238,
   239, 247
National Theatre 217, 244
Natural History Museum 152
NatWest Tower 208
New Scotland Yard 162, 219
New Zealand Chambers 159
New Zealand House 208, 257
Nine Elms 250
North Kensington 124, 216,
   234, 237
Northumberland House,
   Strand 71
Notting Hill Gate 207
Old Deanery, St Paul's
   Cathedral 81
Old Oak Common 176–7
Olympic Park, Stratford 250
One Canada Square, Canary
   Wharf 261
Osterley House 104
Oxford Circus 12
Oxford Street 106, 207, 257
Paddington 141
Palace of Westminster 6, 23, 30,
   42, 57, 82, 134–7, 139–40
Pall Mall 86, 87, 116, 118, 136,
   167, 247
Pantheon, Oxford Street 106
Panton Street 86
Parliament Square 169, 219
Peter Jones (department store) 195
Piccadilly 79, 85, 86, 95, 185, 195
Piccadilly Circus 12, 116, 220,
   232, 266

Index

London – *cont'd*.
  Piccadilly Circus Underground station 189
  Piccadilly Hotel 166
  Pimlico 123, 154, 160, 206, 218, 237
  Pitzhanger House, Ealing 119
  Poplar 214–15, 216
  Portcullis House 247
  Portland Place 204
  Portman Square 104
  Post Office Tower 244
  Queen Anne's Gate 100
  Queen's Gate, Kensington 159, 232
  RAC Club 167
  Ranelagh Gardens, Chelsea 106, 110
  Reform Club 136
  Regent Street 114, 115–16, 118, 129, 156, 169, 185
  Regent's Park 1, 115–18, 133
  Ritz Hotel 166–7, 185
  Robin Hood Gardens, Poplar 214–15, 218
  Ronan Point, Canning Town 213
  Royal Albert Hall 144, 159–60, 232
  Royal College of Art 232
  Royal College of Surgeons 136
  Royal Exchange 69, 75, 81, 140
  Royal Festival Hall 205
  Royal Hospital, Chelsea 90
  Royal Hotel, Paddington 141
  Royal Opera Arcade 257
  Sanderson wallpaper factory, Chiswick 174
  Savile Club 216
  Schomberg House, Pall Mall 87
  Senate House, London University 189
  The Shard 264–5
  Shell Centre, South Bank 208
  Shepherd's Bush 233, 256
  Shoreditch 81, 255
  Simpsons (department store) 195
  Skylon 205
  Sloane Square 195
  Smithfield 32, 74, 212
  Soane Museum 119–20
  Soho 86, 115, 235, 236
  Soho Square 86
  Somerset House 78, 102, 103, 104
  South Bank 205, 208, 217
  South Kensington 144, 152, 162–3
  Southgate Underground station 189
  St Augustine's church, Kilburn 152
  St Bartholomew's church, Smithfield 32
  St Bride's Fleet Street church 83–4
  St George Wharf Tower 249
  St George's church, Bloomsbury 93
  St Giles church, Camberwell 147
  St Helier estate, Morden 180
  St James the Less church, Pimlico 154
  St James's church, Piccadilly 85–6
  St James's Palace 76, 79, 84
  St James's Park 169
  St James's Square 77, 85–6
  St James's Street 159
  St John's church, Bethnal Green 119
  St John's Smith Square church 93
  St Luke's church, Chelsea 122
  St Magnus Martyr church 83
  St Martin-in-the-Fields church 94, 133, 231
  St Mary Abbots church, Kensington 148

Index

St Mary Woolnoth church 92–3
St Mary-le-Bow church 83
St Mary-le-Strand church 94
St Michael's church, Chester Square 146
St Pancras station 150, 234
St Paul's Cathedral 4, 75, 81, 82–3, 84, 89, 93, 170, 184, 263, 264
St Paul's church, Covent Garden 77, 79, 127
St Paul's church, Deptford 93
St Peter's church, Eaton Square 132–3, 146
St Peter's church, Walworth 119
St Stephen's Chapel, Westminster 42, 51–2
St Vedast Foster Lane church 83
Stag Place, Victoria 207
Staple Inn, High Holborn 69
Stepney 205–6, 266
Strand 71, 75, 81, 102, 103–4, 154, 220
Stratford 250
Sudbury Town Underground station 189
Swan House, Chelsea 159
Sydenham 144
Tate Gallery 160
Thamesmead 225–6
Tite Street, Chelsea 157–8
Tooting 187
Tottenham 176
Tower Bridge 263
Tower of London 26, 30, 48
Trafalgar Square 116, 129, 140, 169, 238, 247
Travellers Club 136
Treasury 140, 219

Trellick Tower, North Kensington 216–17
United Services Club (Institute of Directors) 118
University College 129
Upper Thames Street 211
Vauxhall 249, 251
Vauxhall Gardens 110
Victoria and Albert Museum 148, 186, 233, 250
Victoria Memorial 170
Victoria Street 219
Walkie-Talkie building 247, 263
Wanstead 95, 96, 177
Wapping 81
War Office 169
Wardour Street 86
Waterloo Bridge 243
Waterloo Place 115, 116, 118
Waterloo station 196
Westfield shopping centre, Shepherd's Bush 256
Westminster Abbey 23, 37, 41, 48, 54–5, 60, 92, 105, 135, 147, 164, 168
Westminster Cathedral 164, 171
White City 233–4
Whitechapel Art Gallery 174
Whitehall 76, 97, 140, 148–9, 169, 219, 231, 242, 266
Whitehall Palace 79, 84
Wimbledon 177
Wolseley Motors building, Piccadilly 185
Zoo 195
see also Croydon; Greenwich; Kew; Richmond (Surrey); Twickenham
London and Birmingham Railway 141

Index

London Board of Education 163
London County Council *see* LCC
London Underground (Tube)
    177, 188–9
  Jubilee Line extension 261
  stations 189, 249
  see also individual station names
    at 'London'
London University 129, 189, 231, 250
Longleat House (Wiltshire) 5, 64, 65–6, 67, 71
Loos, Adolf 191
Los Angeles 226, 246
Loudon, John Claudius:
  Encyclopaedia of Cottage, Farm and Village Architecture 130
Louis XIV, King of France 79, 200
Louth (Lincolnshire) 55
Lübeck (Germany) 202
Lubetkin, Berthold 191
Luder, Owen 239, 243
Lullingstone (Kent):
  Castle 61
  Roman villa 16
Lutyens, Sir Edwin 4, 162, 170–71, 184–5
Lyminge, Robert 71
Lytham Hall (Lancashire) 97
Lyttelton, George Lyttelton, 1st Baron 105

M8 (motorway) 209, 234
Macclesfield (Cheshire) 232
MacCormac, Sir Richard 252
Macdonald clan 125
Mackintosh, Charles Rennie 174–5, 186, 191, 195, 197
Mackintosh, Margaret Macdonald 175
Macmillan, Harold, 1st Earl of Stockton 208
Madin, John 218, 239
Maesyronnen Chapel (Powys) 127
Maggie's centres (cancer patient centres) 252
magic and mysticism 3, 31, 173
Magna Carta 41
Major, Sir John 261
Malraux, André 218, 260
Manasseh, Leonard 197
Manchester 8, 209, 220, 263
  Albert Square 145
  Ancoats 145
  Art Gallery 136
  Beetham Tower 263
  Deansgate 145, 263
  Free Trade Hall 145
  Hulme 209, 221–2, 266
  Imperial War Museum North 248
  Lowry Centre 248
  Moss Side 209
  Northern Quarter 255
  railway station 140–41
  Salford Quays 242, 248, 249
  synagogue 263
  town hall 6, 145
Manners family 50
Manzoni, Sir Herbert 209
March (Cambridgeshire) 57
Margate (Kent):
  railway station 196
Marlborough, John Churchill, 1st Duke of 91
Marlborough, Sarah Churchill, Duchess of 91
Marney, Henry Marney, 1st Baron 61
Marriott, Oliver:
  The Property Boom 199, 207

Index

MARS (Modern Architectural Research Group) 194–5, 199–200
Marseilles 193
   Unité d'Habitation 206, 214
Martello towers 113
Martin, Sir Leslie 205–6, 219, 231, 244
Mary I, Queen 64, 65
Mary II, Queen 84, 87
Matcham, Frank 168–9
Matthew, Sir Robert 205–6, 216
Mawson, William 145
May, Hugh 79
Maynard, Alan 65
McAslan, John 251
McQueen, Steve 171
Mendelsohn, Erich 191
Merthyr valley (south Wales) 126
Metroland 177
Metropolitan Police 162
Metropolitan Railway 177
Mewès, Charles 167
Michelangelo 55, 74, 97, 155, 167
Midland Railway 150
Mies van der Rohe, Ludwig 241, 246
Milan 4
Millais, Sir John Everett 155
Millennium Experience (exhibition; 2000) 249
Miller, Sanderson 105
mills 145–6, 257
Milne, Oswald 188
Milton Keynes (Buckinghamshire) 226–7, 244
Mintons (pottery manufacturing company) 156
Miralles, Enric 251
model villages 160

Modern Architectural Research Group (MARS) 194–5, 199–200
modernism 6–7, 174, 184, 191–8, 200, 203, 205–6, 211–12, 214–18, 219, 224–6, 231, 240, 241–3, 244–6, 248, 267
see also postmodernism
Moholy-Nagy, László 191
monasteries 20, 21, 22, 23, 26, 28–9, 32, 50
   dissolution 34, 61–2
Monkwearmouth Abbey (Northumberland) 22
Monmouth Castle 26
Montfort, Simon de, 6th Earl of Leicester 41
Moor Park (Hertfordshire) 93
Moore, Charles 246
Moore, Dudley 180
Moore, Henry 13
Moore, Rowan 263
Moro, Peter 205
Morris, Roger 102–3
Morris, William 154, 155–7, 158, 160–61, 162, 163, 165, 166, 174, 241
Morriston (Glamorgan) 153
Mortimer, Blanche 57
Moscow:
   Metro 189
   Vkhutemas academy 191
motorways, urban 208–10, 233–4
Moya, Hidalgo 206, 223
Mozart, Wolfgang Amadeus 110
Much Marcle (Herefordshire) 57
Much Wenlock (Shropshire) 69
Mughal style 108–9, 115
Munstead Wood (Surrey) 170

Index

Muthesius, Hermann:
  Das Englische Haus 173, 191
mysticism and magic 3, 31, 173

Nairn, Ian 230
Nansledan (Cornwall) 240
Napoleon I, Emperor 121, 200
Napoleonic Wars (1803–15) 107, 111, 120, 121, 122, 129
Nash, John 5, 113–18, 119, 121, 122, 130, 133, 138, 188
  All Souls church, Langham Place 116, 118, 121
  Brighton Pavilion 115, 122
  Buckingham Palace 116, 133
  Caerhays Castle 114
  Carlton House Terrace 118, 219
  Cronkhill 114
  Ravensworth Castle 114
  Regent Street and Regent's Park 1, 115–18, 133, 169, 185
  Royal Opera Arcade 257
National Trust 165, 188, 216
Nazism 191, 201
Needham Market (Suffolk) 57
neo-Elizabethan style 135, 141, 143, 172
neo-Georgian style 181–2, 185, 218–19, 241, 242
neo-Jacobean style 141, 159
neo-Tudor style 160, 182, 183, 184, 242
  see also Tudorbethan style
Neville, Gary 263
Neville family (Raby Castle) 49
New House (Sussex) 241
New Lanark (Lanarkshire) 125, 160
New Society (magazine) 242
new towns 201, 204, 209, 210, 223–7, 239–40
  see also garden cities

New Urbanism 239
New Wardour Castle (Wiltshire) 101
New Ways (Northampton) 195
New York 192, 254, 255, 262
  Chrysler building 186
  Soho 255
  Sony Tower 246
  Tribeca 255
Newcastle 7, 14, 132, 209–10
  Byker Wall estate 215
  Eldon Square 210
  Grainger Town 132, 210, 234
  railway station 141
  Royal Arcade 209–10
Newcastle, William Cavendish, 1st Duke of 72
Newmarket (Suffolk) 77
Newnham College, Cambridge 162
Newport (Gwent) 126
Newquay (Cornwall) 240
Nicholas, Rowland 209, 221
Nietzsche, Friedrich 191
Ninian, St 20
Nonconformists 121, 126–7, 153–4
'non-plan' movement 242–3
Nonsuch Palace (Surrey) 62
Normans 23, 24–30, 37
Northampton:
  New Ways 195
Northleach (Gloucestershire) 55
Northumberland, John Dudley, 1st Duke of 62, 63
Norwich 8, 254, 264
  Castle 26, 30, 50
  Cathedral 27, 30, 264
  Goldsmith Street 252
Nottingham 67, 89
  Castle 234
  Maid Marian Way 234

Index

Ockwells Manor (Berkshire) 50–51
Odeon (cinema chain) 187
oil crisis (1973) 229
Oliver, Paul:
  Dunroamin: The Suburban Semi and Its Enemies 181, 183
Olympic Games (London; 2012) 250
Omega Workshops (design studio) 186
Oosthuizen, Susan:
  The Emergence of the English 18
Open University 227
Orkney 13
  Kirkwall Cathedral 29
  Skara Brae 11, 13
Ormonde, James Butler, 1st Duke of 86
Orwell, George:
  1984 189
Ottery St Mary (Devon) 46, 53
Ottoman Empire 108
Ottonian dynasty (Germany) 27
Outram, John 241, 247
Owen, Robert 160
Oxborough (Norfolk) 50, 57
Oxford:
  Castle 26
  Cutteslowe 182
Oxford, Edward Harley, 2nd Earl of 94
Oxford Movement 139
Oxford University 50, 59
  All Souls College 80, 92
  Ashmolean Museum 129
  Christ Church 84
  Divinity School 53
  Examination Schools 172
  Hertford College 172–3

  Keble College 151
  Radcliffe Camera 94
  Sheldonian Theatre 80
  Taylorian library 129
  Worcester College 74

paganism 3, 4, 12, 13, 19, 20, 99, 138, 185
Paine, James 101
Palladio, Andrea 63, 74, 95, 108, 113, 241
Palladianism 66, 68, 75, 77–8, 79–80, 89, 94–5, 96, 97, 102–3, 109, 120, 169, 239
Palmerston, Henry John Temple, 3rd Viscount 149, 154
Palmyra (Syria) 136
Paris 31–2, 41–2, 85, 115, 117, 159, 191, 199, 218, 254, 261
  Beaugrenelle 218
  Champs-Élysées 115, 169
  Chêne Pointu 218
  École des Beaux-Arts 166
  Eiffel Tower 265
  Grand Palais 166
  Hôtel de la Marine 167
  Louvre 76, 80, 84, 89, 102, 136, 149
  Notre-Dame 32
  Petit Palais 166
  Place Royale (Place des Vosges) 77
  Pompidou Centre 245, 246, 264
  Sainte-Chapelle 42, 51
  St-Denis Abbey 5, 31–2, 41
  see also Versailles Palace
Paris, Peace of (1763) 108
Paris Exhibition (1900) 166
Paris Exposition of Decorative Arts (1925) 186
Parker, Richard Barry 176
Parler family (masons) 65

Index

Pathfinder programme 252–3
Patricio (Powys) 56
Patrick, St 20
Patrington (Yorkshire):
   St Patrick's church 46
Paxton, Sir Joseph 143–4
Peabody, George 160, 176
Peabody Trust (housing
   association) 226
Peaky Blinders (television series) 253
Pearson, John Loughborough 151,
   152, 163
Peel, Sir Robert 134–5
pele towers 38
Pelli, César 261
Pembroke, Philip Herbert,
   4th Earl of 76
Pembroke College, Cambridge 80
Peniel Chapel (Powys) 127
Pennethorne, Ann 114
Penshurst Place (Kent) 39
Pepys, Samuel 62
Percy family 49, 105
Perpendicular Gothic style 51–8,
   68, 70, 121
   revival 125, 141, 152, 161, 163, 185
Persimmon (house-builders) 242
Peterborough Cathedral
   (Cambridgeshire) 35
Peterlee (Co. Durham) 223
Peto, Harold 162, 170
Pevsner, Sir Nikolaus 35, 44–5, 183
Philae (Egypt) 136
Piano, Renzo 245, 264
Pick, Frank 189
Picts 14–15, 18, 22, 27
picturesque aesthetic 111–12, 158, 162
pilgrimages 22, 28, 33–4, 35, 51
Pitt, Joseph 123

plague (1665) 80, 81
Playfair, William Henry 125, 131
Plymouth 199, 201, 202
   Drake Circus shopping centre 247
podium construction 200, 205, 211–12,
   214, 220, 236, 265, 270
Pompeii (Italy) 104, 136
Pont Street Dutch style 159
Poor Law (1834) 147
Pope, Alexander 91–2, 97
Porchester Castle (Hampshire) 25
Porphyrios, Demetri 251
Port, M. H. 136
Port Grimaud (France) 226
Port Lympne (Kent) 188
Port Sunlight (Wirral) 160
Portman, Henry Portman,
   2nd Viscount 161
Portmeirion (Gwynedd) 188
Portofino (Italy) 188
Portsmouth:
   Tricorn Centre 218
postmodernism 241, 246–7
Poundbury (Dorset) 239–40
Powell, Sir Philip 206, 223
Powers, Alan 188, 196, 217, 230, 241
Powis Castle (Montgomeryshire) 38
Pratt, Sir Roger 78, 79, 86
prefabs (prefabricated houses) 199
prehistory 11–14
Pre-Raphaelite Brotherhood 155, 166
Prescott, John Prescott, Baron 248,
   249, 252
Preseli hills (Wales) 12
Preston (Lancashire) 240
   Bus Station 218
Price, Cedric 242
Price, Sir Uvedale 111
Prior, Edward 174

Index

Prisoner, The (television series) 188
prisons 26, 58, 69, 98
prodigy houses 60–61, 65–9, 71–2, 78
professionalization of architecture, development of 142, 157
Proud City, The (documentary film; 1946) 202
Pugin, Augustus Welby 125, 137–9, 142, 144, 147, 154, 155, 156, 195, 209, 241
  Contrasts 137–8
Putin, Vladimir 265
pyramids (Egypt) 5, 12

Qatar 264, 265
Quarterly Review (journal) 135
Queen Anne style 6, 93, 94, 121
  revival 159, 160, 161–3, 166, 171, 174, 176, 183
Queens' College, Cambridge 69–70

Raby Castle (Co. Durham) 49
Railtrack 264
railway stations 140–41, 150, 196, 234, 247, 251, 264
railways 6, 140–41, 150, 231
  see also London Underground
Raleigh, Sir Walter 66
Ramsgate (Kent):
  railway station 196
Ranworth (Norfolk) 56
Raphael 97, 155
Raphael, Sir Herbert 177–8
Raunds (Northamptonshire) 46
Rausing family 241
Ravenna (Italy) 20
Ravensworth Castle (Co. Durham) 114

Rayne, Max Rayne, Baron 207
rayonnant style 41–2, 48, 51
Reformation 36, 47, 56, 61, 64, 79, 105, 126
Reilly, Sir Charles 210
Reith, John Reith, 1st Baron 201
Renaissance (12th century) 31
Renaissance (15th–16th centuries) 4, 5, 6, 49, 54–5, 57, 59–60, 62–3, 65, 68, 69, 71, 72, 74, 76–7
Repton, Humphry 111–12, 113, 114, 116, 188
Repton Abbey (Derbyshire) 22
Restoration (1660) 78, 79, 85, 101
Restoration style 79, 85–7, 90, 94, 96
Revett, Nicholas 108
Rheims Cathedral (France) 42
Rhuddlan Castle (Denbighshire) 48
RIBA *see* Royal Institute of British Architects
Richard II, King 57
Richard III, King 54
Richard of Farleigh (mason) 46
Richardson, Sir Albert 185
Richborough (Kent) 14
Riches, Mikhail 252
Richmond (Surrey) 206
  Palace 50
  Riverside 241
Richmond Castle (Yorkshire) 26
Rickards, Edwin Alfred 168
Rickman, Thomas 120–21, 130
Rievaulx Abbey (Yorkshire) 28, 32, 61
Ripon, George Robinson, 1st Marquess of 153
Ripon Cathedral (Yorkshire) 22, 35
Rippon, Geoffrey, Baron Rippon of Hexham 221, 231–2

Index

RMJM (architects' practice) 216, 218
Robson, Edward Robert 163
Rochdale (Lancashire):
   town hall 145
Rochester Castle (Kent) 25
Rogers, Richard, Baron Rogers of
   Riverside 244, 245, 247, 249, 251,
   252, 264
Roman Empire 3–4, 14–18, 19, 22, 39,
   75, 103, 108
   see also Byzantine architecture
Romanesque style 4, 17, 31, 33, 121,
   152, 174
Rome 136, 242, 261
   Arch of Constantine 119
   Arch of Titus 14
   Palazzo Farnese 136, 140
   Pantheon 106, 119
   San Carlo alle Quattro Fontane 89
   Sant'Andrea al Quirinale 89
   St Peter's Basilica 4, 27, 106, 184
   Theatre of Marcellus 80
   Villa Borghese 96
rood screens 56, 147, 148
Roos, Karen 17
Rose, Joseph Jr 104
Rose, Joseph Sr 104
Rossetti, Dante Gabriel 155
Rousham House (Oxfordshire) 96
Rowlandson, Thomas 111
Royal Academy of Arts 95, 102, 120
   New Architecture exhibition
     (1986) 244–6
Royal Fine Art Commission 209
Royal Geographical Society 159
Royal Institute of British Architects
   (RIBA) 142, 157, 164, 229–30,
   238, 239, 243
   Stirling Prize 251–2

Royal Society 80
Rugby School (Warwickshire) 151
Runcorn (Cheshire) 210
rural–urban migration 101, 177, 253
Ruskin, John 3, 154, 155, 156, 157,
   162, 195
   Seven Lamps of Architecture 148
Rutland, Thomas Manners,
   1st Earl of 61
Rutland, Francis Manners,
   6th Earl of 74

Sackville-West, Vita 170
Salisbury, Robert Cecil, 1st Earl of 71
Salisbury Cathedral (Wiltshire) 35,
   36, 46, 107
Salle (Norfolk) 55
Salt, Sir Titus 145–6, 160
Saltaire (Yorkshire) 146, 160
Saltram House (Devon) 104
Samuel, Harold, Baron Samuel of
   Wych Cross, 206
San Francisco 255, 258
Sandwich (Kent):
   The Salutation 171
Sandys, Duncan, Baron Duncan-
   Sandys 229, 230
Sassoon family 188
Saumarez Smith, Otto:
   Boom Cities 213, 220, 224–5
SAVE Britain's Heritage (charity) 233
Scarbrough, Richard Lumley,
   1st Earl of 100
Schinkel, Karl Friedrich 132
School of Art Needlework 156
School of Handicraft 156
schools 157
   Board schools 163
   Bryanston School 157, 247

Index

Eton College 51
Impington College 195
Royal High School, Edinburgh 131
Rugby School 151
Scots baronial style 38, 105, 125, 140
Scott, Elisabeth 196
Scott, Sir George Gilbert 2, 36, 147–50, 151, 152, 156–7, 169
Scott, Sir Giles Gilbert 171–2, 184, 185–6, 196
Scott, James Robb 196
Scott, Keith 240
Scott, Mackay Baillie 178
Scott, Sir Walter 131
Scottish Enlightenment 131
Scruton, Sir Roger 230
Seaton Delaval Hall (Northumberland) 92
Second World War (1939–45) 7, 8, 180, 197–8, 211, 259
   Blitz (1940–41) 199–200, 201, 204, 206, 221
secteurs sauvegardés (France) 260–61
Sedding, J. D. 154, 163, 164
Sedgefield (Co. Durham) 79
Segesta temple (Sicily) 1–2
Seifert, Richard 208, 244
Sellar, Irvine 264–5
Sens Cathedral (France) 33
Serlio, Sebastiano 3–4, 59, 63, 64, 67, 72, 74
Service, Alastair 164–5
Seven Years' War (1756–63) 108
Sezincote House (Gloucestershire) 108–9
Shaftesbury (Dorset) 61
Shakespeare, William 6, 13, 70, 73
Shanghai 262

Shankland, Graeme 210–11, 220–21, 266
Sharp, Evelyn Sharp, Baroness 224–5, 226
Shaw, George Bernard 266
Shaw, Richard Norman 154, 158–62, 163, 164, 166, 170, 171, 173, 175
Shaw, Sandie 180
Sheffield:
   City Hall 185, 219
   Meadowhall shopping centre 255
   Park Hill estate 214, 215, 217, 218, 222
Shell (oil company) 208
Sherborne Abbey (Dorset) 53
Sheringham Park (Norfolk) 111–12
shopping centres 211, 221, 229, 255–6
   Bluewater, Dartford 255
   Bull Ring, Birmingham 249
   Cabot Circus, Bristol 255–6
   The Centre, Milton Keynes 227
   Drake Circus, Plymouth 247
   Eldon Square, Newcastle 210
   Meadowhall, Sheffield 255
   St James Centre, Edinburgh 218
   Tricorn Centre, Portsmouth 218
   Westfield, Shepherd's Bush 256
Shrewsbury (Shropshire):
   railway station 141
Shrewsbury, George Talbot, 6th Earl of 67
Shrewsbury, John Talbot, 16th Earl of 139
Shrewsbury, Elizabeth Talbot, Countess of (Bess of Hardwick) 67, 72
Shute, John 63–4, 74
   First and Chief Grounds of Architecture 63, 67

Index

Sicily:
   Casale Roman villa 16
   Segesta temple 1–2
Silkin, Lewis Silkin, 1st Baron 223
Silures (tribe) 15
Silver, Nathan 233
Simpson, John 241
Skara Brae (Orkney) 11, 13
Skelmersdale (Lancashire) 210, 224
Skipton Castle (Yorkshire) 48
slum clearance 160, 179, 221–2, 230, 253, 266
Smirke, Sir Robert 120, 121, 129, 133, 134–5, 137
Smith, Adam 131
Smith, T. Dan 209–10
Smith, Sir Thomas 64
Smith of Warwick, Francis 97
Smithson, Alison and Peter 200, 203, 214–15, 216
Smythson, John 72
Smythson, Robert 65, 67–8, 69, 72, 73
Soane, Sir John 5, 113, 118–20, 121, 133, 137, 140, 146
socialism 156, 160, 174, 176, 189, 194
Society for the Protection of Ancient Buildings 21, 156, 185
Society of Antiquaries 95–6
Society of Dilettanti 95–6, 108
Somerset, Edward Seymour, 1st Duke of 62–3, 72, 75, 102
Sonning (Berkshire):
   Deanery Gardens 170
South Queensferry (West Lothian):
   Hopetoun House 102
Southampton, Thomas Wriothesley, 4th Earl of 86
Southern Railway 196

Southwell Minster (Nottinghamshire) 44–5
spa towns 122–3
   see also Bath (Somerset)
Spectator (magazine) 134
Spence, Sir Basil 216, 219, 244
Spenser, Edmund:
   The Faerie Queen 72
Split (Croatia) 103
St Albans, Henry Jermyn, 1st Earl of 85, 86
St David's Cathedral (Pembrokeshire) 27–8
St Neot (Cornwall) 57
St Petersburg 117, 134, 265
   Hermitage 91
Stafford 167
stage design 72, 74–5, 158
Stalag Luft III (prisoner-of-war camp) 202
Stamp, Gavin 190
'starchitects' 246, 249, 251
Starr, Sir Ringo 253
stations *see* London Underground; railway stations
Staunton Harold (Leicestershire) 79
Steinbach family (masons) 65
Stephenson, Robert 141
Stevenage (Hertfordshire) 223
Stevenson, J.J. 159, 163, 164
Stewart, James 168
Stirling, Sir James 244, 245–6
Stirling Ackroyd (estate agents) 254
Stirling Castle 60
Stirling Prize 251–2
Stockholm 189
Stockport (Cheshire) 167
Stoke-on-Trent (Staffordshire):
   railway station 141

Index

Stone Age 11–13
Stonehenge 11–13, 75, 99
Stoneleigh Abbey (Warwickshire) 97
Stourhead (Wiltshire) 96
Stout's Hill (Gloucestershire) 105
Stowe House (Buckinghamshire) 96, 105, 110
Stratford-upon-Avon (Warwickshire):
  Shakespeare Memorial Theatre 196
Street, George Edmund 151, 154, 155, 157, 158
'streets in the sky' construction 211, 214
Stuart, James 'Athenian' 108, 131
Studio (magazine) 157
Studley Royal Park (Yorkshire) 153
Stukeley, William 12
Stuttgart (Germany):
  Staatsgalerie 245–6
Sudjic, Deyan 245
  The Edifice Complex 262
Suffolk, Thomas Howard, 1st Earl of 71
Suger, Abbot of St-Denis 5, 31–2, 41
Sumerians 12
Summerson, Sir John 72, 90–91, 117, 194
  The Classical Language of Architecture 3
Suntrap style 196, 197
Surbiton (Surrey):
  railway station 196
Survey of London 163
Sussex, University of 216
Sutton Place (Surrey) 61
Sutton Scarsdale Hall (Derbyshire) 97
Swansea (Glamorgan) 126, 153
Swift, Jonathan 86

Sydney:
  Opera House 246
Synod of Whitby (664) 4, 21, 22
Syon House (Middlesex) 63

Tallis, John:
  London Street Views 129–30
Talman, William 89, 90
Tattershall Castle (Lincolnshire) 50
Tatton Brown, William and Aileen 200, 203
Taunton (Somerset) 56
taxation 42, 92, 203, 252, 254, 262, 263
Taylor, Nicholas 230
Taylor, Sir Robert 101–2, 109
Taylor Woodrow (house-builders) 182
Taymouth Castle (Perthshire) 125
Tchaikovsky, Pyotr Ilyich 189
Tecton Group 197, 200
telephone kiosks 186
Telford (Shropshire) 224
Terry, Dame Ellen 157
Terry, Quinlan 241
Tewkesbury Abbey (Gloucestershire) 28, 30, 57
Thatcherism 255, 261
theatres 74–5, 157, 168–9, 227
  London Coliseum 168
  National Theatre 217, 244
  Sheldonian Theatre, Oxford 80
  see also stage design
Thetford (Norfolk) 27
Thirties Society (charity) 217
Thirty Years' War (1618–48) 78
Thomas of Witney (mason) 43, 44
Thomson, Alexander 'Greek' 146
Thorneycroft, Sir Hamo 167
Thornhill, Sir James 84, 93

Index

Thurlby, Malcolm:
 Romanesque Architecture and Sculpture in Wales 28
Thurley, Simon 98
Thynne, Sir John 62–4, 65, 74, 75
Tickencote (Rutland) 29
Tilden, Philip 188
Tintern Abbey (Monmouthshire) 112
Tite, Sir William 140
Torquay (Devon) 122
Torrigiano, Pietro 55
Toryism 94, 95, 99, 120, 134–5
tourism 2, 48, 106, 120, 122–3, 188, 253, 254, 256
 see also grand tour
Town and Country Planning Act (1947) 203, 204–5
town planning 7–8, 39–40, 81–2, 84–5, 109, 116, 117, 180–81, 199–205, 208–12, 220–23, 227–8, 229–32, 234–7, 242–3, 260
 see also building acts
Townsend, Charles Harrison 174
Tremadog (Gwynedd) 127
Tre'r Ceiri (Gwynedd) 13–14
Trinity College, Cambridge 84, 128–9
Tristram, Ernest William 37, 43
Truro Cathedral (Cornwall) 152
Tudorbethan style 6, 69, 184, 190, 196, 232, 267
Turner, J. M. W. 13, 112
Tuscan order 4, 63
Twentieth Century Society (charity) 217
Twickenham (Middlesex):
 Orleans House 94
 Strawberry Hill House 106, 125

UNESCO 202
University College London 129, 250
Unwin, Sir Raymond 176, 178
Up Marden (Sussex) 58
Upcher, Abbot 112
Uppark (Sussex) 94
Uxbridge (Middlesex) 218

Van Dyck, Sir Antony 6
Vanbrugh, Sir John 5, 90–92, 93, 94, 96, 106
Vaux-le-Vicomte Château (France) 89
Venice 148
 Ca' d'Oro 152
 St Mark's Square 146
Venturi, Robert 246–7
Vernon family 93
Verrio, Antonio 93
Versailles Palace (France) 79, 84, 91, 96, 118, 133
Vertue, Robert 53
Vertue, William 53, 54, 55, 105
Victoria, Queen 140, 143, 144, 167, 170
 coronation 101
Victorian Society 229, 234
Vienna 85, 191, 261
 Hofburg Palace 118
Vienna, Congress of (1815) 120
Vienna Secession exhibitions 175, 191
Vikings 22, 25
Villa Rotonda (Italy) 241
Villa Ventorum (Somerset) 16–17
Viñoly, Rafael 247, 263
Viollet-le-Duc, Eugène 159
Vitruvius 3–4, 74, 81, 95, 113, 138, 185
 De architectura 63
Vkhutemas academy (Moscow) 191

Index

Voltaire 91
Voysey, Charles 174, 175, 186, 195, 197
Vredeman de Vries, Hans 64
Vyne, The (Hampshire) 79

Wagner, Otto 175
Wakefield (Yorkshire) 167
Walker, Derek 226
Wallis, Gilbert and Partners (architects' practice) 186–7
Walpole, Horace, 4th Earl of Orford 92, 93, 97, 106
Walpole, Sir Robert, 1st Earl of Orford 109
Walsingham, Sir Francis 66
Walters, Edward 145
Wanstead House (Essex) 95, 96
Warkworth Castle (Northumberland) 49
Wars of the Roses (1455–87) 53–4, 57, 59
Warsaw 202, 222
Warwick 97
  Castle 26
  Lord Leycester Hospital 69
  St Mary's church 57
Washington, DC:
  Capitol 120
  national cathedral 152
  White House 120
Wastell, John 54
Waterhouse, Alfred 145, 151, 152, 162, 166
Waterloo, Battle of (1815) 121
Waterloo churches 121–2, 130, 133, 136
Waterloo University (Canada) 256
Wates (house-builders) 182, 196
Watkin, David 129, 138, 151
Waugh, Evelyn 203

Webb, Sir Aston 169–70
Webb, John 79–80, 84
Webb, Philip 154, 155–6, 158
Wells (Somerset):
  Cathedral 34, 43–4, 45
  St Cuthbert's church 56
Welwyn Garden City (Hertfordshire) 225
Wentworth Woodhouse (Yorkshire) 96
West Molesey (Surrey) 197
West Stow (Suffolk) 19
West Wycombe Park (Buckinghamshire) 96
Westminster, Richard Grosvenor, 2nd Marquess of 123
Westminster Review (journal) 134
Weston, Sir Richard 61
Westphalia, Peace of (1648) 78
Whiggism 90, 94–5, 108, 120
Whistler, James McNeill 157–8
Whitby, Synod of (664) 4, 21, 22
Whitfield, Sir William 242
'Why is British Architecture so Lousy?' (seminar; 1979) 233
Wigmore Castle (Herefordshire) 26
Wilde, Oscar 158
Wilds, Amon 122
Wilds, Amon Henry 122
Wilford, Michael 248
Wilkins, William 128–9, 133, 247
William I (the Conqueror), King 23, 24, 25–9, 31
William II (Rufus), King 29–30
William III, King 84, 87, 94
William and Mary style 84, 93, 94
William the Englishman (mason) 33, 34
William of Sens (mason) 33
William of Wykeham, Bishop of Winchester 53

Index

Williams, Sir Owen 187
Williams-Ellis, Sir Clough 178, 188
Willoughby, Sir Francis 67
Wilson, Sir Colin St John 238–9
Wilson, Hugh 222, 224, 225
Wilson, Robin 218
Wilton House (Wiltshire) 76–7
Wimpey (house-builders) 182, 242
Wimpole Hall (Cambridgeshire) 94, 105, 119
Winchcombe, Richard 53
Winchester 23
    Cathedral 27, 53, 57, 70
    Hospital of St Cross 28
    King's House 84, 90
Windsor (Berkshire) 140
    Castle 52, 133, 142
    Great Park 133
    St George's Chapel 53
Wodehouse, P. G. 39, 184
Wolfe, Tom:
    From Bauhaus to Our House 240
Wollaton Hall (Nottinghamshire) 67
Wolsey, Thomas 59, 60, 62
Womersley, J. Lewis 214, 222
Wood, John, the Elder 12, 99
wool trade 32, 55
Woolf, Virginia:
    A Room of One's Own 162
Worcester:
    Cathedral 26
    guildhall 99

Worcester College, Oxford 74
Wordsworth, William 13, 112
workhouses 147
Wren, Sir Christopher 5, 80–81, 89–90, 93, 95, 115, 144, 168, 171, 203
    City of London churches 83–4, 89, 264
    St James's church, Piccadilly 85
    St Paul's Cathedral 82–3, 84
Wren, Christopher, the Younger 84
Wright, Frank Lloyd 175
Wulfstan, Bishop of Worcester 26
Wyatt, James 5, 106–8, 113, 122, 128, 133, 137, 147
Wyatt, Sir Matthew Digby 141, 149
Wyatt, Samuel 106
Wyatville, Sir Jeffry 133
Wynford, William 53

Yeavering (Northumberland) 19
Yevele, Henry 53
York 8, 15, 22, 46
    assembly rooms 98
    Castle 26, 98
    courthouse 97
    Fairfax House 97
    Minster 42
    railway station 141
York, University of 216
Young, Thomas 87
Young, William 169